First World War
and Army of Occupation
War Diary
France, Belgium and Germany

42 DIVISION
Divisional Troops
Royal Army Service Corps
Divisional Train (428-429-430-431 Companies A.S.C.)
9 April 1916 - 14 April 1919

WO95/2653/2

The Naval & Military Press Ltd
www.nmarchive.com
Published in association with The National Archives

Published by

The Naval & Military Press Ltd

Unit 10 Ridgewood Industrial Park,

Uckfield, East Sussex,

TN22 5QE England

Tel: +44 (0) 1825 749494

www.naval-military-press.com

www.nmarchive.com

This diary has been reprinted in facsimile from the original. Any imperfections are inevitably reproduced and the quality may fall short of modern type and cartographic standards.

Contents

Document type	Place/Title	Date From	Date To
Heading	WO95/2653/2 Div. Train 428/9/30/1 Cos. A.S.C. Mar 17-Apr 19		
Heading	42nd Division 42nd Divl Train A.S.C. Mar 1917-Apr 1919 428-431 Coys Ase		
Heading	War Diary O.C. Headquarters Company. 42nd Divisional Train.		
War Diary		28/02/1917	29/03/1917
War Diary	Trek	30/03/1917	31/03/1917
War Diary	Mericourt	01/04/1917	16/04/1917
War Diary	Fontaine	17/04/1917	21/04/1917
War Diary	Peronne	22/04/1917	01/05/1917
War Diary	Tincourt	03/04/1917	21/04/1917
War Diary	Bus	22/04/1917	11/07/1917
Miscellaneous			
Heading	WO95/2653		
War Diary		21/07/1918	10/04/1919
Heading	Army Book 152. Correspondence Book (Field Service)		
Miscellaneous			
War Diary	Bus	25/07/1917	15/08/1917
War Diary		16/08/1917	20/07/1918
Miscellaneous	D.A.G. G.H.Q. 3rd Echelon	18/04/1919	18/04/1919
Miscellaneous	D.A.G., 3rd. Echelon. B.E.F.	10/04/1917	10/04/1917
War Diary	Larkhill Salisbury Plain. and Havre	25/02/1917	01/03/1917
War Diary	Havre	02/03/1917	04/03/1917
War Diary	Hallencourt (Sheet 3 Borden Tuis J.K.6.)	04/03/1917	05/03/1917
War Diary	Hallencourt	06/03/1917	30/04/1917
Heading	War Diary Of 42nd Divisional Train From 1/4/17 To 30/4/17. (Volume 2)		
War Diary	Hallencourt.	01/04/1917	01/04/1917
War Diary	Mericourt Sur-Somme	02/04/1917	16/04/1917
War Diary	Mericourt Sur-Somme & Peronne	17/04/1917	17/04/1917
War Diary	Peronne.	18/04/1917	30/04/1917
Heading	War Diary Of 42nd Division Train From 1/5/17 To 31/5/17 Volume 3		
War Diary	Peronne.	01/05/1917	03/05/1917
War Diary	Tincourt	04/05/1917	22/05/1917
War Diary	Tincourt & Bus.	23/05/1917	31/05/1917
Heading	War Diary Of 42nd Division Train A.S.C. 1st. June To 30th June 1917. Volume 4		
War Diary	Bus	01/06/1917	30/06/1917
Heading	War Diary Period 1st July 17 To 31st July 17 Volume V 42nd Divisional Train Army Service Corps.		
War Diary	Bus	01/07/1917	08/07/1917
War Diary	Bus & Achiet-Le-Petit.	09/04/1916	09/04/1916
War Diary	Achiet-Le-Petit	09/04/1917	31/07/1917
Heading	War Diary. 42nd Division Train. A.S.C. Volume VI. Period 1st August To 31st August 1917		
War Diary	Achiet Le Petit	01/08/1917	21/08/1917
War Diary	Acheux	22/08/1917	23/08/1917
War Diary	Watou	24/08/1917	30/08/1917

War Diary	Watou & H7c92	31/08/1917	31/08/1917
Heading	War Diary. 42nd Divisional Train Army Service Corps. Period September 1917. Volume No. VII		
War Diary	Sheet 28 H4.c98	01/09/1917	03/09/1917
War Diary	HA.c.9.8 Brandhoek	04/09/1917	15/09/1917
War Diary	Brandhoek	16/09/1917	18/09/1917
War Diary	Poperinghe	19/09/1917	21/09/1917
War Diary	La Panne	22/09/1917	25/09/1917
War Diary	Stidesbalde	26/09/1917	30/09/1917
Heading	War Diary. 42nd Divisional Train. Army Service Corps. Volume XIII. Period 1-X-1917 To 31-X-1917		
War Diary	St. Idesbalde	01/10/1917	06/10/1917
War Diary	Coxyde Bains	07/10/1917	31/10/1917
Heading	War Diary 42nd Divisional Train A.S.C. Period-1-XII-1917-30-XII-1917. Volume IX.		
War Diary	Coxyde. Bains.	01/11/1917	18/11/1917
War Diary	Aire	19/11/1917	28/11/1917
War Diary	Bethune. Locon.	29/11/1917	30/11/1917
Heading	War Diary. 42nd Divisional Trains. A.S.C. Period-1-XII-1917 To 31-XII-1917. Volume X.		
War Diary	Bethune. Locon.	01/12/1917	31/12/1917
Heading	War Diary. 42nd Division Train. A.S.C. Period. 1-1-1918 To 31-1-1918. Volume XI		
War Diary	Bethune. Locon	01/01/1918	31/01/1918
Heading	War Diary 42nd Divisional Train. A.S.C. Period 1-2-1918 To 28-2-1918 Volume-XII		
War Diary	Bethune Locon.	01/02/1918	14/02/1918
War Diary	Gonneham	15/02/1918	28/02/1918
Heading	War Diary. 42nd Divisional Train. A.S.C. Period 1-3-1918 To 31-3-1918. Vol XIII		
War Diary	Gonneham	01/03/1918	21/03/1918
War Diary	Hautrieux	22/03/1918	22/03/1918
War Diary	Monchy-Au-Bois	23/03/1918	24/03/1918
War Diary	Bienvillers. Au. Bois	25/03/1918	25/03/1918
War Diary	St.Rmand	26/03/1918	27/03/1918
War Diary	Couin.	28/03/1918	31/03/1918
Heading	War Diary. 42nd Divisional Train A.S.C. Period-1-4-1918 To 30-4-18. Volume XIV.		
War Diary	Couin.	01/04/1918	02/04/1918
War Diary	Henu	03/04/1918	06/04/1918
War Diary	Pas	07/04/1918	15/04/1918
War Diary	Couin.	16/04/1918	30/04/1918
Heading	War Diary. 42nd Divisional Train. A.S.C. Period-1-5-1918 To 31-5-18. Volume XV.		
War Diary	Couin	01/05/1918	05/05/1918
War Diary	Pas-En-Artois.	06/05/1918	31/05/1918
Heading	War Diary. 42nd Divisional Train. A.S.C. Period-1-6-1918 To 30-6-1918. Volume XVI.		
War Diary	Pas. En. Artois	01/06/1918	06/06/1918
War Diary	Bus Les. Artois	07/06/1918	30/06/1918
Heading	War Diary. 42nd Divisional Train. A.S.C. Period 1-VII-18 To 31-VII-1918. Volume. XVII.		
War Diary	Bus-Les-Artois	01/07/1918	08/07/1918
War Diary	Sarton.	09/07/1918	15/07/1918
War Diary	Authie	16/07/1918	31/07/1918

Heading	War Diary 42nd Divisional Train. A.S.C. Period 1-8-18 To 31-8-18. Volume XVIII		
War Diary	Authie	01/08/1918	14/08/1918
War Diary	Bus. Les. Artois	15/08/1918	27/08/1918
War Diary	Miraumont	28/08/1918	31/08/1918
Heading	War Diary 42nd Divisional Train. A.S.C. Period 1-IX-18. To 30-IX-1918. Volume XIX.		
War Diary	Miraumont	01/09/1918	03/09/1918
War Diary	Warlencourt	04/09/1918	21/09/1918
War Diary	Velu	22/09/1918	30/09/1918
Heading	War Diary 42nd Divisional Train. A.S.C. Period 1-X-1918-31-X-1918. Volume XX.		
War Diary	Velu	01/10/1918	08/10/1918
War Diary	Trescault And Esnes	09/10/1918	09/10/1918
War Diary	Esnes	10/10/1918	11/10/1918
War Diary	Beauvois-Cambresis	12/10/1918	23/10/1918
War Diary	Beauvois. En Cambresis.	24/10/1918	31/10/1918
Heading	War Diary. 42nd Divisional Train. A.S.C. Period 1-XI-18-30-XI-1918. Volume XXI.		
War Diary	Beauvois. En Cambresis	01/11/1918	04/11/1918
War Diary	Beaudignies And Potelle	05/11/1918	05/11/1918
War Diary	Potelle	05/11/1918	10/11/1918
War Diary	Hautmont	11/11/1918	14/12/1918
War Diary	Binche	15/12/1918	15/12/1918
War Diary	Fontaine L'Eveque	16/12/1918	17/12/1918
War Diary	Charleroi	18/12/1918	31/12/1918
Heading	War Diary 42nd Divisional Train. 1st January 1919 To 31st January 1919 Volume 23		
War Diary	Charleroi	01/01/1919	31/01/1919
Heading	War Diary. 42nd Divisional Train. R.A.S.C. Period-1-2-1919-28-2-1919. Volume XXIII.		
War Diary	Charleroi	01/02/1919	28/02/1919
Heading	War Diary. 42nd Divisional Train. R.A.S.C. Period-1-3-1919-31-3-1919. Vol XXV.		
War Diary	Charleroi	01/03/1919	12/04/1919
War Diary	Antumps.	13/04/1919	14/04/1919

WO95/2653 (2)

Div. Train

428/9/30/1 Cos. A.S.C

Mar '17 – Apr '19

42ND DIVISION

42ND DIVL TRAIN A.S.C.

MAR 1917-APR 1919

428-431 Coys

ASC

Opened on February 28th 1917

Closed on ....

The Squares in this book are $\frac{1}{4}$ inch.

(S.O. 1089) W79.2/M891. 100,000. 12/16. —McC. & Co., Ltd.– E 646.

WAR DIARY

O.C. HEADQUARTERS COMPANY.
42nd DIVISIONAL TRAIN.

WAR DIARY

O.C. HEADQUARTERS COMPANY

42nd DIVISIONAL TRAIN

WAR DIARY

Wednesday. February 28th 1917

5 Officers 85 other ranks 94 horses and 40 four wheeled vehicles of Hd. Qrs. and Hd. Qrs Company, 42nd Divisional Train entrained at Amesbury Station and proceeded to Southampton.
The above embarked at Southampton on S. S. Manchester Importer.

MARCH 1st 1917. Thursday.

5 Officers 85 other ranks 94 horses and 40 four wheeled vehicles of Hd. Qrs. and Hd. Qrs. Company 42nd Divisional Train which embarked yesterday, disembarked at HAVRE and proceeded to No 2 Rest Camp SANVIC, HAVRE.
One H. D. horse admitted to Veterinary Hosp, Larkhill, suffering with colic.

---

9 Officers 88 other ranks, 78 horses, 29 four wheeled vehicles and 2 two wheeled vehicles entrained at Amesbury and proceeded to Southampton.
Two H. D. horses cast by Veterinary Officer at Southampton Docks and replaced by Remount Officer at Southampton.
9 Officers 88 other ranks 78 horses embarked at Southampton on S. S. Londonderry and Volumnia leaving 5 other ranks, 29 four

wheeled vehicles and two 2 wheeled vehicles at Southampton Docks.

MARCH 2nd 1917. Friday.

9 Officers, 83 other ranks and 78 horses which embarked at Southampton yesterday disembarked at HAVRE and proceeded to No 2 Rest Camp SANVIC HAVRE.

29 four wheeled vehicles 2 two wheeled vehicles and 5 other ranks embarked at Southampton on S.S. Hunsgrove.

MARCH 3rd 1917 Saturday.

1 Riding Horse and 1 H.D. horse admitted to Veterinary Hospital, HAVRE. 1 Riding Horse and 2 H.D. Horses drawn from Remount Depot HAVRE to complete establishment.

29, 4 wheeled vehicles and two 2 wheeled vehicles and 5 other ranks disembarked at HAVRE from S.S. HUNSGROVE today and proceeded to No 2 Rest Camp, SANVIC, HAVRE.

MARCH 4th 1917 Sunday.

4 H.D. Horses admitted to Veterinary Hospital, HAVRE.
4 H.D. Horses drawn from Remount Depot, HAVRE to complete establishment.
7 Officers, 170 other ranks, 173 horses, 62 four wheeled vehicles, 16 two wheeled vehicles and 16 Bicycles entrained at POINT 1. HAVRE in two trains at 7 p.m. and 11.30 p.m.

MARCH 5th 1917. Monday.

The above personnel, horses and vehicles of Hd. Qrs. and Hd. Qrs. Company, 42nd Divisional Train detrained at PONT REMY today and proceeded to Billets at HALLENCOURT, arriving at HALLENCOURT in two parties at 7 p.m. and 10 p.m.

MARCH 6th 1917 Tuesday.

Company routine. Settling down in Billets. Arranging and putting down horse lines etc.
1 Saddler Staff Sgt. and two Drivers of old 42nd Divisional Train home on leave from EGYPT attached to Headquarters Company for duty.

WAR DIARY

MARCH 7th 1917 Wednesday

Refilling for Divisional Troops commenced at SOREL today at 10·0 a.m.

Company routine etc.

MARCH 8th 1917 Thursday.

Refilling at SOREL for Divisional Troops. Time altered to 7·30 a.m.
Drivers Cook and Ferguson with Supply Wagons of the 427th & 428th Field Companies R.E. detached for duty with No 3 Company, 42nd Divisional Train, LIMERCOURT.
Company routine etc.

MARCH 9th 1917 Friday

Refilling for Div. Troops at SOREL at 7·30 a.m.
C.O. Inspected Company Billets etc this morning.
1 Corpl. and 1 Pte. reported from D.H.Q. as loaders for Supply Wagon of Div. H.Q.

Company routine etc.

W. P. Reynolds Major, MAJOR,
COMMANDING 428 COY. A.S.C.

WAR DIARY.

MARCH 10th 1917 Saturday.

Refilling for Divisional Troops at SOREL at 7.30 a.m.
One man reported from H.Q. Div. Signals as loader for Supply Wagon of Divl. Signals.

Company Routine.

MARCH 11th 1917 Sunday.

Refilling for Divisional Troops at SOREL at 7.30 a.m.
One Officer and 30 N.C.O.s and men attended Church Parade at Hotel du Ville Hallencourt at 9.30 a.m.
2 Officers, 43 other ranks, 44 Horses and 19 vehicles comprising whole of Supply Details and Divisional Artillery Supply Vehicles of Train proceeded from HALLENCOURT to billets at CAOURS today for supply and transport duties for 42nd Divisional Artillery.

One man from each of the following units reported as loaders:- 1/2nd E. Lanc Fld. Amb. 429 Field Coy. R.E., 19th Mobile Vet. Section

Company Routine.

WAR DIARY.

MARCH 12th 1917 Monday

Divisional Troops attached to 127th Infantry Bde. for Supplies on this date. Refilling for Divisional Troops now taking place at 127th Bde. Refilling Point HUPPY at 8.30 a.m.

Refilling for Divisional Artillery commenced this morning at L'HEURE beyond ABBEVILLE at 8.30 a.m.

T4/123961 Dr. Bain A. Transferred to 429 Company A.S.C.

T4/244870 Dr. Jones P. from 42nd Divl. Train, Egypt taken on strength of Company to replace No. T4/123961 Dr. Bain transferred.

Company Routine

MARCH 13th 1917 Tuesday

Refilling for Divisional Troops and Divisional Artillery as yesterday.

The Train Baggage Wagons of R.A. Hd. Qrs. and 210th & 211th R. F. Artillery Brigades handed over to their units today (G.S. Wagons in all) Horses, Drivers and harness for these vehicles retained with Company.

1 N.C.O. and 2 men of R.E. reported as Train Postal Section. Postal Equipment handed

over to the N.C.O. and an office found for them in HALLENCOURT.

Company Routine.

MARCH 14th 1917 Wednesday

Refilling for Divisional Troops and Divisional Artillery as yesterday.

Supply Wagon of 427 Field Coy. R.E. with driver and horses attached to 429 Coy. A.S.C. from 430 Coy. A.S.C.

8 Drivers 16 H.D. horses and 8 Train Supply Wagons of Divisional Ammunition Column proceeded from HALLENCOURT today to join Artillery Supply Section Detachment at L'HEURE under Lieut. W.W. Yeats, A.S.C.

Company Routine.

Company Paid.

MARCH 15th 1917. Thursday.

Refilling for Divisional Troops and Divisional Artillery as yesterday. D.A.C. commenced refilling at Artillery Refilling Point this morning.
Train Supply Wagon of 429 Field Coy. R.E. with Driver Loader and Horses attached to 431 Coy. A.S.C.
T4/244872 Sadd. S. Sgt. Medlock, attached from 42nd Divisional Train, Egypt admitted to Hospital today and struck of ration strength of company from 17th instant inclusive.

Company Routine.

MARCH 16th 1917 Friday

Refilling as yesterday.
One man reported as loader from 1/3rd E Lanc. Field Ambulance.
One Horse L.D. No L.1. 129 died from pneumonia.
A stampede of horses occurred on the Company horse lines at 10:30 p.m. tonight. 17 draught horses have escaped from the lines and have

WAR DIARY

made off along the HALLENCOURT – CITERNE Road towards CITERNE. All N.C.Os and men turned out and standing to their horses. 2 cyclists and a party of 1 officer and 6 N.C.Os and men despatched to follow up horses. A double picquet has been mounted on horse-lines.

11.30 p.m. Search party has returned. Officer i/c reports that owing to darkness horses cannot be traced. A strong search party ordered to turn out at daybreak.

In the Field
17.3.17

W. P. Reynolds MAJOR,
COMMANDING 428 COY. A.S.C.

WAR DIARY

MARCH 17th 1917. Saturday

Refilling as yesterday.
Search parties started off at 4.00 this morning in search of 17 horses lost last night and after searching all day have recovered 7 horses. 2 further horses found by O.C. 431 Coy. A.S.C. at FRUCOURT. Train Headquarters, D.H.Q and A.P.M. supplied with report and full particulars of 8 horses still missing.
T4/244872 Sadd. S. Sgt. Medlock discharged from hospital today and taken on ration strength of Coy.

Company Routine

MARCH 18th 1917. Sunday.

Refilling as yesterday.

Further search made for 8 missing horses, but without result.
Bathing parade for all N.C.Os & men of Coy. at Divisional Baths, HALLENCOURT from 2 p.m to 5 p.m. today.
Company Routine.

MARCH 19th 1917 Monday.

Refilling as yesterday.

T/37868 Dr. Orman C. admitted to No 2 Hospital, Abbeville suffering with mumps. All men occupying the same billet as Dr. Orman isolated and billet disinfected.

Company Routine. 8 H.D. still missing

MARCH 20th 1917. Tuesday.

Refilling as yesterday.

T4/244925 Dr. Ellison R. T4/2449262 Dr. Robinson W.H., T4/244884 Dr. Gamble. J. and T4/246512 Dr. McDonagh, A.E. from 42nd Divisional Train, Egypt taken on ration strength.

Company Routine.

8 H.D. Horses still missing

MARCH 21st 1917 Wednesday.

Refilling as yesterday.

A Board of Officers assembled at Hd. Qrs Coy. Office at 9-0 a.m. this morning to enquire into the loss of the 8 H.D. Horses missing from this Company. The necessary evidence (6 witnesses) was produced. Board sat from 9-0 a.m. to 6-0 p.m.

Company Paid.

Company Routine. 8 H.D. Horses still missing

WAR DIARY

MARCH 22nd 1917 Thursday

Refilling as yesterday.

Called on A.P.M. to enquire if he had heard anything of 8 missing H.D. horses. A.P.M. states that search ~~~~ is still being made and that Headquarters of other formations have been notified, but nothing has yet been heard of the horses. T4/244876 Dr. Dyson R. taken on strength.

Inspected Supply Section Detachment at L'HEURE this afternoon. Four pairs of horses looking poor though stated to be eating and working well. Instructed Section Officer to rest the poor conditioned animals and arranged to send him 6 pairs of spare horses from Baggage Section to enable this to be done.

Other animals in good condition. Harness good. Camp generally clean and tidy.

MARCH 23rd 1917 Friday

Refilling as yesterday.

6 Pairs Horses H.D. and 7 Drivers of Artillery Baggage wagons sent to Supply Section Detachment at L'HEURE to relieve work of Supply Section horses.

Company Routine.

8 H.D. horses still missing.

W.P. Reynolds MAJOR, A.S.C.
O.C. HD. QRS. COMPANY 42nd DIVL. TRAIN.

WAR DIARY

MARCH 24th 1917 Saturday

Refilling as yesterday.

Bathing Parade for all N.C.Os & men at Divisional Baths at 2-0 p.m.

Company Routine

MARCH 25th 1917 Sunday.

Refilling as yesterday.

Church Parade at Officers' Mess at 3-0 p.m.

7/34707 Dr. Morgan H.H. admitted to Hospital.

O.C Company made a further search this afternoon for 8 missing horses visiting Remount Depot, Base Commander & French Cavalry Barracks Abbeville, also French Veterinary Hospital, BLANGY and the villages of SENARPONT and OUISEMONT, but without results.

Company ordered to be prepared to move at short notice. Verbal instructions received from O.C. Train to have company in readiness to move by 6 a.m tomorrow.

MARCH 26th 1917 Monday.

Instructions received from Adjutant at 3-0 a.m this morning that move of Company will not take place, but that Supply Section will move from HALLENCOURT and L'HEURE today to LA CHAUSSEE. Supply Section to continue to trek tomorrow, halting for the night at FOUILLOY, and will proceed on the 28th from the latter place to ESTREES.

Units to be fed by Mechanical Transport and their own 1st Line until further notice.

The Supply Section of H.Q. Company left HALLENCOURT and L'HEURE for ESTREES, via LA CHAUSSEE and FOUILLOY, this morning as follows:-

HALLENCOURT party:- (S.S.M. Hanwood in ch)
8 Wagons G.S. 2 Limbered G.S. 16 Horses H.D.
4 Horses L.D. 1 Rider, 1 W.O. and 13 other ranks

L'HEURE party:- (Lieut W.W. Yeats in charge)
24 Wagons G.S. 2 Limbered G.S. 50 Horses H.D.
4 Horses L.D. 4 Riders, 1 Officer, 2 Sgts
and 39 other ranks.

Total Supply Section at ESTREES:-
1 Officer, 1 W.O. 2 Sgts. 52 other ranks,
66 Horses H.D. 8 Horses L.D. 5 Riders
32 Wagons G.S. 4 Limbered G.S.

A.P.M 42nd Division called to report that

he had sent out mounted police and gendarmes yesterday to make a further search for the 8 horses missing from this Company. They enquired at NEUFCHATEL, GAMACHES and numerous villages between these places and HALLENCOURT, but met with no result.

T4/186806 Dr. Murphy A. admitted to Hospital at Abbeville from ST. HEURE with broken leg.

MARCH 27th 1917 Tuesday.

All loaders attached to the Company returned to their units.

Company Routine.

MARCH 28th 1917 Wednesday.

Refilling at SOREL at 8-30 a.m.
1 limber with driver and horses attached to 431 Company A.S.C. for A.P.M's use.
T4/244925 Dr. Ellisba R. and T4/249262 Dr. Robinson W.H. taken on strength to replace Drivers Monger and Murphy admitted to hospital.

Company Routine.

MARCH 29th 1917 Thursday.

Refilling at cross roads on Limercourt-Limeux Road at 10-0 a.m

Company Routine.

MARCH 30th 1917 Friday: on Trek

Refilling at SOREL at 7-30 a.m.
9 Drivers and 9 pairs of H.D. horses with harness of Baggage Section also one G.S. Wagon of Headquarters Section attached to 430 Company A.S.C.

Headquarters of Company and portion of Baggage Section moved today by road to ST. SAUVEUR together with Transport and Horses of Divisional Headquarters troops.

MARCH 31st 1917 Saturday. on Trek

7/244870 Dr. Jones [illegible] admitted to Hospital at CHUIGNOLLES

Headquarters of Company, portion of Baggage Section and Transport and Horses of Divisional Headquarters Troops moved by road today from ST. SAUVEUR to HAMEL.

54/043988 Cpl. Randall W.A. admitted Hospital.

W.P. Reynolds Major
O.C. H.Q. Coy. 42nd Divisional Train

APRIL 1st 1917 Sunday. on Trek and at MERICOURT

Headquarters of Company, portion of Baggage Section and Transport and horses of Divisional Headquarters Troops moved from HAMEL into Billets at MERICOURT.

Supplies for whole of above party drawn from Railhead at CHUIGNES and issued by 428 Coy. A.S.C.

Settling down in Billets, etc.

APRIL 2nd 1917 Monday. at MERICOURT

Supplies for Company drawn at CHUIGNES

2 3 ton M.T. lorries reported from D.S.C. for duty at MERICOURT under O.C. Train

The two Baggage Wagons of Pioneer Battn. with horses and drivers attached to Supply Section at FOYCAUCOURT for duty with 59th Div. Train.

No 186129 Driver James. H. T. admitted Hospital

APRIL 3rd 1917 Tuesday. at MERICOURT

Supplies for Company drawn by lorry from CHUIGNES.

Company routine.

S4/140249 Cpl. Treasure G. admitted to hospital.

APRIL 4th 1917 Wednesday. at MERICOURT

Supplies drawn by Horse Transport from CHUIGNES Railhead.

No T/13822 Dr Lemins W. admitted hospital

Company Routine.

Company Paid.

APRIL 5th 1917 Thursday at MERICOURT

Supplies drawn by H. T. from CHUIGNES Railhead.

Lt. W. W. Yeats with Supply vehicles of Div. R.A and D.A.C. moved from FOUCAUCOURT to CAPPY. Strength as follows:- 1 Officer, 39 other ranks, 54 draught horses, 3 Riders, 24 Wagons G.S and 2 Limbers.

S. S. M. Harwood moved from FOUCAUCOURT to join Company at MERICOURT with portion of Supply Section as follows:- 18 other ranks, 26 draught horses, 2 riders, 11 G.S. Wagons & 2 Limbers.

Baggage Limber of Headquarters R.E. detached with C.R.E at HERBECOURT.

Supply Wagon of 428 Field Coy. R.E. returned to Company from 430 Company A.S.C.

APRIL 6th 1917 Friday at MERICOURT

Supplies for consumption on the 8th instant for Divisional Troops stationed at MERICOURT drawn in bulk by H.T. at CHUIGNES Railhead and issued by me to units at MERICOURT.

Train Post Office and Postal Wagon moved by order of A.D.P.S. from MERICOURT to CAPPY and attached to Lieut. Yeats' detachment.

No T/13822 Dr. Timms W. discharged from hospital

Company Routine

W. P. Reynolds MAJOR, A.S.C.
O.C. HD. QRS. COMPANY 42nd DIVL. TRAIN.

WAR DIARY

APRIL 7th 1917 Saturday. at MERICOURT

Supplies for Divisional Troops at MERICOURT drawn at Railhead by H.T. and issued by me to units, for consumption on the 9th instant.
4 Baggage Wagons of D.A.C. 4 pairs horses and 5 Drivers attached to Lieut. Yeats' section at CAPPY.
Supply Limber of H.Q. R.E. with driver and pair of L.D. horses attached to Supply Section of 429 Coy. under Lt. Morphy.
50 Officers N.C.Os and men attended lecture on Gas Defense.

APRIL 8th 1917 Sunday. at MERICOURT

Supplies for Divl. Troops drawn at Railhead and taken to 126th Bde. Dump at MORCOURT. No issue to units today.
Officers, N.C.Os and men who were unable to attend Gas lecture yesterday attended special lecture today.
1 Supply and 1 Baggage Wagon of D.A.C. and 8 Supply and Forage Wagons of 211th Bde. R.F.A. 10 pairs horses, 1 rider, 10 drivers and 1 Corporal

from Lieut. Yeats Section at CAPPY left today with 211th Bde. R.F.A. These vehicles etc. to be attached to 48th Divisional Train.

7/261140 Dr. Johns admitted to Hospital

Company Routine.

APRIL 9th 1917 Monday. at MERICOURT

Supplies for Divisional Troops from Railhead to MORCOURT. Coy. Rations drawn from 126th Bde. Dump at MORCOURT. 2 of the 8 missing H.D. horses which were found at Remounts ABBEVILLE and brought to MERICOURT by 430 Coy. A.S.C., were handed over to me by 430 Coy. today. One Wagon G.S. sent to 430 Coy. on March 30th returned to me today.

One Wagon G.S. with pair H.D. horses and driver attached permanently to 42nd Divl. Reinforcement Camp at MERIGNOLLES. One limber with pair of L.D. horses and driver returned from detachment with 431 Coy. A.S.C.

T/2016868 Dr. Charlish, W.A. admitted to hospital.

WAR DIARY.

APRIL 10th. 1917 Tuesday. AT MERICOURT

Supplies for Divisional Troops drawn as yesterday.

One H. D. Horse No 108 evacuated to Mobile Veterinary Section and struck off strength of Coy.

T4/123868 Dr. Boatwright admitted to hospital.

D. D. of S. & T. IIIrd Corps called and inspected the Company horses. He considered all horses were looking well.

Company Routine

APRIL 11th 1917 Wednesday. AT MERICOURT

Supplies drawn from divisional troop dump at Cappy (CAPPY)

Company Routine.

APRIL 12th 1917 THURSDAY. AT MERICOURT.

Supplies as yesterday from CAPPY.

The supply wagon of 428 Field Company R.E. with horses and driver sent to 429 Company A.S.C.

One Batman No T4/186301 Green G.F. sent to 429 Company A.S.C. in exchange for No T4/257535 Dr Cunningham G. posted to this Company.

APRIL. 13th. 1917 FRIDAY AT MERICOURT.

Supplies from CAPPY at 10.A.M.
Court Martial on Sadd. St. Sgt. Todd and Sergt. Vince at 2.30 pm
Company Routine.

APRIL 14th 1917 SATURDAY AT MERICOURT.

Supplies as yesterday.
One pair of horses with driver sent to divisional Hd. Qrs this morning, also one G.S. wagon with horses and driver and one G.S. limbered wagon.
One G.S. limbered wagon sent to A.P.M. complete with horses and driver.
These wagons to be used for moving D.H.Q. and the A.P.M. The spare pair of horses for D.H.Q. water cart.

Company Routine.

G.L. Stimson Capt.
for Major
O.C. Hd-Qrs Coy A.S.C. 42nd Divisional Train.

WAR DIARY

APRIL 15th 1917. SUNDAY at MERICOURT.

Supplies as yesterday. One G.S. wagon and 1 G.S. limbered wagon, complete, also 1 pair of horses returned by Divisional Hd-Qrs.

Company Routine.

APRIL 16th 1917. MONDAY AT MERICOURT.

Supplies as yesterday two days rations drawn. Baggage horses for C.R.A. have been sent to C.R.A. Hd-Qrs wagon for same already there. One G.S. limbered supply wagon sent to C.R.A. complete. No T/278625 Dr LOVE. A. and No 219822 Pte DONOHUE. H. sent to for eye treatment.

Company Routine.

APRIL 17th 1917 TUESDAY AT FONTAINE LES CAPPY.

2 G.S. wagons (supply) and 1 G.S. wagon (baggage) complete sent to No 2 section of D.A.C.

HD-QRS of company with portion of supply and baggage section moved to day to FONTAINE LES CAPPY. by road.
Capt CALDERWOOD A.V.C. remained at MERICOURT with the 19th mobile veterinary section.

APRIL 18th 1917 WEDENSDAY AT FONTAINE LES CAPPY.

This morning I destroyed horse No 106 belonging to [illegible] Coy A.S.C. This horse was left in my care as it was unfit to travel but had to be destroyed for debility.
The promulgation of the sentence of the F.G.C.M held on [illegible] Sgt Todd and [illegible] Vause was read to the company yesterday each was awarded "reduct to the ranks and imprisonment for [illegible] ~~days~~ months without hard labour" the sentence being commuted to "reduct to the ranks and [illegible] days field punishment No 2.

Company Routine.

APRIL 19. 1917 THURSDAY AT FONTAINE.

Company Routine.

Supplies from railhead CHOIGNES.

APRIL 20th 1917 FRIDAY. AT FONTAINE.

Lieut W. H. TAYLEUR joined the Company to day from 430 Company A.S.C.

Company Routine.

G.L. Stinnes Capt

O.C. 40-QRS Company A.S.C. 40th Div Train

APRIL 21st SATURDAY. AT FONTAINE-LES-CAPPY.

RATIONS DRAWN FROM DIVISIONAL TROOPS SUPPLY DUMP AT CAPPY.
1 PAIR OF H.D. HORSES WITH WAGON AND DRIVER WHICH HAS BEEN DETACHED AT THE REINFORCEMENT CAMP MERICOURT SINCE 7.4.17. HAS RETURNED TO THE COMPANY TO-DAY.

APRIL 22nd SUNDAY AT PERONNE.

RATIONS AS YESTERDAY.
HD-QRS OF COMPANY WITH PORTION OF SUPPLY AND BAGGAGE SECTIONS MOVED TO-DAY TO PERONNE.

APRIL 23rd MONDAY AT PERONNE.

RATIONS DRAWN FROM 125 BDE DUMP AT LE MESNIL BRUNTEL.
COMPANY ROUTINE.

APRIL 24th TUESDAY AT PERONNE.

RATIONS AS YESTERDAY. 12 LOADERS REPORTED FOR DUTY, FOR UNITS WHICH ARE TO BE RATIONED BY DIVISIONAL TROOPS SUPPLY OFFICER.
WAGON FOR 429 FIELD COMPANY R.E. RETURNED TO COMPANY FROM 431 COMPANY A.S.C. ALSO WAGON G.S. FOR No1 SECT D.A.C. AND LIMBERED WAGON FOR C.R.E. RETURNED FROM 430 COMPANY A.S.C.
COMPANY ROUTINE.

APRIL 25th Wednesday at Peronne.

Rations from divisional Troops dump at Peronne.
Lieut Yeats, after transporting supplies from railhead to divisional Troops dump, reported to company for duty with part of supply section.
Company Routine.

APRIL 26th Thursday at Peronne.
Company rations as yesterday.
Supply wagons at railhead at 11a.m. instead of 9.30a.m. as yesterday.
2 wagons reported for duty from 431 Company A.S.C. These wagons to draw rations for 1/5th Manchester Regiment which is at present being rationed by Divl. Troops Supply Officer.

APRIL 27th Friday at Peronne.
Company rations as yesterday.
Supply column wagons as yesterday.
The 2 supply wagons belonging to 431 Coy A.S.C. returned to day as the 1/5 Manchester Regiment is not to be supplied by Divl. Troops Supply Officer.
1G.S. Baggage wagon returned to the Company from C.R.A.

G.L. Plummer

APRIL 28th Saturday AT PERONNE.

Company rations as yesterday.
Supply column wagons as yesterday.
No T4/18129 Dr James. H.T. returned from Corps rest station Cerisy
No S4/08538 Pte Copie A and No S/312045 Pte Dingley S. H and No S/312306 Pte Brewis H H reported for duty as supply reinforcements.

APRIL 29th SUNDAY AT PERONNE

Company rations as yesterday.
Supply column wagons as yesterday.
Four R.A.M.C. men have reported for duty and have been disposed of as follows. No 350032 Cpl Howell. W.H. reported 29.4.17. posted to 428 Coy A.S.C. No 281 Pte Goddard reported 25.4.17. posted to 429 Coy A.S.C. No 350125 Pte Mattock reported 28.4.17 posted to 430 Coy A.S.C. No 621 Pte Fitzgerald reported 25.4.17 posted to 431 Coy A.S.C.
No T3/132 Dr Warburton. A, who has been on duty with the A.R.M. with a Limbered G.S. wagon and a pair of L.D. horses returned to duty with the company.
No T/34954 Dr Palmer. W.E. with the supply Limbered G.S. wagon for the C.R.A. has returned from that unit and reported to the company for duty.

APRIL 30th Monday at Peronne.

Company rations as yesterday.
The supply wagons of divisional Troops, in this vicinity proceeded to the divisional Troops dump this morning for the purpose of transporting rations and forage direct to units. In many cases these wagons were not required as units sent their 1st Line Transport
The supply reinforcements which reported for duty on the 25th inst have been disposed of this morning as follows Pte Capie to 429 Coy A.S.C. Pte Dingley to 430 Coy A.S.C. and Pte Brewis to 431 Coy A.S.C.
S.Q.M.S. Field No S/16051 evacuated to 1/2 field ambulance for debility
No T4/244870 Dr Jones. P. proceeded to Flixecourt this morning to attend a cookery class
No WT4/069939 S/Sgt Parkinson. A.V. proceeded to Mericourt-Sur-Somme. to attend a course of instruction at the divisional gas school.
No 354349 Pte Pearson. T. R.A.M.C. reported for duty.

~~April~~ May 1st Tuesday at Peronne.

No T1/3096 Dr Jordan has been detailed for duty at the reinforcement Camp Peronne.
No T4/244 C.S.M. Kershaw has been

evacuated to 1/2 Field Ambulance.
Pte Pearson R.A.M.C. who reported for duty yesterday has been sent to 429 Coy A.S.C. for duty.
Those wagons of the supply section which are actually being used at present have moved to TINCOURT to-day. The ration dump for Divisional troops has also moved and is now on the TINCOURT-DRIENCOURT road.
The second blanket which was drawn from ordnance stores some time ago for the men of this Company has been returned to ordnance.
The baggage wagon of the C.R.A. has reported to that unit for duty.

May 2nd Wednesday at TINCOURT.
Supplies from TINCOURT.
HD-Qrs of Company with portion of supply and baggage sections moved to-day to TINCOURT.
Cpl Heard together with 4 G.S wagons horses and drivers also 4 loaders has returned to the company from the 59th Divisional Train A.S.C.
2 G.S wagons 8 mules 4 drivers & 2 loaders have reported to me for duty from

"C" squad IIIrd Corps Cav. Regt.
Sec 5 / 7 G.S. wagons with horses drivers and loaders under a N.C.O. have reported for duty from the 48th Divisional Train.
No. 1/5786 [illegible] Love and No. 2/198 22 Pte Donoghue have been despatched to the base to-day under instructions received from train head-quarters office as being unfit for further active service in the field owing to physical unfitness.

APRIL 3rd Thursday. At Tincourt.
Rations as yesterday.
This morning we moved from our last nights position to the North Side of the Boire–Tincourt road map ref sheet 62c J.23.
The wagon for the 1/1st Field Ambulance complete with horses and driver has been sent to O.C. 429 Coy A.S.C. The Supply wagon for the 427th Field Company R.E., which is at present with that unit has been ordered to report to O.C. 429 Coy A.S.C.
The supply wagon complete for the 1/3rd Field Ambulance and loader has been sent to O.C. 430 Coy A.S.C. The Supply wagon detailed for 428 Field Company R.E. which is at present with that unit has been

ordered to report to O.C. 430 Coy A.S.C.
The supply wagon detailed for the 1/3rd Field Ambulance and the wagon detailed for 429 Field company R.E. together with 1 Ambulance loader and 2 R.E. loaders has been sent to O.C. 431 Coy A.S.C.
The wagons for 310 Bde R.F.A. with loaders which were attached to 431 Coy A.S.C. have returned to this Company for duty.
Horse No L-124 was destroyed to-day for debility.

APRIL 4th FRIDAY. AT TINCOURT.

No 254841 Pte Rearns P. and No 44?245 Dr Percival W. Hawes reported here to attend a course in cold shoeing, from 429 Coy R.E.
Supplies as yesterday.

C.H. Plummer

APRIL 5th Saturday at TINCOURT.

No WT4/069939 A/Sgt. Parkinson returned to-day from the divisional gas school Morcourt-sur-SOMME where he has been attending a Course.
3 Loaders from the Canadian Rly troop reported to the Company ~~yesterday~~ to-day for duty.
A loader reported for duty from "D" Bty 211th Bde.
Company Routine.
Rations as yesterday.

APRIL 6th Sunday at TINCOURT.

The loader from the "D" Bty 211 Bde has been sent to 1/2 Field Ambulance. Another loader has been applied for from this unit.
Rations as yesterday.

APRIL 7th MONDAY. AT TINCOURT.

No T4/186405 Dr Wolsey G.E. has been sent to 1/2nd Field Ambulance.
Rations as yesterday
Company Routine.

APRIL 8th Tuesday at TINCOURT.

Rations as Yesterday.
The refilling point moved this afternoon to the Station yard at Roisel.
Horses and drivers of 210th Bde R.F.A. and 42nd D.A.C. for baggage wagons have returned to the Company.
Company Routine.

APRIL 9th Wedensday at TINCOURT.

Refilling this morning at 10 A.M. at Roisel.
No T1/3104 14 C.S.M. Hirshaw returned to duty from 1/2nd Field Ambulance

APRIL 10th Thursday at TINCOURT.

Rations as yesterday.
Company Routine.

APRIL 11th. Friday at TINCOURT.

Supply wagons for artillery reported at refilling point at 10 A.M. all other wagons at 11 A.M.
No 169163 Gunner Burny reported from 'B' Bty 211 Bde for duty as a batman
No 75581 9 Pte Hunt evacuated to 1/2 Field Ambulance.

Company Routine.

G. L. Plummer

APRIL 12th 1917 Saturday at Tincourt

Refilling as yesterday.

No [illegible] Pte Middleton was admitted to 1/2 Field Ambulance this morning. The [illegible] have reported for duty No [illegible] Gnr. O'Sullivan T from No 2 Sect D.A.C. No 715539 Gnr Ware H from D Bty 210 Bde No 1263 Gnr Middlehurst from C Bty 210 Bde. Some shells fell in the vicinity this afternoon starting at about 2 p.m. Owing to this we have temporarily moved the horse lines about 1 mile S.W. of our present position. No damage was inflicted.

Company Routine.

APRIL 13th 1917 Sunday at Tincourt.

Refilling as yesterday

No 14/186129 Dr Jones was admitted to 1/2 Field Ambulance this morning.

Company Routine

Horse lines have now been brought back to the original position

APRIL 14th 1917 MONDAY AT TINCOURT.

Refilling as yesterday.

There was a violent thunderstorm in the vicinity this morning starting at about 3.45 A.M. and finishing about 4.30 A.M. The men of the Company suffered considerable discomforts owing to the fact that little or no shelter of any description has been provided for them.

The transport attached to this Company from the 48th Divisional Train has returned to that train to-day i.e. 5 G.S. wagons complete with drivers horses and leaders and one mounted Corporal.

H.D. horse No 78 evacuated to 19th Mob. Vet.

No 715293 Bdr. Staunton [illegible] reported for duty from "D" by 211th Bde for duty as loader.

APRIL 15th 1917 Tuesday AT TINCOURT.

Refilling as yesterday.

H.D. Horse No 148 evacuated to 19th Mob. Vet.

Company Routine.

APRIL 16th Wednesday at Tincourt.

Refilling as yesterday
No 104435 Pte McKay Canadian Rly Troops who is attached to this company as a loader has been admitted to the 1/2nd Field Ambulance.
H.D. horse No 25 strayed from grazing at 5 P.M to-day.

APRIL 18th Friday at Tincourt.

Refilling as on 16th.
Transport belonging to Surrey Yeomanry has been returned to that unit today, this consists of 4 drivers 8 mules 2 loaders and two wagons.
Company Routine.

APRIL 19 Saturday at Tincourt.
Refilling as yesterday
H.D horse No 525 was destroyed this morning with a compound fracture of the off hind.
The supply wagon of the signal company after refilling this morning followed on after the unit, it will report to night to OC 430 Coy A.S.C.

G.T. Hammond

APRIL 20th Sunday at Tincourt.

Refilling as yesterday.
All the baggage horses for the R.F.A. and D.A.C. have been sent to their respective units. Two supply wagons for 'D' Battery 210th Bde have been sent to that unit.

Company Routine.

APRIL 21st ~~Sunday At~~ Monday at Tincourt.

Refilling as yesterday.
After refilling the wagons which are detailed for those units which are moving to-day proceeded to the new area. After delivering the supplies they will report to O.C. 430 Coy A.S.C. and will refill to-morrow at the dump of the 126 Bde. These wagons will return to the company when we move to the new area.

Company Routine.

APRIL 22nd Tuesday at Bus

Refilling at 6 a.m. this morning
The Head-Quarters of the company moved to-day to Bus (map of Sheet 57C D30a 6.9.)
The supply section of the Company moved under O/C supply sect and reported to the Company in the evening. Those wagons which were with 430 Coy A.S.C. have

(Tues. Cont)
also returned to the company.

APRIL 23rd 1917 Wednesday at Bus.

Rations have been drawn by the supply section from Railhead at Rocquigny and taken to the R.P. situated at (sheet 57c) 24.B.9.2. These rations were then taken on to the units at 2p.m.

Company Routine.

APRIL 25th 1917 Friday at Bus.

Refilling as on 23rd.

No 16472 Gnr Wood W.H. admitted to the Field Ambulance.

No T/4 156129 Dr James J. admitted to No 5 C.C.S. from 92 Field Ambulance.

Company Routine.

Saturday 26th May 1917 at Bus.

I moved the lines to-day and took up a position vacated by the no company of the 20th Divisional Train. Map ref (Sheet 57c) O30 a 6.9
Refilling as yesterday.

Sunday 27th May 1917 at Bus.

Refilling as yesterday
No T/244570 Dr Jones P. returned to the company for duty from a cooking course at Flixecourt
Company Routine

Monday 28th May 1917 at Bus.

No 6312 Gnr Turner J. reported for duty as a loader from No 3 sect. D.A.C.
Refilling as yesterday
Company Routine.

Tuesday 29th May 1917 at Bus

Refilling as yesterday
Company Routine.

Wednesday 30th May 1917 AT BUS.

Refilling as Yesterday.

No 1272 Gnr Hampson J.V. reported for duty with the company as loader from No 3 Sect D.A.C.

No TSR/462 C.Q.M.S. Hatherley J. admitted to 1/3 Field Ambulance.

Company Routine.

Thursday 31st May 1917 AT BUS.

Refilling as Yesterday.

No T4/036635 Dr Hulme J. admitted to 1/3 Field Ambulance

Company Routine.

Friday 1st June 1917 AT BUS.

Refilling as Yesterday

No 126909 Lc Corp Munn. A.W. and No 127344 Pte Turner. R.G. and No 127321 Pte Symonds. S. reported to the company for duty from the Royal Fusiliers Labour Company, as loaders

Company Routine.

C.H. Turner.

Saturday 2nd May 1917 AT Bus.

Refilling as Yesterday
Some Gunners who was attached to the company as loaders have been sent back to their units to-day
Company Routine

Sunday 3rd May 1917 AT Bus.

Refilling as Yesterday.
S2SR/04223 Staff Sgt Osborne H admitted to Field Ambulance.
Company Routine.

Tuesday 5th May 1917 AT Bus.

Refilling as on the 3rd
No T4/162059 Dr Denby A. admitted to Field ambulance
H.D. horse No L1-151 sent to Mobile Vet. Section and riding horse No L1-3 sent to mobile vet section
Company Routine

Wednesday 6th May 1917 AT Bus.

Refilling as Yesterday.
Company Routine.

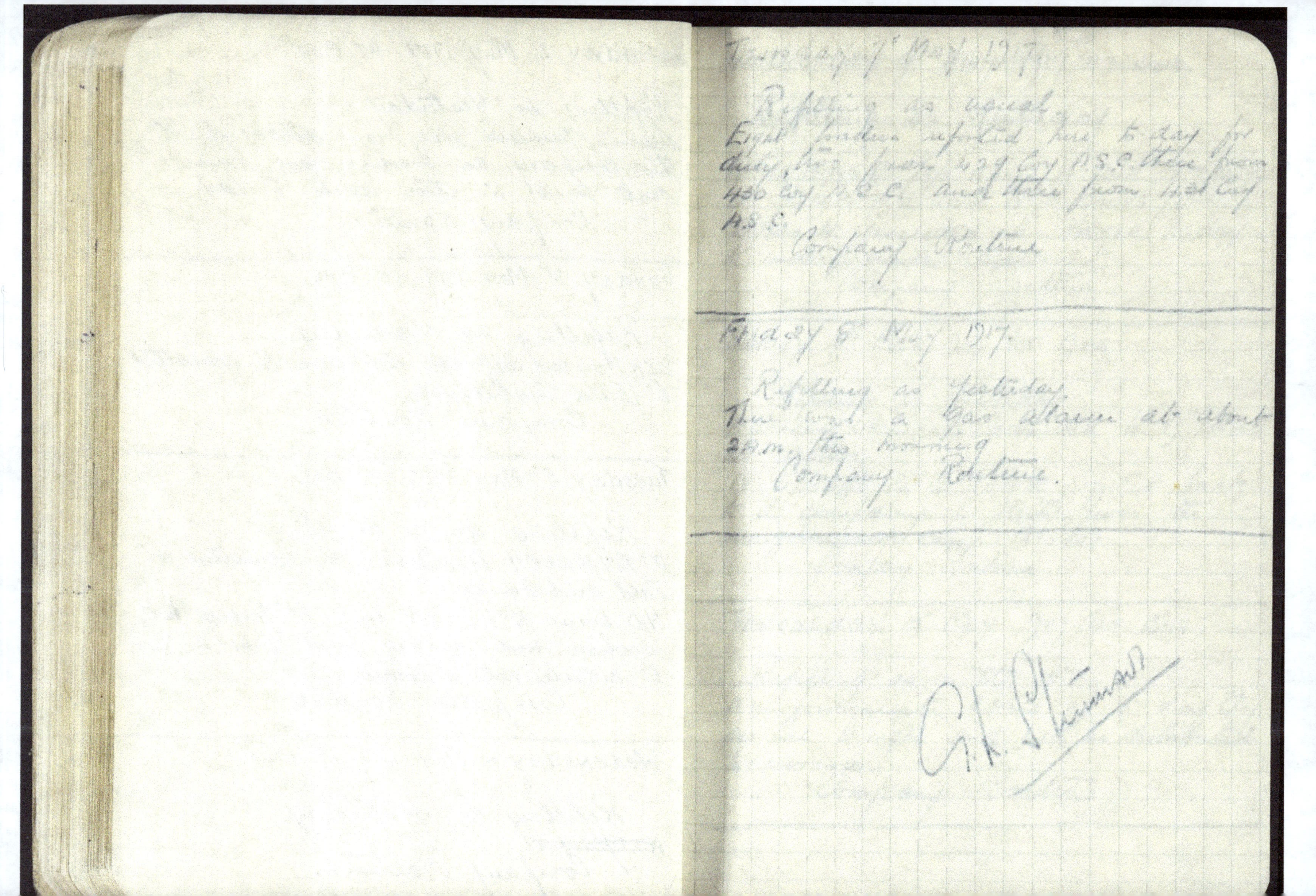

Thursday 4th May 1917.

Refilling as usual.
Eight Sadlers reported here to day for duty, two from 429 Coy A.S.C. three from 430 Coy A.S.C. and three from 431 Coy A.S.C.
Company Routine

Friday 5th May 1917.

Refilling as yesterday
There was a Gas alarm at about 2 a.m. this morning
Company Routine.

G.A. Stimson

Saturday 9th May 1917 At Bus.

Refilling as Yesterday

No T4/039887 S/Cpl White H and No T34594 Dr Palmer W.E. and No T4/244876 Dr Dyson W. proceeded to Havre to-day to undergo dental treatment.

Company Routine

Sunday 10th May 1917 At Bus

Refilling as Yesterday

HD horse No L1-166 admitted to 19th Mobile Vet section.

No T4/3296 Dr Jordan W reported back to the company for duty from the reinforcement camp Peronne.

Company Routine

Wednesday 13th May 1917 At Bus.

Refilling as on the 10th.

Reinforcements came up to-day they are here to-night and will be distributed to-morrow.

Company Routine

Thursday 14 May 1917 AT Bus.

Refilling as yesterday
The following men have been posted to the company:-
N° T/259647 Dr Simkin H., T/260890 Dr Fletcher
N° S/217698 Pte Huish H. E. J. S/290654 Pte Evans. D.
and S/367209 Pte Mayo A.G.

Company Routine

Friday 15th May 1917 AT Bus.

Refilling as yesterday
N° T1/317 Dr Henry. E.C. admitted to Field Ambulance.
The following have reported here for duty as loaders:-
N° 588 Cpl Taylor, N° 241393 Pte Turner N° 281739
Pte Hoole N° 3644 Pte Joy. These men will be transferred to the 239th Labour Company
Company Routine.

C.H. Stimson.

Saturday 16th May 1917 at Bus.

Refilling as yesterday.

The following have reported to the Company for duty as loaders, No 30444 Pte Joy 1/5 Manchester Regt. No 1688 Cpl Taylor 42nd Divisional Signal Coy No 241393 Pte Turner 1/6 Lancs Fus. No 281739 Pte Hook 1/7 Lancs Fus. No 280693 Pte Taylor 1/7 Lancs Fus No 282195 Pte Cryer J. 1/7 Lancs Fus. No 706408 Dr Smith A Bty 210 Bde No 700316 Dr Wheele B Bty 210 Bde

The have replaced the following who have returned to their units

No 2488 Gnr Thorpe Hd. Qrs D.A.C No 97395 Gnr Tylke No 3 Sect D.A.C. No 6310 Gnr Turner No 3 Sect D.A.C. No 444382 Sapper Sidebottom 42nd Divisional Sig Coy No 700865 Gnr Tasker "A" Bty 210 Bde No 700333 Dr Urmston "A" Bty 210 Bde. No 700455 Dr Sharples "B" Bty 210 Bde No 598 Gnr Strahan W "C" Bty 210 Bde

Company Routine.

Sunday 17th May 1917 at Bus.

~~No 305~~ Refilling as yesterday

The following have reported to the Coy for duty as loaders.

No 305671 Pte Hussey 1/8 Lancs. Fus.

No 11530 Pte Lowe 1/5 Lancs Fus.
No 305671 Pte Goodwin 1/5 Lancs Fus.
No 210016 Pte Barron D.H.O.
No 200053 Pte Moulds D.H.O.
They have replaced the following who have been returned to their units
No 169163 Gnr Emery "B" Bty 211 Bde.
No 1587 Gnr Forshaw "C" Bty 211 Bde
No 1077 Gnr Hayes "C" Bty 211 Bde
No 715393 Bdr Spainton "D" Bty 211 Bde
No 201429 Pte Clewort[illegible] C.R.E.
Company Routine

Monday 15 May 1917 at Bus.

Refilling as yesterday.
The NCO and one man for the day have [illegible] accompanied for the purpose of bringing back remounts
The following have reported here as loaders
No 306970 Pte Jackson 1/5 Lancs Fus.
He replaced the following who has been returned to his unit
No 2073 Gnr Wood W. N Mid D.A.C.
Company Routine.

Tuesday 19 May 1917 At Bus

Refilling as yesterday

The following have reported here for duty as loaders

No 273560 Pte Trowbridge 1/7 Manchesters in relief the following who has been returned to his unit.

No 18660 Pte Bignell 19th Mob Vet Sect

No S/307259 Pte Mayo was admitted to hospital this morning

4 H.D. remounts have been taken on the strength of the company today.

Company Routine

Friday 22 May 1917 At Bus.

Refilling as yesterday

No 305970 Pte Jackson admitted to hospital this morning

Company routine.

Saturday 23 May 1917 At Bus

Refilling as yesterday

Company Routine

The following have been sent

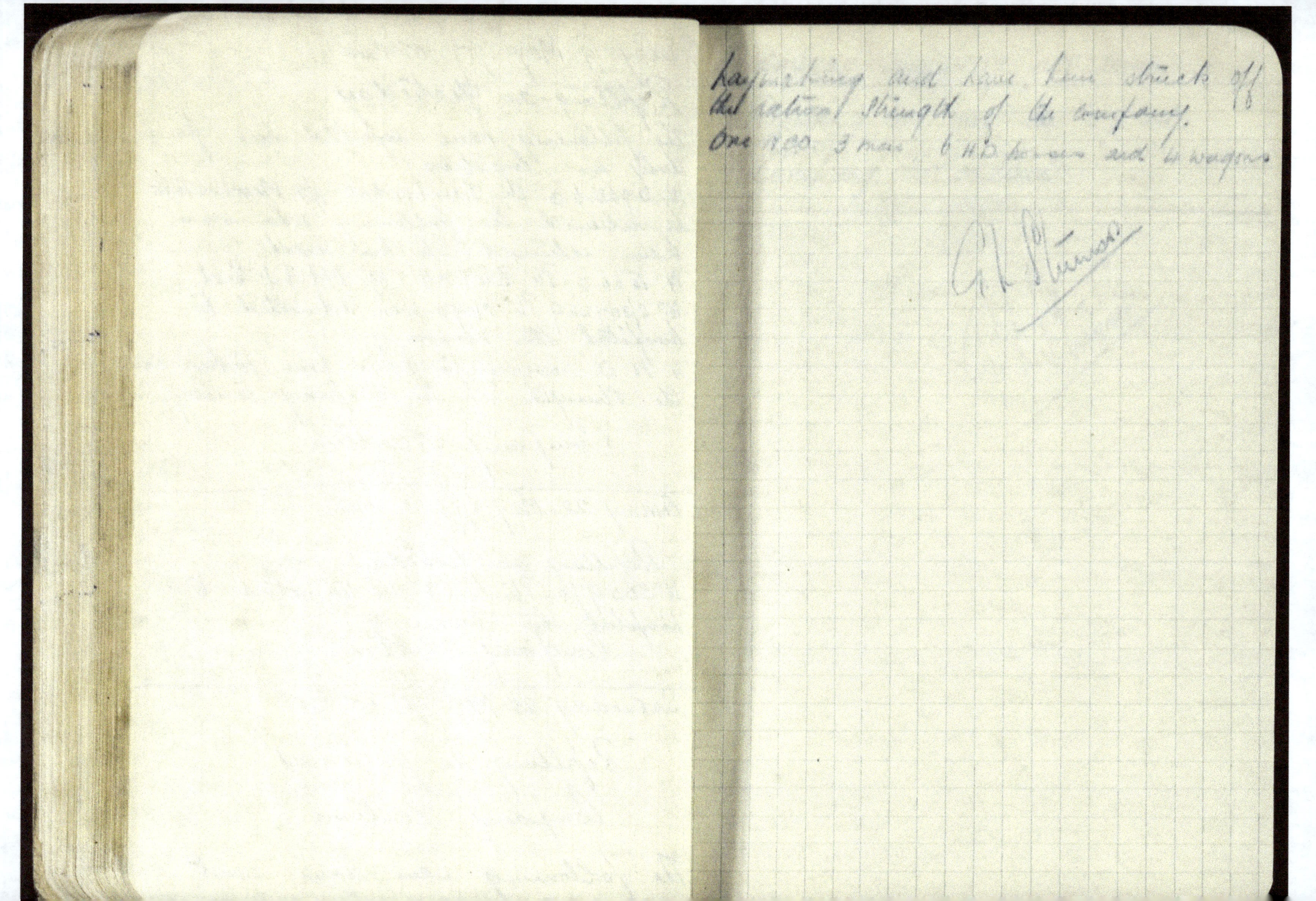

haymaking and have been struck off
the ration strength of the company. 16
One N.C.O. 3 men, 6 H.D. horses and 4 wagons

Friday 29 June 1917 at Bus.

Refitting as on the 27 and

Company Routine.

SATURDAY 30th JUNE 1917 AT BUS

Refilling as yesterday
No 350646 Pte COLLINS 1/9 MANCHESTERS has reported to the company for duty as a loader and has replaced No 2741 Dr Robinson "A" Bty 210 Bde who has been returned to his unit
Company Routine

SUNDAY 1st JULY 1917 AT BUS.

Refilling as yesterday.
No T4/86 448 Dr Smith F who was on duty at D H Q has been admitted to hospital. He has been replaced by No T4/186418 Dr Wilton H.F.
Company Routine

MONDAY 2nd JULY 1917 AT BUS.

Refilling as yesterday
No 11530 Pte LANE F admitted to hospital
No T4/206594 Dr LIVINGSTONE F.S. attached to the company with effect from the 1st inst.
Gas Alarm was given last ~~night~~ to-night at about 11 p.m. and lasted till about 1 A.M. the following morning
Company Routine.

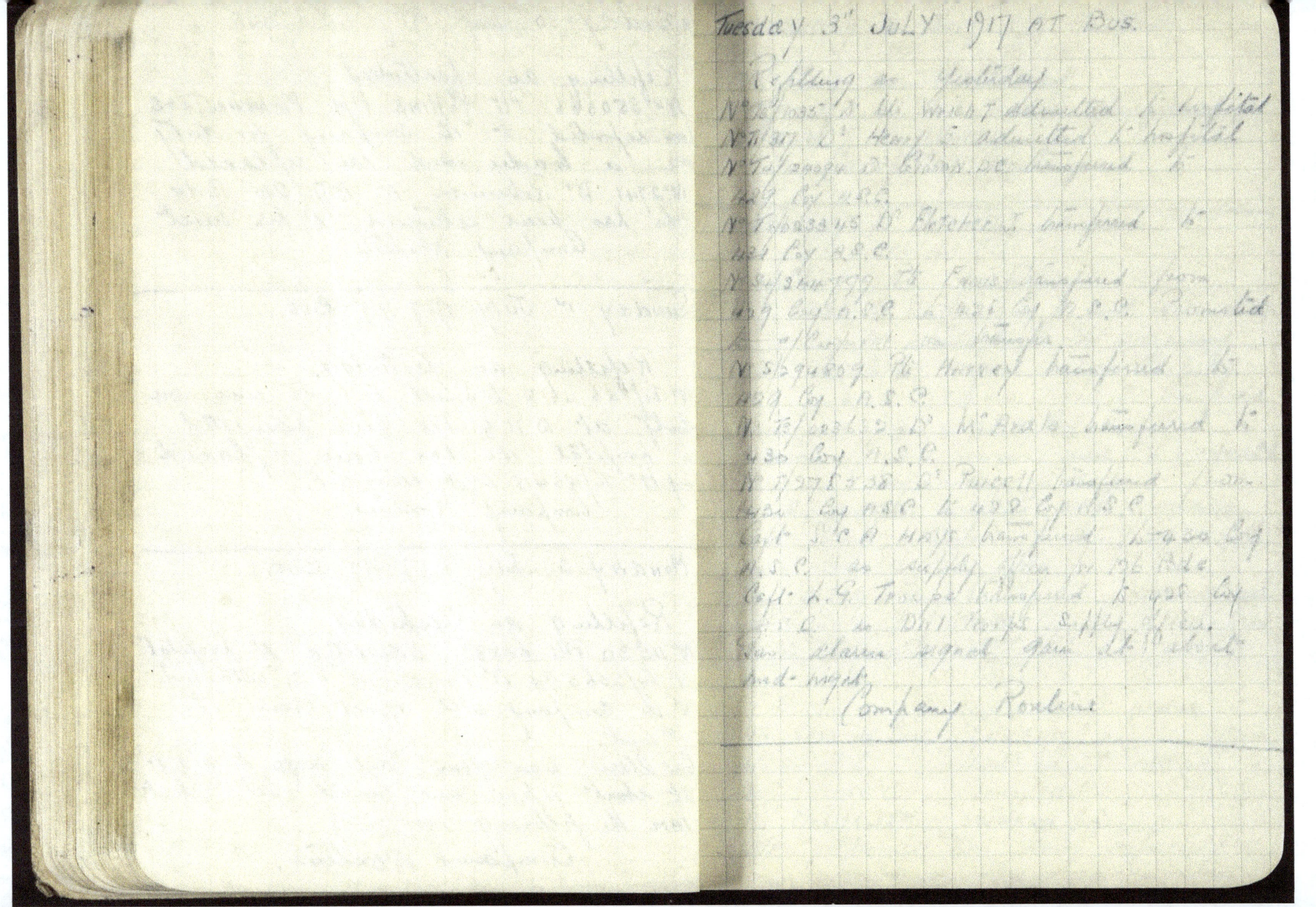

Tuesday 3rd July 1917 at Bus.

Refilling as yesterday

No T4/1035 Dr W. Wright admitted to hospital

No T1/317 Dr Henry [illegible] admitted to hospital

No T4/2909 Dr Brown [illegible] transferred to 429 Coy A.S.C.

No T4/053345 Dr Fletcher transferred to 424 Coy A.S.C.

No S4/244779 Pte Evans transferred from 429 Coy A.S.C. to 426 Coy A.S.C. Reverted to Pte at own request.

No S4/094807 Pte Harvey transferred to 429 Coy A.S.C.

No T3/022672 Dr McArdle transferred to 430 Coy A.S.C.

No T/29788 Dr Purcell transferred from 430 Coy A.S.C. to 428 Coy A.S.C.

Capt J. C. A. Hays transferred to 430 Coy A.S.C. as supply officer in 136 Bde.

Capt L. G. Trouse transferred to 428 Coy A.S.C. as Div. Troops Supply Officer.

Gas alarm signal given at 11 o'clock mid-night.

Company Routine

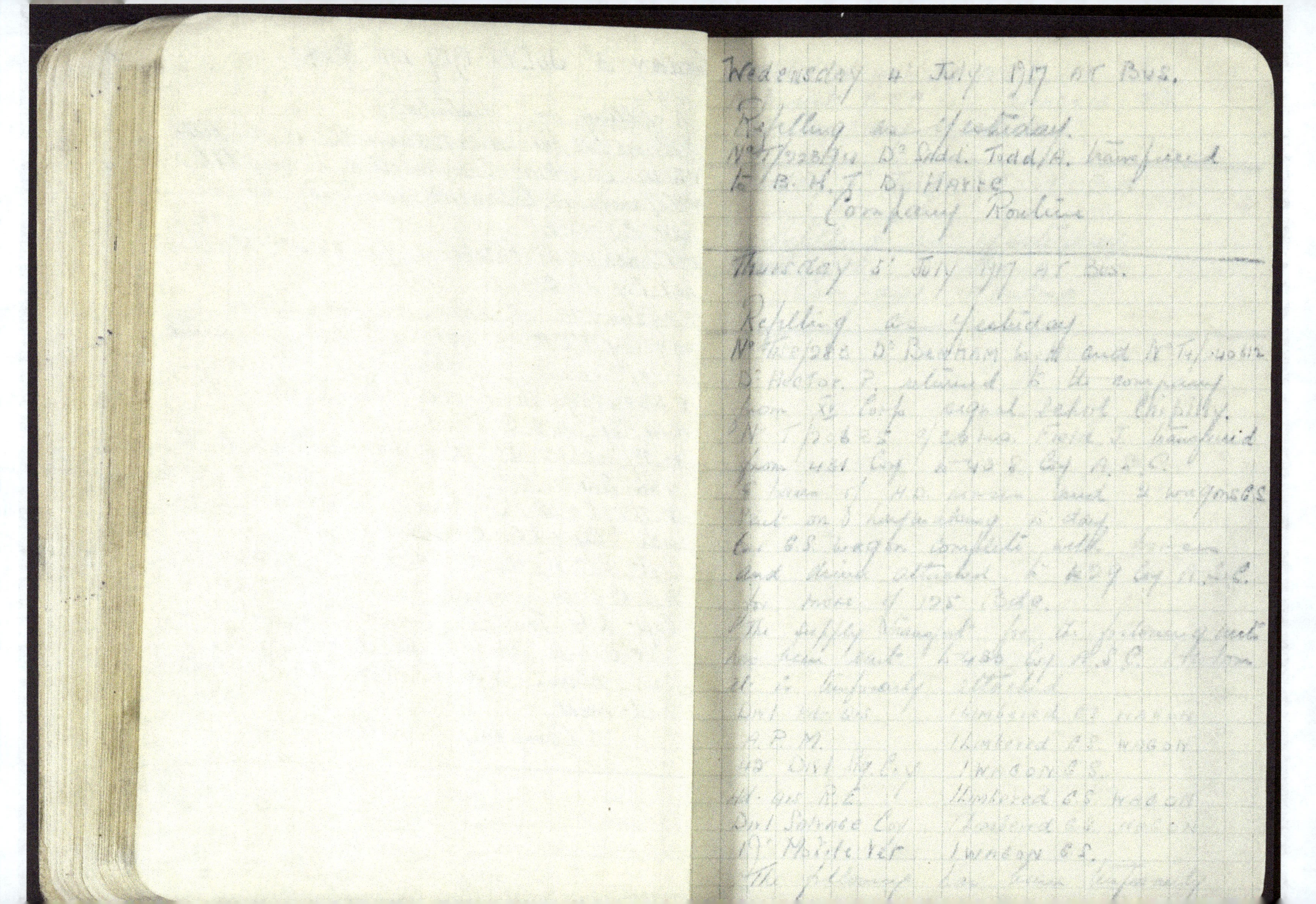

Wednesday 4 July 1917 At Bus.

Refilling as yesterday.
No T/228?4 Dr Sadd. Todd/A. transferred
to B.H.T. D. Havre
Company Routine

Thursday 5 July 1917 At Bus.

Refilling as yesterday
No T4/2822 Dr Bedham [illegible] and No T4/40612
Dr Hector P. returned to the company
from [illegible] Corps signal school Chipilly.
No T/[illegible] [illegible] transferred
from 481 Coy to 426 Coy A.S.C.
[illegible] H.D. [illegible] and 2 wagons G.S.
[illegible] on [illegible] today
[illegible] G.S. wagon complete with [illegible]
and driver attached to 427 Coy A.S.C.
[illegible] 125 Bde.
The supply [illegible] for the following units
has been [illegible] to 426 Coy A.S.C. [illegible]
[illegible] temporarily attached
Dvl [illegible] [illegible] G.S. wagon
A.P.M. Limbered G.S. wagon
42 Dvl [illegible] 1 wagon G.S.
[illegible] R.E. Limbered G.S. wagon
Dvl Salvage Coy Limbered G.S. wagon
1/1 Mobile Vet 1 wagon G.S.
The following [illegible] temporarily

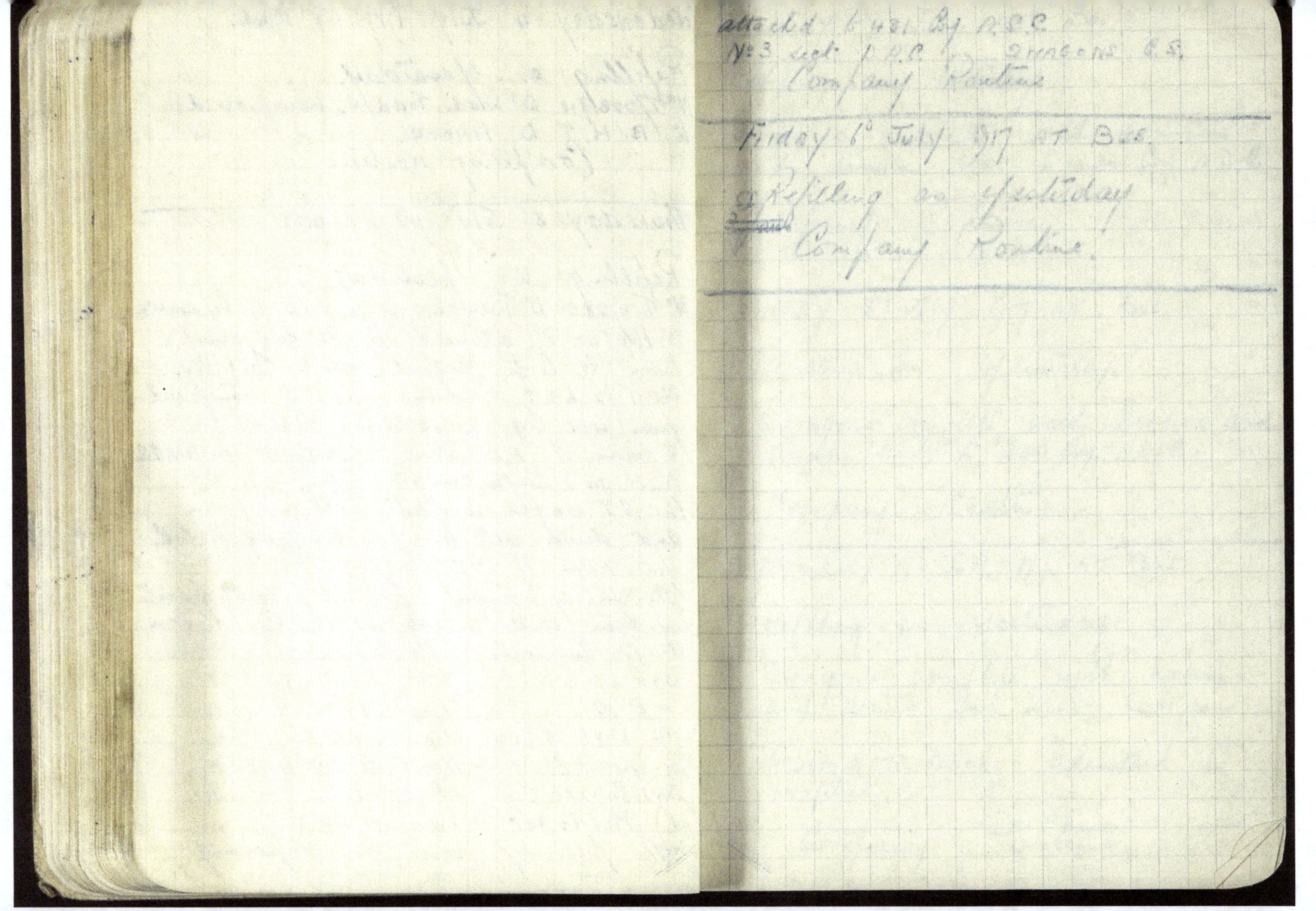

attached 6 431 By R.S.C.
No 3 sgt R.S.C. 2 masons R.S.
Company Routine

Friday 6th July 917 at B.cs.

Refilling as yesterday
Company Routine!

Saturday 7th July AT Bus.

Refilling as yesterday

3 wagons complete with horses and drivers sent to 430 Coy A.S.C.

Company Routine

Sunday 8th July 1917 AT Bus.

Refilling as yesterday.

8 wagons complete with horses and drivers sent to 431 Coy A.S.C.

Company Routine.

Monday 9th July 1917 AT Bus.

Refilling as yesterday

2 wagons complete with horses and drivers sent to 4th D.H.Q.

No 200013 Pte Barker admitted to hospital.

Company Routine.

Tuesday 10 July 1917 AT Bus.

Refilling as yesterday

3 wagons complete with horses and drivers returned from 430 Coy A.S.C.

2 wagons complete with horses and drivers returned from 42 D.A.C.

Company Routine

Wednesday 11 July 1917 AT Bus.

Refilling as yesterday

8 wagons complete with horses and drivers returned from 431 Coy A.S.C.

Company Routine

Friday 13 July 1917 AT Bus.

Refilling as on the 11 inst.

No 2/244799 Cpl Ennis H admitted to hospital.

No 1228 C/L Taylor F. returned to 239 labour company.

No 127332 Pte Thurgood reported to the company for duty from 239 labour company

Company Routine

C. J. Pimm[?]

25
20
———
500
═══

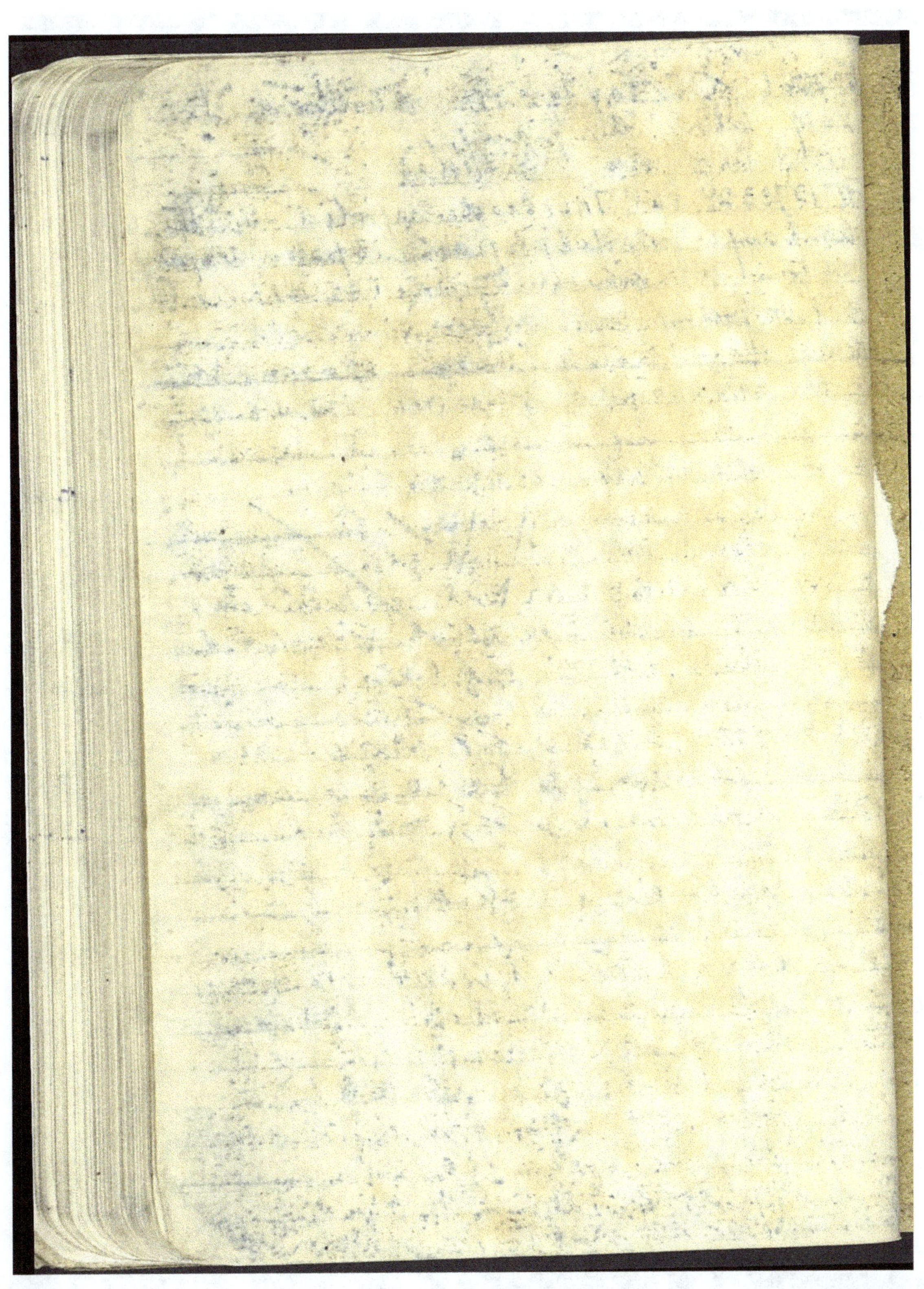

War Diary

428–31

Sunday 21/7/1918

T/32304 a/Sgt. SWEENEY W. applied for Temporary Commission in Infantry.
Company routine.

H.P.

Monday 22/7/1918

2nd Lieut. J.P. BLACKMORE proceeds on leave to England
Company routine

H.P.

Tuesday 23/7/1918

Two Farrier Cpls. arrived as reinforcements from the Base.
Dvr. J. Hunt applying for Commission is passed medically unfit. (eyesight). Company routine.
Box Respirator drill at night.

H.P.

Wednesday 24/7/18
Thursday 25/7/18
Friday 26/7/18.
Company Routine.
D.A.D.V.S. Saw horses

H.P.

Saturday 27/7/18.

H.D. 211 evacuated to 19th M.V.S
Board of Officers to test Shoeingsmiths
T.R.O. 471. d. 25/7/18. Heavy Rain.
General routine

H.P.

Sunday 28/7/1918

General Routine.

HPW/

Monday 29/7/1918.

Bathing parade for Loaders. Board assembled at No 2 Coy. for audit of Company accounts.

Conference at Bns on "Canteens", attended by O.C., and report rendered to I.H.Q.

General Routine.

HPW/

Tuesday 30/7/1918.

Farr. Cpl. HARTIN G.F. surplus to establishment, transferred to Bn. Bathing parade for Company.

Whr. LONERGAN returned from duty at No 28 Light Mobile Workshop.

HPW/

Wednesday 31/7/1918.

Bathing parade Coy.

General routine.

HPW/

Thursday 1/8/1918.

Major H.P. Williams M.C. proceeded on leave to England. Lieut. W.W. Yeats in temporary command. One N.C.O. with driver to Abbeville for remounts.

General Routine.

E.J.

Friday. 2/8/1918.

Capt. E.F. SPRECKLEY and Capt. J.L. GRAHAM returned from leave.

General Routine.

E.J.

Saturday. 3/8/1918

Capt. E.F. SPRECKLEY assumed command of the Company.

7 Riders and 1 L.D. remounts for the Train arrived.

General Routine

E.J.

Sunday 4/8/1918.

Remounts which arrived on 3/8/18 allotted to Companies. 3 Riders taken on strength.

General Routine

E.J.

Monday 5/8/1918.

G.S. Wagon complete, with Horses and driver, arrived from ABBEVILLE, as authorised additional transport for the

E.J.

Machine Gun Btn.
4 Drivers, reinforcements, arrived from Base.

General Routine.

Tuesday 6/8/1918

Sdr. LOOKE. C.R. to 3rd. Army Rest Camp. Bathing parade.

General Routine

Wednesday 7/8/1918

Sgt. SWEENEY. W. tried by C.O. for "neglect of duty" and severely reprimanded. Bathing parade.

General Routine

Thursday 8/8/1918

2nd. Lieut. J.P. BLACKMORE returned from leave.

General Routine.

Friday 9/8/18

Company parade. Inspection of arms, equipment and clothing.
Lieut. W.W. YEATS returned to No 4 Coy.

General Routine

Saturday. 10/8/1918.

1 N.C.O. + driver to PUNCHEVILLERS, returning same day with 3. H.D. — taken on strength.

General Routine. E.D.

Sunday. Aug. 11/1918. E.D.

General Routine

Monday. Aug. 12/1918. E.D.

General Routine

Tuesday. Aug. 13/1918. E.D.

Pay Parade. Bathing parade.

General routine

Wednesday Aug. 14/1918. E.D.

Bathing parade.

General routine

Thursday. Aug. 15/1918. E.D.

General routine.

Friday. Aug. 16/1918. E.D.

Company parade: inspection of arms, clothing + equipment. General Routine.

Saturday Aug. 17. 1918
Inspection of E.D.
Horses by. D.A.D.V.S.
General routine

Sunday Aug. 18. 1918
General routine E.D.

Monday Aug. 19. 1918
Two wagons, complete, for Divl. Salvage Officer, attached to 2 Company E.D.
General routine.

Tuesday Aug. 20. 1918
Bathing parade. E.D.
General routine.

Wednesday Aug. 21. 1918.
Bathing parade E.D.
Baggage Wagons + Horses sent to the Pioneer Bttn.

Thursday Aug. 22. 1918 E.D.
Capt. J.L. Graham to Croisilles i/c Agriculture detachment.

Friday Aug. 23rd.

General Routine.

E.D.

Saturday Aug. 24

E.D.

2 Baggage Wagons returned from Pioneer Btn.
Company parade, inspection of equipment, Arms, & clothing.
General routine

Sunday Aug. 25. Company moved at 4.p.m. to BERTRANCOURT

E.D.

Monday Aug. 26 Company moved at 7.30 a.m., and camped on MIRAUMONT - IREES road. Supply dump on camp.

E.D.

Tuesday Aug. 27 General Routine and arranging camp. Vicinity of camp shelled at 5 p.m

E.D.

Wednesday 28/8/18.

General routine. E.D.

Thursday. 29/8/18

General routine E.D.

Friday. 30/8/18.

Intermittent hostile shelling of area in proximity of camp, from 10/30a.m to 5/30 p.m E.D.

MAYFIELD. W. Dvr. Wk wounded in the head by shrapnel, and detained in Dressing station. Company moved at 6 p.m, nearer to Miraumont, and camped near the railway.

Saturday. 31/8/18. E.D.

One H.D. horse found dead at Reveille. General routine work in Camp.

Sunday Sept 1/1918. General Routine

H.P.W.

Monday Sept 2/1918. General Routine

H.P.W.

Tuesday Sept 3/1918. General Routine

H.P.W.

Wednesday Sept 4/1918. Major H P WILLIAMS returned from leave, and assumed command of the Coy.

Coy. moved to camp on ALBERT.-BAPAUME road. Sheet 57. C. N.6.c.8.3. Dump near to Camp.

H.P.W.

Thursday Sept 5 1918. Camp being required by the C.H.M.C., Coy. moved to opposite side of the road.

H.P.W.

Friday Sept. 6. 1918. No refilling at dump, owing to the late arrival of supplies. Driver STANLEY placed in arrest, for drunkenness.

H.P.W.

Saturday Sept. 7. 1918.
Coy. moved at 10 a.m to VILLERS au FLOS. Map ref. Sheet 57. C. O.7. C.1.1.
HPL

Sunday Sept. 8. 1918.
Dvr. Stanley. W. charged with drunkenness, remanded by C.O. for F.G.C.M.
Company moved to camp near BAPAUME Dump near to camp on the BAPAUME-PERONNE road.
HPL

Monday. Sept. 9. 1918.
Pte. BARNES. P. found medically unfit to undergo sentence of F.P. No1. at A.P.M.
Dvr. W. STANLEY — summary of evidence taken.
HPL

Tuesday. Sept. 10. 1918
General Routine
HPL

Wednesday Sept. 11. 1918.
T/26513 S/Sgt. GLOVER. T. attached to 1/8th Manchesters for one months' probation for Commission
HPL

Thursday Sept. 12. 1918.

General Routine.

H.P.W.

Friday. Sept. 13. 1918.

Farrier RAYBOULD. W.T. remanded by C.O., for "absent off leave to U.K. H.D. Horses 109 and 209, lost on 10/9/18 when on detachment with Divl. Mobile Canteen, and struck off strength. Auth:- 42nd Div. Q. 2/556

H.P.W.

Saturday Sept. 14. 1918.

Dvr. STANLEY. W. tried by F.G.C.M: 2 H.D. Horses slightly wounded by shrapnel, when in B/210 supply wagon.

H.P.W.

Sunday Sept. 15. 1918.

Farrier RAYBOULD. W.T awarded 21 days. F.P. No 1. by. C.O. for absence from leave.

2nd Lieut. J.P. BLACKMORE treated at 1/1. E.L.F.A. and afterwards evacuated to 3rd C.C.S, suffering from serious injuries received when out riding on duty.

Company parade. Inspection of Arms and equipment, also Field dressings, and identity discs.

H.P.W.

Monday. Sept. 16. 1918.

Farrier RAYBOULD sent to A.P.M. to undergo sentence.

Company paid

H.P.W.

Tuesday. Sept. 17. 1918.

One remount H.D. received and taken on strength.

H.D. 262 Killed by shell fire, when attached to "C/210".

Driver. W. STANLEY, promulgation of sentence. Awarded 90 days. F.P. No 2, and fined £1, by F.G.C.M. 14/9/18.

H.P.W.

Wednesday. Sept. 18. 1918

Dvr. W. STANLEY sent to A.P.M. to undergo sentence.

H.D. Horses. 229 + 237 to 19th M.V.S. for casting.

H.D. 225 to M.V.S.

H.P.W.

Thursday. Sept. 19. 1918.

General routine.

H.P.W.

Friday. Sept. 20. 1918.

General routine.

H.P.W.

Saturday. Sept. 21. 1918

General routine. H.P.W.

Sunday 22nd Sept. 1918.

General routine H.P.W.

Monday. 23rd. Sept. 1918.

General routine H.P.W.

Tuesday. 24th. Sept. 1918.

Baggage wagons returned from Units

H.D. 95 admitted to M.V.S. 1 Wheeler and 1 driver, taken on strength from Base. General routine. H.P.W.

Wednesday. 25th. Sept. 1918

7 H.D. remounts received General routine. H.P.W.

Thursday. 26th. Sept. 1918

General Routine. H.P.W.

Friday 27th Sept. 1918

Preparations for a probable move at short notice. H.P.W.

Saturday 28th. Sept. 1918.

Baggage wagons sent to Units: Company moved at 9.45 a.m to Sheet 57C. - O.23.a.5.8 - BUS-BARASTRE Road. Refilling point in Camp. Fair accommodation and stabling H.P.W.

Sunday. 29th Sept. 1918.

Dvr. STRIPLING. A. awarded 21 days. F.P. No1, by C.O., for absence from leave.

General routine

HRC

Monday. 30th Sept. 1918.

Company moved at 9.30 a.m. to NEUVILLE-BOURJONAL. Ref:- Sheet 57C. R22. b. 8. 8. Good accommodation Refilling point. P.23. c. 6. 5.

Company paid.

HRC

Tuesday 1st Octr. 1918

Driver HANSON. C. to Rest Camp ST. VALERY.

Divisional Troops dept. of Ordnance attached to the Company, + dump established at Supply refilling point

First blanket issued to N.C.O's and men.

Driver HADLEY. J. to 1/1st. E.L.F.A. - Accidental injuries received when on duty.

HRC

Wednesday 2nd. Octr. 1918

Dvr. CAMBLE T. to DOULLENS. for interview with Officer of the Royal Air Force respecting transfer.

HRC

Thursday. 3rd. Octr. 1918.

Dvr. LEWIS. awarded 7 days. C.C. by. C.O. for making a disrespectful reply to a N.C.O.

General routine

Inspection of Salvage Coys transport

Friday. 4th. Octr. 1918

H.B.

General routine.

Inspection Bde. Coys detached wagons

Saturday. 5th. Octr. 1918.

H.B.

Dvr MASON. P. admitted to 1/3rd E.L.F.A. suffering from a scalded foot

Dvr. WELSH. R admitted to 1/3rd E.L.F.A. suffering from injuries to feet & legs caused by the explosion of a shell fuse

General Routine

H.B.

Sunday 6th Octr. 1918.

At Neuville.

General Routine. Driver MASON P evacuated to 29. C.C.S.

HPW

Monday 7th Octr. 1918.

Notification received that Dvr. STRIPLING, undergoing F.P. had been evacuated to 56. C.C.S.

Leather Jerkins issued to Company. General Routine

HPW

Tuesday 8th Octr. 1918.

One H. D. Remount taken on strength.

Company stands to for probable move at short notice.

HPW

Wednesday 9th Octr. 1918

Company moved at 09.00, and camped near BEAUCAMP. Accommodation – sunken road and dug-outs. Supply dump at Beet factory in village, ½ mile from Company. Map Refs. Sheet 57C. Coy. Q.17.d. central. Dump Q.17.d.3.3.

Authority received for 2nd Lieut J.P. BLACKMORE to be struck off strength.

HPW

Thursday. 10th Octr. 1918.

Company moved at 08·00 and camped on LESDAIN – ESNES Road. Supply dump on camp. No accommodation. Coy in tents. Map ref. Sheet 57.B N.2.a.4.8.

Ordnance detachment returned to D.A.D.O.S.

H.P.L.

Friday. 11th Octr. 1918.

Company moved at 09·00 and camped near FONTAINE-au-PIRE. No accommodation. Dump on camp. Map Ref. Sheet 57.B I.20.b.3.4. No refilling, owing to late arrival of supplies.

Heavy rain.

H.P.L.

Saturday. 12th Octr. 1918.

Refilling at 05·00. General work on Camp.

H.P.L.

Sunday. 13th. Octr. 1918

T4/249312. TAYLOR.E. Driver awarded 28 days F.P. No1 by. C.O., and sent to A.P.M.
T4/244884. GAMBLE T. Driver sent to England, for transfer to the R.A.F.
10 turnouts from 8th A.A (H.T) Coy attached. HRG

Monday. 14th. Octr. 1918

Company moved at 13.00 to camp on. BEAUVAIS. - BEVILLERS road. Map references, sheet 57.B.
Company. I.4.c.3.9
R. Point. I.4.a.3.7 HRG

Tuesday. 15th. Octr. 1918

General routine

Wednesday. 16th. Octr. 1918. HRG

Company paid. Baggage turnouts returned to Coy. from Hd. Qrs. 1 and 2 Sections D.A.C.
General routine.
D.A.D.V.S. inspection. HRG

Thursday 17th. Octr. 1918

Bathing parade at BEAUVAIS.
T/26513. GLOVER. T. Sgt. returned from probation with 1/8. Manchesters, for Commission.
HRG

Friday. 18th Octr. 1918 T4/114567 Dvr. TAYLOR. W. absent from leave to U.K., remanded for further enquiries for the Northampton Military Hospital.

2 Stewart Clipping machines received from D.A.D.O.S. One sent to No4. Company

WMG

Saturday 19th. Octr. 1918 Baggage turnouts sent to Hd. Qrs. 1 and 2 Sections of the D.A.C.

10 Wagons attached from No8 Army Aux. Horse Coy. returned to their Company.

Shelling in vicinity of camp at 23.00 hours.

Company stands to for probable move.

WMG

Sunday. 20th October. 1918.

At. BEAUVAIS.

General routine.

HPW

Monday 21st October 1918.

General routine

T4/186700 MASON. R. Dvr. injured ankle when on duty, and admitted to 1/2nd E.L.F.A

HPW

Tuesday 22nd October 1918.

Heavy rain, and camp in very bad condition.

HPW

Wednesday. 23rd. October 1918.

Company moved at 10.00 to AULICOURT. FARM. Refilling point in Camp. Good accommodation. Sheet 57B. J.1. a. 4.5

20 Wagons stand to to draw supplies from railhead (CAUDRY) if required.

HPW

Thursday 24th. October. 1918

Company stand: to and moved at 11.00 via QUIEVY. to SOLESMES. No accommodation. Map refs. Sheet 57. B. Camp. E.13.c.4.9. R.P. E.13.c.3.7. Supplies for consumption on 25th did not arrive until 22.00 hours. 211 Brigade supply wagons out all night

HPW

Friday. 25th Octr. 1918.

General routine work in camp. Site for camp at ROMERIES provisionally taken. HHo

Saturday 26th Octr. 1918.

Routine work. Weather good. Following changes in grouping of supply vehicles

Hd. Qrs. R.A. from No. 1. Coy. to No. 4 Coy.
3. Sect. D.A.C. " " 2 " " 1 "
1/7th. N.F. " " 4 " " 1 "

HHo

Sunday. 27th Octr. 1918.

General Routine. HHo

Monday. 28th Octr. 1918.

6 Reinforcements arrive from Base.

General Routine. HHo

Tuesday. 29th Octr. 1918.

Supplies for consumption on the 30th inst. arrive at 20.00 hours. Baggage vehicles return to Company from the Pioneer Btn. HHo

Wednesday 30th Octr. 1918.

Shelling in vicinity of Camp from 03.00 hours to 06.00 hours.

Report rendered to T.H.Q. respecting the inefficiency of recent reinforcements to the Coy.

Thursday 31st Octr. 1918

HPW

Driver BARTLETT. F.J. decorated by the Divisional Commander – Military Medal.

F.S. Boots issued.

General routine

HPW

Friday 1st November 1918.

General Routine

HPW

Saturday 2nd November 1918

Lieut. V. STEER admitted to Hospital.

General Routine

HPW

Sunday. Nov. 3. 1918.
At. Solesmes.
General Routine

Monday. Nov. 4. 1918.
General Routine

Tuesday. Nov. 5. 1918.
Baggage & Supply
Wagons to Pioneers.
Company moved to
LE QUESNOY. Sheet 51^{a}. L. 23. d. 3. 8.
No accommodation. Heavy rain
210th Brigade supplies for consumption
6th inst. not delivered, owing to Units not
being located.

Wednesday Nov. 6. 1918.
Heavy rain.
210 Brigade supplies for todays
consumption, delivered by mid-day

Thursday. Nov. 7. 1918.
Company moved
to vicinity of R.P. near LE QUESNOY station.
Good accommodation for all ranks
in villas.

Friday. Nov. 8. 1918.

Company moved at 09.00 hours to Eastern boundary of FOREST. de MORMAL, in vicinity of HAUTE. RUE. Sheet. 51. O.22. C. 6.0

Good accommodation.

Lieut. V. STEER rejoined from Hospital

Lieut. C. EDWARDS reported for duty, from 2 Company.

K.R.

Saturday. Nov. 9. 1918.

No Hay ration with forage for consumption on 10th.

Refilling at Foresters Cottage. MORMAL. WOOD.

4. driver reinforcements taken on strength.

K.R.

Sunday Nov. 10. 1918.
At La Haute Rue.
General Routine.
T4/249312. TAYLOR E. Driver, sent to Camp Commandant.
HPW

Monday. Nov. 11. 1918.
General Routine.
HPW

Tuesday. Nov. 12. 1918.
1 N.C.O. and 2 drivers to Divl. Clipping Depot.
General Routine.
HPW

Wednesday Nov. 13. 1918.
Refilling point moved to BERLAIMONT.
HPW

Thursday Nov 14 1918.
Company parade. Inspection of Arms, equipment, and clothing.
1 Rider with set of N.C.O's saddlery to T.H.Q.
HPW

Friday. Nov. 15. 1918.
Company moved at 09.00 hours to BOUSSIERES. Good billets and stabling.
HPW

R.P. remains at BERLAIMONT.

Saturday Nov. 16. 1918.
7 Tents retd. to D.A.D.O.S.
Winter clothing received from Baths.
General routine.
KAW

Sunday Nov 17. 1918

At BOUSSIERES. Lieut LIVINGSTONE Learmonth reported for duty from No 4 Company.
1 Rider from No 4 Company.
KAW

Monday Nov 18 1918
2 Tents returned to D.A.D.O.S.
General Routine.
KAW

Tuesday Nov 19. 1918
Bicycle 8522 (Driver STANYER) reported lost, to I.H.Q.
General Routine
KAW

Wednesday Nov 20. 1918
Court of Enquiry to investigate loss of bicycle No 8522.
25 Maps returned to Base. KAW

Pairs and drivers for the Divl. competition
Sergt. WAGDIN. W. admitted to 1/1 E.L.F.A.

H.M.

Thursday Nov 21 1918

General Routine

H.M.

Friday Nov 22 1918

Company pay parade.
Driver HAYES. E.J. to 1/1 E.L.F.A.

H.M.

Saturday Nov 23 1918

General Routine in Camp.
Supplies drawn from R.P. and delivered to Units by D.H.C. transport.

H.M.

Sunday. Nov. 24. 1918.

General Routine

H.A.W.

Monday. Nov. 25. 1918.

General Routine

Belgian Interpreter (C. RAES.) reported from G.H.Q. and attached to the Company

H.A.W.

Tuesday. Nov. 26. 1918.

Train eliminating competition for Wagon limbered G.S. at HAUTMONT. No2 Company successful by 1 point over this Company.

Court of Enquiry reassembled to enquire into loss of Bicycle 8522

H.A.W.

Wednesday Nov. 27. 1918.

General Routine

H.A.W.

Thursday Nov. 28. 1918.

Bicycle No 8522 found in the possession of French Civilians

H.A.W.

Friday. 29th Nov. 1918.

R.P. moved to ST. REMY - MAL - BATU.
map reference Sheet 51. V.3 central
7/32304 Driver. a/Sergt. SWEENEY. W.
reverted to act/Corporal, and
transferred to 4 Company
(inefficiency for rank of Sergeant.)

H.B.

Saturday. 30th Nov. 1918.

Company parade. —
inspection of clothing, arms,
and equipment
General Routine
Horses (other than H.D.)
paraded

H.B.

Sunday December 1. 1918.

Driver HYDE.T. granted special leave to U.K.

1 Officer and 20 O.R. to HAUTMONT on occasion of the KING'S visit.

HHW

Monday. December 2. 1918

General routine.

HHW

Tuesday December 3. 1918

General routine

HHW

Wednesday December 4. 1918

Sergt. WAGDIN. W. admitted to 1/1. E.L.F.A.

General routine

HHW

Thursday December 5. 1918

6 Reinforcements (Drivers) taken on strength.

HHW

Friday December 6. 1918

General Routine

HHW

Saturday December 7. 1918.

Surplus water cart sent to Salvage General Routine.

HHW

Saturday, Decr. 8. 1918.

Company parade. inspection of clothing arms and equipment.

Sergt WAGSIN discharged from Hospital

Monday Decr. 9. 1918.

Dvr ELLISON with turnout returned from D.A.P.M and replaced by Dvr HAYES.

Sergt. WAGSIN admitted to Hospital

Tuesday Decr. 10 1918.

S.S.M HARWOOD proceeds on leave to U.K.

General routine

Wednesday Decr. 11 1918

Bathing parades at HAUTMONT. Capt. GRAHAM with advance party proceeds to new area.

Company Pay parade

Thursday Decr. 12. 1918.

Dvr. FULKER with turnout returns from Reinforcement Camp.

Dvr STANLEY rejoins from detention

Friday Dec. 13. 1918.

Baggage turnouts sent to Units.

Advance party sent to JEUMONT.

H.Pho

Saturday Dec 14. 1918

Company moved to JEUMONT. – good accommodation

H.Pho

Sunday Decr. 15. 1918

Company moved to THUIN. (Belgium). Good accommodation for all ranks.

R.P. near to Coy. at THUIN-WEST. station.

H.Pho

Monday Decr. 16. 1918

General routine

Advance party ⅟c. Capt. J.W. GRAHAM proceeds to new area

H.Pho

Tuesday Decr. 17. 1918

General routine

H.Pho

Wednesday Decr. 18. 1918

Company moved to MONTIGNIES-SUR-SAMBRE, arriving at 17.00 hrs

Good accommodation for personnel.

Horses distributed over a wide area.
Heavy rain all day.

Thursday Decr. 19. 1918.

Baggage turnouts ordered to rejoin Company forthwith. Lieut. V. STEER granted 14 days extension of leave.

Friday Decr. 20 1918.

2nd. Lieut. T.T. SIMMS, education and demobilisation Officer attached to Company.

Saturday Decr. 21. 1918.

Baggage turnouts rejoin from Units. Company parade, Divisional Educational scheme fully explained.

Sunday. Decr. 22.

Lieut. SIMMS – Education Officer – attached to the Company Capt. E.F. SPRECKLEY assumed duties of S.S.O. vice Major REYNOLDS. on leave

Monday. Decr. 23.

3. O.R. – Coalminers – sent to England for demobilisation.

General routine

Tuesday Decr. 24.

C.S.M. BURDON T.J. proceeds on 14 days special leave to U.K.

One Sergeant, and one driver, reinforcements, from. Base. General routine, + preparations for Xmas. Day.

Wednesday Decr 25.

G.O.C. Division visits the mens dining room and cookhouse, expressing his satisfaction, with what had been done.

No wagons required for Railhead.

Thursday Decr. 26

3. O.R. – Coalminers – sent to England for demobilisation, while attached to No 2 Company

Friday. Decr. 27.

General Routine

Saturday. Decr. 28.

General Routine

Inspection by D.A.D.M.S.

Sunday. Decr. 29.

General Routine

Monday Decr. 30.

Coy. Bathing parade.

General Routine.

Tuesday Decr. 31.

Pay Parade. General Routine

Wednesday. 1st. January. 1919

S.S.M. HARWOOD A.H., returned from leave to U.K.
General Routine

W.P.

Thursday 2nd. January. 1919

Driver SCOLLICK. J. with turnout, attached from No8 Army Aux. (Horse) Coy. returned to that Unit.

W.P.

Friday. 3rd. January 1919

General Routine.
Company Parade, inspection of clothing, arms, and equipment.
Bathing parade.

W.P.

Saturday. 4th. January 1919

W.P.

General Routine.

Sunday. 5th Jan. 1919.

Farrier TAYLOR. J. returned from detachment with No2 Coy.
General Routine

Monday. 6th Jan. 1919.

Driver PARKER C.W. interviewed by C.O. with reference to his debtor balance
General Routine. Bathing parade

Tuesday. 7th Jan. 1919.

2 Reinforcements - drivers - from Base
Lieut. V. STEER granted extension of leave pending his appointment to S.D.8.
H.D. 31 stolen.

Wednesday. 8th Jan. 1919.
General Routine

Thursday. 9th Jan. 1919
General Routine

Friday. 10th Jan. 1919
Bathing parade.
Company parade. inspection of clothing arms and equipment.

Court of Inquiry to investigate loss of H.D. 31 on the 7th. inst.

President. Capt. G.T. BLACKWELL.
Member. 2nd. Lt. J.A. JAMES

Saturday. 11.1.1919

General Routine.

Sunday. 12. 1. 19

T/16307. BURDON T.J. C.S.M. returned from leave
General routine.

Monday. 13. 1. 19.
General Routine.
Bathing parade.

Tuesday 14. 1. 19
Pay parade.

Wednesday. 15. 1. 19.
General Routine

Thursday. 16. 1. 19
Horses paraded for classification by a Veterinary Board.
General routine.

Friday 17. 1. 19.

Company parade — inspection of clothing, arms, and equipment.

Bathing parade

Saturday 18. 1. 19

517722 CLARKSON J. Pte absent from duty - deprived of 14 days pay by C.O., and returned to the Divl. Emp. Coy.

Sunday. 19. 1. 19.

Corporal H.D.N. EVANS appointed Local Sergeant.

T.S/522 SOUTHALL L. S.Sgt. Whr. evacuated. (sick.)

Monday. 20. 1. 19.

Company Books inspected by the Commanding Officer

General Routine

Tuesday. 21. 1. 19.

General Routine

Wednesday 22. 1. 19

Two H.D. Horses 119. 260, stolen, while attached to No 2 Company.

General Routine. [initials]

Thursday. 23. 1. 19.

Court of Enquiry to investigate loss of 2 Horses.

Company Canteen a/c audited by a Board of Officers. [initials]

Friday. 24. 1. 19.

Major H.P. WILLIAMS. M.C. assumed temporary command of the Train, vice Lieut. Col. J. COULSON D.S.O. on leave to U.K.

Capt. J.L. GRAHAM assumed temporary command of the Company. [initials]

Bathing parade.

Company parade – inspection of arms, clothing and equipment.

Saturday. 25. 1. 19.

General Routine [initials]

Sunday. 26. 1. 19

Divisional Commander visits the horse lines.
Slight fall of snow.
General routine.

Monday. 27. 1. 19

Sergt. LEES. D. to Divl. Employment Coy. for demobilisation.
General routine.

Tuesday. 28. 1. 19

First lot of material drawn from the R.E's. for construction of a stable.

Wednesday. 29. 1. 19

General Routine.

Thursday. 30. 1. 19

General Routine

Friday. 31. 1. 19

Marching Order Parade. Bathing parade.
R.E's. commence stables. Fall of snow.

Saturday. 1/2/1919. Fall of snow.

General Routine

Sunday. 2/2/1919. General routine

Monday. 3/2/1919. Bathing parade.

General routine

Tuesday. 4/2/1919. CHEW. A.J. Driver, returned to Company, motor tractor course having been cancelled.

Wednesday. 5/2/19.
Thursday. 6/2/19.
Friday. 7/2/19.
Saturday. 8/2/19.
} General Routine

Sunday. 9/2/1919.
General Routine.
HPW

Monday. 10/2/1919.
Major H. P. WILLIAMS. M.C
returned from T.H.Q. and assumed
command of the Company.
HPW

Tuesday. 11/2/1919.
General Routine.
HPW

Wednesday. 12/2/1919.
General Routine
HPW

Thursday. 13/2/1919.
Personnel returned to Coy.
from the Central Purchase Board.
Captain T.L. GRAHAM proceeds on leave
to U.K.
HPW

Friday. 14/2/1919.
General Routine
HPW

Saturday 15/2/1919.
11. H.D. 6. L.D. and 2 Riders
demobilised.
General Routine
HPW

Sunday. 16/2/19.
New stables completed.
All. Emp. Coy. personnel with the 3 Brigade Coys. reported for duty.

HMC

Monday. 17/2/19.
General Routine.

HMC

Tuesday. 18/2/19
General Routine

HMC

Wednesday. 19/2/19.
Lieut. C. EDWARDS. to No 3 Coy. for temporary duty.
Stores surplus to Mob. Equip. returned to D.A.D.O.S.

HMC

Thursday. 20/2/19.
6. H.D. Horses to 19th M.V.S. for sale.

HMC

Friday. 21/2/19
General Routine

HMC

Saturday. 22/2/19
General Routine.

HMC

Sunday 23/2/19.

6 Turnouts complete rejoined from 2 Company.
4 Drivers, reinforcements, from Base, taken on strength.

Monday. 24/2/19.
12 H.D. and 4. L.D. despatched to the Base.
4. L.D. and 2 Riders to M.V.S. for sale
Dvr GUNNING. F. awarded 21 days F.P. No 2 absent from leave.

Tuesday. 25/2/19. General Routine

Wednesday. 26/2/19
1 H.D. and 1 Rider to 19. M.V.S. for sale.
Following turnouts rejoined from detachment:-
C.R.E. A.P.M. M.V.S. Reception Camp 1/3rd. E.L.F.A.

Thursday. 27/2/19. S.Q.M.S. WILKINSON. S.A. posted to H.Q. IV Corps.

27/2/19 Pay Parade.

3½ H.D. and 1 Rider to Base. [inserted above: "ditto"]

6 Driver reinforcements taken on strength.

JMO

Friday. 28/2/19.

Lieut. C. EDWARDS rejoined from 3 Company.

30 Wagons parked at the Infantry Barracks CHARLEROI

JMO

Saturday. 1/3/1919.

12 H.D. Horses to Base.

9 O.R. taken on strength from 1/1. E.W.F.A.

General Routine

Sunday. 2/3/1919.

4. O.R. to Guards Divl. Train

Monday. 3/3/1919.

General Routine

Tuesday. 4/3/1919.

General Routine

Wednesday. 5/3/1919.

6. H.D. Horses to M.V.S. Base. General Routine.

Thursday. 6/3/1919.

12 G.S. Wagons & Harness to 210 Bgde. R.F.A.
12 " " " " 211 " "
(2) 2 " " " " to Field Coys. R.Es.

Friday. 7/3/1919.

1. G.S. Wagon & Harness. to 427 Field Coy. R.E.
General Routine.

Saturday. 8/3/1919.

4. O.R.'s taken on strength from 1/2.
E.L.F.A.
General Routine

Sunday. 9. 3. 1919

12 G.S. Wagons. 24 sets harness handed over to D.A.C.
40. O.R's. to Corps Concentration Camp for demobilisation.
4 drivers trans. from 2 Coy
8 " " " 3 "

Monday. 10. 3. 1919.

2 limbers with harness to C.R.E
5 drivers transferred from No 4. Coy.
24. H.D. Horses with harness and 12 drivers posted to Div. Artillery
C.S.M. Burdon T.J. to 46th Div. Train.
Lieut. W.W. YEATS. posted to Coy.

Tuesday. 11. 3. 1919.

Ford Car. 59441 trans. to 42nd. Divl. M.T. Coy.
25. O.R's. demobilised.

Wednesday. 12. 3. 1919

24. H.D. Horses, with harness and 12 drivers to 42nd. Divl. Artillery

Thursday. 13/3/19.

10 H.D. Horses with harness and 5 drivers posted to Machine Gun. Btn

Friday. 14/3/19.

9 drivers posted to 21st. Army. Aux. Horse Coy.
Major H.P. WILLIAMS. M.C. handed over command of Company to Capt. A.F. AKIS.

Saturday. 15/3/19.

8. O.R's. demobilised.
Major H.P. WILLIAMS. M.C. proceeds on leave to U.K

Sunday. 16/3/19.

Driver WICKS. G. transferred from 93 Brigade R.F.A. General Routine

Monday. 17/3/19.

Sergt. D.H.S. MITCHELL rejoined from leave
General Routine

Tuesday. 18/3/19

General Routine

Wednesday. 19/3/19

Dvr. BENNETT. J. A. admitted to Shorncliffe Military Hosp. whilst on leave.

Dvr. WILLIAMS. G. demobilised whilst on leave to U.K

Thursday. 20/3/19

Drivers. WILTON. H. F. and WEBSTER. C. W. C. G. posted to 4th Corps Cyclists Btn.

Friday. 21/3/19

Drivers attached to Divl. Artillery rejoin Company. Horses, harness, and wagons remain with Artillery.

Saturday. 22/3/19

S. S. Sdr. FORD. W. and 4 drivers demobilised.

Sunday. 23/3/19. General Routine

Monday. 24/3/19. 2 Drivers transferred to No 4 Company.

Tuesday. 25/3/19. 2 L.D. Horses transferred to 42nd. Machine Gun Btln.
General Routine

Wednesday 26/3/19. 20 Drivers. 1. Dvr. Whr. 1 Dvr. Sdr. transferred to 21st. Army Aux. Horse. Coy.
Dvr. HISCOCK to Hosp.

Thursday 27/3/19. S.S. GAVES. C. transferred to No 2 Coy. Cadre

Friday. 28/3/19. General Routine

Saturday. 29/3/19.
Capt W.H. TAYLEUR } To Company
" E.H. MANNERS. }

Sunday 30/3/19

8 O.Rs demobilised
Capt. E.F. Spreckley assumed command of Cadre

Monday 31/3/19

General Routine

Tuesday 1/4/19

4 O.Rs demobilised

Wednesday 2/4/19

2 Supply Details transferred to Base Supply Depot Calais

Thursday 3/4/19

General Routine

Friday 4/4/19

TH/059883 Regan C.E. Driver.
Sentence of 3 months I.H.L. awarded by F.G.C.M. commuted to 90 days F.P. No2

Saturday 5/4/19

General Routine

Monday 6/4/19
Tuesday 7/4/19
Wednesday 8/4/19 } General Routine

Thursday 9/4/19

Ration drawn for 10th and 11th also "Train ration")
Supply Dump closed

Friday 10/4/19

Wagons loaded, and sent to station for entraining.

ARMY BOOK 152.

Correspondence Book.

(FIELD SERVICE.)

Parcel No. 14

Opened on ....

Closed on ....

The Squares in this book are ¼ inch.

546) Wt.4496-M642 40,000 Books 9/16 B.,M.&S.

ARMY ORDER.

WAR OFFICE,
24th July, 1916.

VII.—Leakage of Military Information.—There is reason to believe that information concerning operations is being conveyed by officers and men of the British Army in the Field to their relatives at home either personally, by letter or by telegram, and that, in some cases, a code has been elaborated to facilitate the communication of information which would otherwise be stopped by the Censors. 121/8583

It is to be regretted that at this stage of the war it is necessary to explain to all ranks that the sole object of the field censorship and of all the other steps taken to prevent the leakage of military information is to secure substantial gains with the least possible loss.

Each officer or man who privately transmits information (even to those on whose discretion he may have the most complete reliance) inevitably facilitates the task of the enemy's agents and indirectly sacrifices the lives of his comrades.

This fact should be impressed on all officers and men, so that all ranks may co-operate to ensure that the progress of the Army is not imperilled or rendered more costly by the criminal folly of a few individuals, who if discovered will be severely dealt with.

By Command of the Army Council,

R. H. Brade

NOTE.—A copy of this Army Order will be issued to every officer serving in the Army, who will bring it continually to the notice of those serving under him.

50000 8/16 4808 A.O. 3485wo

Wednesday 25th July 1917 At Bus

Refilling as Yesterday

No T/4607 Dr Kay F. and T/4119

Dr Salvage transferred to 125 Infantry

Bde Hd-Qrs.

Company Routine.

Friday 27 July 1917 At Bus.

Refilling as on the 20

Company Routine.

Saturday 28th July 1917 AT Bus.

Refilling as yesterday

No M/210414 Cpl. Kershaw, S. proceeded to-day on one months furlough.

Company Routine

Tuesday 31st July 1917 AT Bus.

Refilling as ~~yesterday~~ on the 28th inst.

No 1/24536 C/C Adams admitted to hospital

No 8080 Pte Lang J. admitted to hospital

Company Routine

Wednesday 1st August 1917 AT Bus.

Refilling as yesterday.

The following has returned to the company from No 1 Haymaking company. 36 S. wagons complete 1 N.C.O. 30.R. and 3 riding horses also 1 officer 2Lt CHITTENDON

Lt H.V. HENROTIN and 2 Lt C.C. CHITTENDON were proceeded to ENGLAND on duty and are struck off the company strength accordingly.

Capt. E.F. Spreckley taken on the strength of the Coy as supervising officer No 1

Thursday 2 August 1917 AT Bus.

Refilling as yesterday

The following has returned from No 2 haymaking company:- 7 G.S. wagons Comp 4 pairs H.D. horses 1 riding horse 1 NCO. 12 O.R.

Company Routine.

Friday 3 August 1917 AT Bus.

Refilling as yesterday

Company Routine

Saturday 4th August 1917 AT Bus.

Refilling as yesterday.

No T4/244584 Dr Crabbe admitted to hospital to-day.

No T4/162069 Dr Dixby [illegible] sent to 3rd Army School of Cookery [illegible] Course.

Company Routine.

Wednesday 5th August 1917 AT Bus

Refilling as on the 4th

No T4/186165 Dr Baston B. returned to Company from 3rd Corps convalescent depot

Company Routine.

Thursday 9th August 1917 AT Bus.

Refilling as yesterday

No T4SR/01323 Dr Goodyear admitted to hospital.

The baggage wagons of the batteries of 26th & 9th Bdes R.F.A. have been sent to

Thursday (contd.)

than to-day. The horses and drivers being retained by the company.

Company Routine

Friday 10 August 1917 at Bus.

Refitting as yesterday

Company Routine.

[illegible]

Saturday 11th August 1917 at Bus

Refilling as yesterday.

H.D. horse No.441 transferred to Mobile Veterinary Section

Company Routine.

Sunday 12th August 1917 at Bus

Refilling as yesterday

No T4/043343 Dr Ferguson D and No T4/045
Dr Henry N transferred
Dr Ferguson to 4/4 Field Ambulance and
Dr Henry to 429 Coy A.S.C.

Company Routine

Monday 13th August 1917 at Bus

Refilling as yesterday

No T4/34388 Lce Corp Brown L A to hospital

Company Routine

Tuesday 14th August 1917 AT Bus.

Refilling as yesterday.

No T5/715 Corpl Bullock to hospital

No T4/39559 Corpl White H reported back to company from B.H.T.D. Havre

Company Routine

Wedensday 15th August 1917 AT Bus.

Refilling as yesterday.

Major E.W. Alderson taken over the company.

C. A. Pimm[illegible] Capt.

A.S.C.

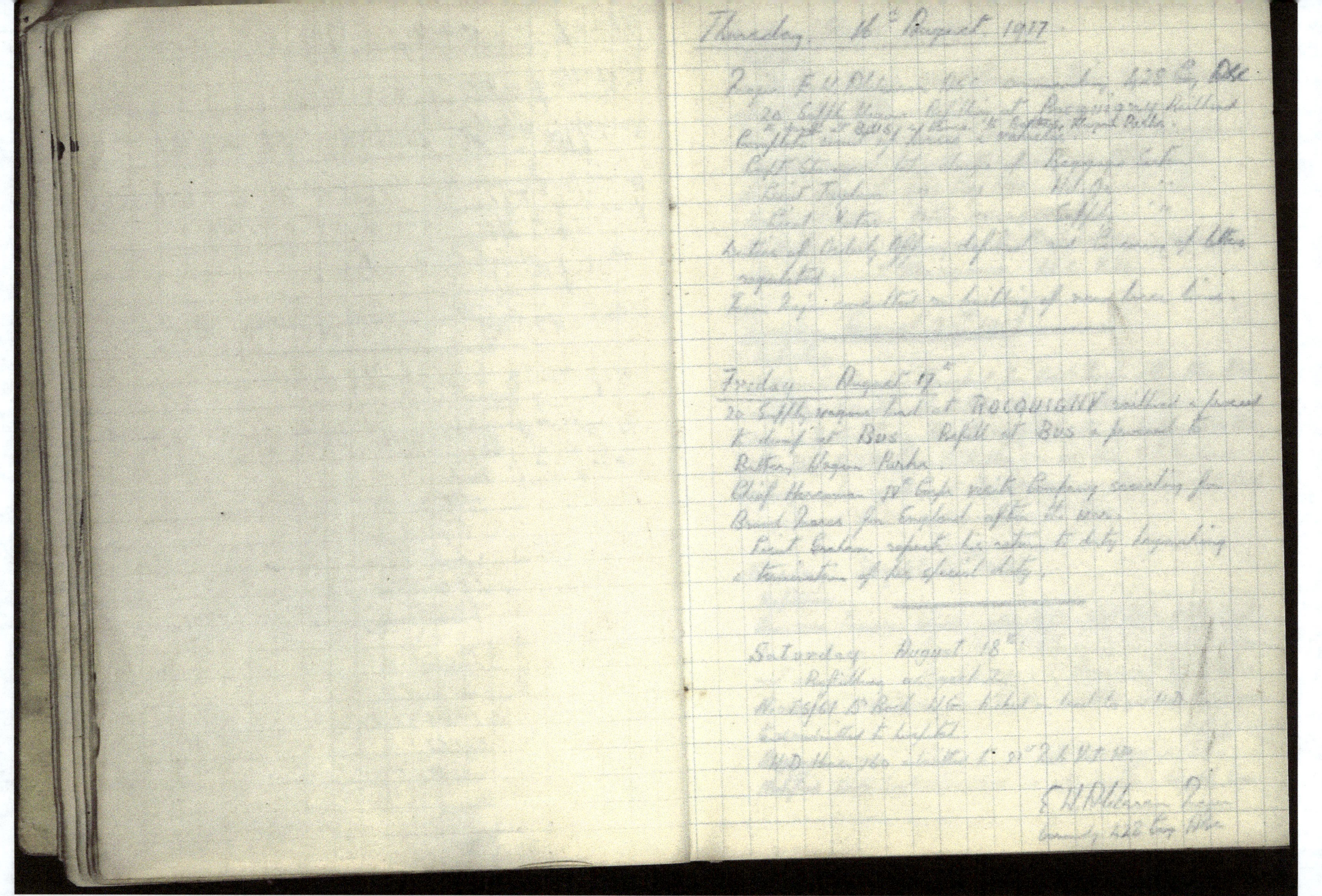

Thursday 16th August 1917

Major E. W. Oldman D.S.O. assumed command 428 Coy A.S.C.

20 Suffolk Wagons [illegible] at [illegible] [illegible]

Complete [illegible] of [illegible] [illegible]

Capt. [illegible] [illegible] [illegible] [illegible]

[illegible] [illegible] [illegible]

[illegible] [illegible] [illegible] Suffolk

[illegible] [illegible] [illegible] [illegible] [illegible] [illegible] regulations.

[illegible] [illegible] [illegible] [illegible] [illegible] [illegible] [illegible]

Friday August 17th

20 Suffolk wagons [illegible] at ROCQUIGNY [illegible] [illegible] to dump at Bus. Refill at Bus [illegible] to Bn. Wagon Parks.

Chief [illegible] 18th [illegible] [illegible] [illegible] [illegible] [illegible] for [illegible] [illegible] for England after the war.

Capt. Graham [illegible] his return to duty [illegible] termination of his special duty.

Saturday August 18th

Refilling as [illegible]

[illegible] [illegible] [illegible] [illegible] [illegible] [illegible] [illegible]

[illegible] [illegible] [illegible]

[illegible] [illegible] [illegible] [illegible] [illegible]

E. W. Oldman Major

Comdg 428 Coy A.S.C.

Sunday. August 19th 1917

Refilling

Instructions through OC 9th Divisional Train re withdrawal of 42nd Div R.A.

Owing to pending move of Division (less R.A.) baggage & supply wagons for all other Divisional troops to be handed over to 431 Coy ASC.

Visited C.R.A re future arrangements.

D Battery 210 Bde goes to Bapaume & requires one lorry at Marquaix 62.C. K.14.

Monday. August. 20th 1917

Refilling

7.30 a.m Paraded transport for Divl Troops other than R.A & Hd Qrs & 2 sections of D.A.C. to go to Achiet.

10 a.m Motor Lorry to Marquaix to D Battery 210 Bde.

210 Bde R.F.A (less D Battery) & 211 Bde R.F.A hand over guns for refitting at Bapaume & Hamel respectively & return to their own wagon lines at Bus.

Tuesday. August. 21st 1917.

Refilling.

One more baggage wagon & spare man despatched to Achiet 10 a.m to join 431 Coy. Train Hd Qrs wires in evening wagon not arrived evidently train (now at Acheux) left before it reached. Notified Town Major & R.T.O. to return wagon to me.

Baggage wagons to be made up with R.A before 25th.

Notified Staff Capt train requirements for Coy & Supply Sec.

Wednesday. August. 22nd

Refilling

Wagon & spare man returned from Achiet.

Telephone to Traffic Albert re train arrangements & requirements for this Company. Baggage and Supply wagons to go with units. Coy to entrain Bapaume.

Advance parties leave Rocquigny 10 a.m 23rd & report Area Commdt Waton

No orders have been received.

Thursday. August. 23rd

Refilling

Sergt Reid sent to Watou as advance party.

Programme of move from 3rd to 5th Army received from D.A.D.R.T. Albert

A.Q.M.G IVth Corps states Lorries have been ordered to join & orders come through R.A. HdQrs.

Friday. August. 24th

Refilling

8 Motor Lorries 42nd Div Supply Col report for duty under Sergt Capron.

4 HdQrs baggage & supply wagons will entrain apart from the Coy. 1 in No 5 train with B batt 210 Bde

2 in No 7 train with C. 210. 1 in No 9 train with D. 210

Rations for 26th on the man for 27th on Supply Train for 28th to be drawn from new railhead.

2 more motor lorries join in evening.

Saturday. August. 25th
Supply Column fills up at Railhead Rocquigny, 8 a.m
Train wagons refill at dump 8 a.m & deliver rations for 26th to units then return to dump load rations for 27th & are posted to their respective units with whom they Entrain. Of the H^d Qrs wagons 1 travels on train 5 2 on train 7. 1 with 4 officers & riders on train 9 and the remainder on train 11 from Bapaume.
~~10 h~~

Sunday. August. 26th
H^d Qrs of Company parade 5 a.m and march to Bapaume Station entraining & leaving at 9.15 a.m and 3.45 p.m. arriving Proven at 7.15 P.M 1st train only camping with H^d Qrs 211 Bde R.F.A. Weather conditions very bad from evening onwards & ground sodden.

Monday. August 27th
Second H^d Qrs train arrived Proven 1.30 a.m & camped on Watou - Abelle Road; 27. K.11.a.
Supply wagons collected from units & ~~refilled at 27. L.14.c central crossroads~~
drew from Railhead L.28.c Hoppenlock
dumping at refilling point 27. L.14.c cross roads.
Coy H^d Qrs collected & with supply wagons camped at L.19.c.3.4.
Weather very bad continuously & ground sodden Strong wind.

Tuesday. August. 28th

Supply wagons refilled at point I.14.c and distributed to units round Watou.
Inspected camps to be taken over by this train from 15th Division with OC.429 & OC 430 Coy ASC & later again with OC. train.
Position of H^d Qr Coy to be 28. G.9.c central.
Improvement in weather towards evening.

Wednesday. August. 29th

H^d Qrs of Company parades at 8.30 a.m and moves to new camp. 28 G.9 c central. POPERINGHE
Supply wagons refill as yesterday distributing to units in advanced positions west of VLAMERTINGHE
Improvement in weather partially continues.
New camp provides rough accomodation for officers & men & for half the horses.

Thursday. August. 30th

Supply wagons at Railhead Wippenhoek to refilling point 28 G.9 c. central and thence to wagon parks.
Area Commd^t Major Hamilton visits camp.
Difficulty in obtaining good water for horses & washing.
2 Wagons & 2 limbers required for Salvage duties.

Friday August. 31st

New railhead EDENHARTHOEK 28 G.4 a 8.10 am
Thence to refilling point & to units.
Irregularity in dealing with charge against Dr Lewis on part of Section Officer & N.C.O's. Case dismissed.

Hostile aircraft overhead twice about 9 PM & midnight.

Saturday. September. 1st 1917.
Supply wagons to Railhead, thence to Refilling Point.
From refilling point to units twice, a double issue
of rations.
Railhead shelled. Casualties in Infantry Bn alongside.
1 Wagon damaged by shell fire returned from R.D
and replaced also 1 sick horse.

E.W. Aldersen Major
OC 428 Coy ASC

Sunday. September. 2nd
Supply wagons to Railhead thence to Refilling Point thence to units.
Driver Henry joins from 429 Coy to replace Dr Munday servant to Capt Blackwell.
Sergt Bullock reports sick, difficulty as to medical treatment.
C.Q.M.S. Field sick.
Hostile aircraft overhead from 9 P.M throughout night.
Improved weather conditions from sundown.

Monday. September. 3rd
Wheeler S.S. Southall and Interpreter Jaffreo proceed on leave.
Refilling. 4 wagons to YPRES 7 P.M. Gas shells forward,
Medical Officer & Veterinary officer detailed & visit the Company.
Requirements for winter accomodation: standings for 100 horses huts for 75 men.
Hostile aircraft overhead at night.

Tuesday. September 4th
Refilling
2 Riding Horses transferred to 127 Bde H^dQrs
3 H.D. Remounts arrive PROVEN. to be allotted by the HQ
Measures to suppress vermin: Bathing, washing of clothes, preparation of washing soap.
Draining of camp renders water for horses fit for use.
Enemy Aircraft overhead. Weather good.

Wednesday 5th September. 17.
Refilling 8.30 a.m.
Two remounts join from ROUEN
Dr Lee goes on leave
Hostile aircraft overhead at night. Fair. Hot.

Thursday 6th September 1917
Thunderstorm in early morning and evening
Refilling.
Good water now available for horses due to clearing of filter pit & opening of surface drains.

Friday 7th September. 17
Refilling
Pte Huntley on leave.
Pte Hardman. A. taken on strength & posted to Train H^d Qrs.
Hostile aircraft overhead about 11 P.M

Saturday 8th September
Refilling
One horse Rider Z. 115 transferred to remounts

E. H. Alderson MAJOR, A.S.C.
O.C. HD. QRS. COMPANY 42nd DIVL. TRAIN.

Sunday. 9th September. 17
Refilling.
Tents & huts to be surrounded by a wall of sand bags 2 feet high.
Drivers must report all mishaps to vehicles or horses on return from duty.
O.C. Train visited company lines. Horses to be picketed apart as far as possible.
All tail boards to be strengthened.

Monday. 10th September. 17
Refilling
Medical Inspection 50 men and all loaders.
Weather Fine, night clear.
Hostile aircraft overhead from 9.30 P.M and during day.

Tuesday. 11th September. 17.
Refilling. 31 wagons.
Weather fine.
No T/4 244872
Saddler S.S. MEDLACK. W. wounded at 8.30 P.M. by a tracer bullet from a friendly Lewis Gun firing at overhead aircraft, admitted to 17 Casualty Clearing Station.

Wednesday. 12th September 1917
Refilling
Weather cooler & slightly overcast.
Medical Inspection of all men with Coy H^d Q^rs. completed
1 Remount H.D. Chestnut joins.
Driver HENRY before OC. Train applying for Commission

Driver HANSON Drunk. 10 days F.P. No. 2
Driver MASON Leaving Wagon unattended 7 days F.P. 2
Forfeit 7 days pay.

Thursday. September 13.
Train at Railhead 3 hours late. Refilling
Sergt REID admonished for not parking Supply
Wagons properly.
Weather wet & stormy

Friday September 14.
Refilling
Dr HENRY before Brig Gen FARGUS 125 Bde
as applicant for a commission.

Saturday September 15.
Refilling
Corpl HOWELL RAMC on leave
Interpreter JAFFRED returns off leave.

Sunday September 16
Refilling
S.S. Southall returns off leave.
Dr Bedford returns off leave
Captain L.G. TROUP on leave to ENGLAND.
Area Commandant visits camp.

Monday. September. 17.
Refilling
Sergt PARKINSON severely reprimanded improperly dressed in POPERINGHE.
V^th Corps require boundary fixed between Company and M.T. lines.
GREENWICH time not to be resumed to day.

Tuesday September. 18
Refilling
7 Supply wagons to 431 Coy
1 to 429
1 to 430
on alteration of supply arrangements.
General MITFORD visited company lines.
Driver LEE returns off leave.

Wednesday September 19
Refilling at SHELLHOEK for R.F.A & D.A.C only. Attached to 55th Div Train.
Lieut TAVLEUR on leave.
Pte HUNTLEY returns off leave.

Thursday September 20.
Refilling
Driver HENRY reports on probation for a commission to 1/7 E. LANCS.
Capt STEVENSON member of board auditing Divisional Canteen a/cs

Friday September 21
Refilling
4 Wagons 1 Water Cart 14 horses with Train
H^d Qrs to WORMHOUDT on Division leaving this area. Corpl SEVERN on leave
2 Remounts drawn from Rail at PROVEN
Hostile aircraft overhead about 9 P.M.

Saturday September 22.
Refilling
1 Loader joins from 429 Coy.
Drivers EDGE and ROB~~D~~SON for re-engagement with the colours for the duration of the war.
E.W.A.

Sunday September 23
Refilling
To be attached for supplies to 59th Div after to-day
C.Q.M.S. FIELD admonished for leaving camp without permission.
Visited C.R.A. 42nd Div at POPERINGHE re future arrangements.

Monday September 24.
Refilling at EDEWAARTHOEK
Driver ROBSON 7 days F.P. No.1 leaving horses unattended.
Weather Fair & still.
Hostile aircraft overhead during day.

Tuesday. September. 25.
Refilling at SHELLHOEK under arrangement with 3rd Div Train. Remainder of 42nd Div in this area attached to 3rd Division.
Driver CAMPBELL 14 days F.P. No 1 and deprived 14 days pay. Insolence
Wheeler LONERGAN deprived 2 days pay dirty on parade.
Hostile aircraft overhead during day & early evening.

Wednesday. September 26
Refilling as yesterday
Baggage wagons need more care.
Weather fresh & cooler, very dusty.

Thursday September 27
Refilling.
Farriers BEST and THORPE complaints as to balance and pay statement.
Horse No died. Inflammation of Bowels.
Corpl HOWELL returned off leave.
Gen WALSH wounded. Hostile aircraft overhead in evening.

Friday September 28
Refilling
Instructions to move on Sunday.
Hostile aircraft overhead during day & evening
S.C.R.A. concerning movement of remainder of 42nd Division.

Saturday. 29th September. 1917.
Refilling. Supply wagons park loaded in Coy Lines
Hd Qrs Coy 3rd Div Train wish to take over this
camp on our move.
Ten motor lorries report as Supply Column for
Divisional Troops marching on 30th inst.
Hostile aircraft overhead from 9 P.M till 3 A.M
in number many bombs dropped all round.

Sunday 30th Sept.
Motor lorries draw from Railhead EDEVAARDHOEK
Supply wagons march with Coy Hd Qrs
parading at 10 a.m and marching in rear of D.A.C
halting West of HOUTKERQUE for 1½ hours
at 3 P.M. arriving in WORMHOUDT area
at 7 P.M officers being billeted, men accomodated
in huts & horses on lines for the night.
Supply wagons deliver to units on arrival at
WORMHOUDT. Motor lorries bring forward
supplies and dump at WORMHOUDT

Monday 1st October.
Motor lorries draw from ARNEKE at 7 a.m.
Supply wagons refill at WORMHOUDT. 8 a.m
Company marches 12.30 P.M. and arrives in
billetting area beyond TETEGHEM 400 yds
short of DUNKIRK - ADINKERKE canal
road, officers & men billetted, horses on lines
round a barn, wagons on ploughed field.
Weather very fine. Hostile aircraft overhead from 9 P.M

Supplies delivered to units on arrival in TETEGHEM area.
Motor lorries dump supplies by roadside of Company billets and then proceed to rejoin their unit.

Tuesday October 2nd
Supply wagons refill at 8 a.m.
Company parades at 12.15 P.M and marches via Canal Road and ADINKERKE to St IDESBALD and camps on Sand Dunes; on arrival supply wagons deliver to units each wagon requires leaders from unit to enable wagon to reach the units lines across the thick sand.
Lieut MORPHY ceases to be attached to company.
Captain L.G. TROUP rejoins from leave.

Wednesday October 3rd.
Refilling at dump in Camp 10.30 a.m & delivers to units. Supplies brought from railhead by DECAUVILLE Railway.
C.Q.M.S. FIELD brought up for smoking on parade on 30th inst and absence on the line of march on same date.
Lieut PAIN & supply details of D.S.C attached to Company for discipline.
Clipping Machine not received from 431 Coy
1 Horse received from 19th MOB. VET. H.P.

Thursday October 4th

Refilling

Lieut TAYLEUR returns off leave.

C.Q.M.S. FIELD Severely Reprimanded by O.C. Train

Pte BUTLER Remanded for trial by F.G.C.M. for Drunk, Striking an N.C.O. Resisting Escort.

1 Horse received from 19th MOBILE Vet. H.

Friday. October 5th

Refilling

Weather Cold. Windy. Wet. Thunderstorms.

Company moves into camp vacated by No. 1 Coy 66th Div Train on S[t] IDESBALD Road. Camp is dirty but affords fair accomodation for officers & other ranks in huts & [illegible] and for half the horses.

Summary of Evidence on Pte BUTLER taken by Adjutant.

Lieut TAYLEUR & 5 wagons to front line.

Saturday October 6th

Refilling

Fixing up the camp & arranging for improvements in accomodation & stabling.

1 N.C.O. & 7 wagons to NIEUPORT at night return about 10.30 P.M.

10 wagons of 72nd A.F.A. Bde report with loaders.

429. 431 Coys move to LA PANNE

Sunday October 7.

Refilling

Very wet & stormy & cold

Pte BUTZER under arrest taken over by Coy H^d Qrs.

5 Loaders deprived 2 days pay parading late on dump.

Monday. October. 8.

Refilling

Fair till 5 P.M then heavy rain.

10 men innoculated.

Strong gale & heavy rain during the night.

Tuesday October. 9th

Refilling

Camp under water instituted drainage & moved 10 pairs of 72nd A.F.A. Bde to Supply lines:

Stabling in Supply Lines completed.

9 bicycles at Coy H^d Qrs inspected & verified.

Lieut TAYLEUR member of board auditing Canteen Accounts.

Wednesday. October. 10th.

Refilling

Lce Cpl BROWN deprived of appointment for neglect of duty.

Driver CROWTHER joins the Coy from 19th Mob Vet.

Rifles of Supply det inspected.

Thursday. October 11th.
Refilling.
Company Routine.
Weather cold & fair but threatening.

Friday October 12th
Refilling at W. 18 a. 4.3. FURNES map for last time
After refilling Supply dump moves to NEW
ZEALAND Camp W. 18 c 4.7.
Office men & horses move during afternoon
taking over from H^d Q^s Coy 32nd Div Train.

Saturday. October. 13th
Refilling at NEW ZEALAND dump.
Camp W. 18. a. 4.3 handed over to 41st Div Train.
Arranging accomodation at new camp.
Weather very wet and stormy.

Sunday October 14.
Refilling.
Dr. W. MAYFIELD 14 days F.P. No.1. insolence
to an N.C.O.
OC Train visited & inspected company quarters, stables
& horses.

Monday. October 15.
Refilling
Pte BUTLER tried by F.G.C.M. 10 a.m.
Company Routine
Weather Fair. Cold

Tuesday. October. 16.
Refilling
Lieut J.A. PAINE. S.O.D.S.C. before O.C. Train.
Weather. Fair.

Wednesday. October. 17
Refilling
Lieut YEATS on leave to ENGLAND.
Drs SILK & WADDINGTON deprived 2 days pay
Lights after Lights-out.
S.S. HARDY reverts to rank Sergt from
15.10.17.
Camp shelled by enemy from 9 P.M to 11.15 P.M
Part of one hut blown up 3 men killed. one died
of wounds, 5 wounded all of 42nd D.S.C.
excepting Sergt KING slightly at duty of 428 Coy
& Pte MAYO. 428 Coy attached D.S.C
4 shells burst in the camp area.

Thursday. October. 18
Refilling. Pte MAYO died 3 A.M of wounds.
Visited J.A. PAINE and Div'l H.Qrs with O.C
Train as to the possibility of moving the camp.
No better place & no accommodation available.
Ordered all men to evacuate huts as sleeping
accommodation and sleep in bivouac shelters.

Friday. October 19.
Refilling
Three loaders late at Supply Dump fined 2 days pay
One fine remitted owing to good behaviour on Wednesday.

Weather fine.

Saturday. October 20.
Refilling
Pte Brown neglect of duty in office.
Dr Craig drunk on duty.
Supply wagons of 72nd R.F.A. to return to their unit.
Company paid out.

Sunday. October 21.
Refilling
C.R.A to arrange for return of baggage horses to the company head quarters and one wagon per week for overhaul.
Hostile aircraft overhead 7.P.M. onwards.
Weather fair frost at night
D.C. Train interviewed Lieut PAYNE
Adjutant promulgated F.G.C.M on Dr BUTLER one year with hard labour.
Driver CRAIG. R. remanded for trial

Monday. October. 22.
Refilling. Baggage horses & 3 wagons return to Coy H.Q.
Adjutant takes summary of evidence re CRAIG.
3 drivers reinforcement posted to Company.
FRANKUM. GRAHAM. GUNNING.
6 B Type and 1 C Type huts received for company accomodation.

and for repair of Water Cart.
Company paid out. Limitation of payments.
Enemy shells fall in vicinity of camp from
5.45 P.M. to 7 P.M.
Promulgation of F.G.C.M. on Dr CRAIG. 28 days F.P. No 1. Imd.

Sunday October 28
Refilling
Capt STEVENSON to report for Infantry
at BEDFORD on 21st November proceeds
to England.
Shells fall in vicinity of camp about noon and in
afternoon. Lieut J.P. BLACKMORE joins the Coy.
14 men from D.S.C. report to join Lieut PAYNE
detachment.

Monday October 29th 1917
Refilling
Lieut YEATS returns off leave.
Dr CAMPBELL from detention.
Weather Fine. cold.

Tuesday October 30th 1917
Refilling
Wet and cold.
Company routine. Report on advisability of
moving from this camp.
Slight clouds.

Wednesday 31st October

Refilling

With O.C. Train to LA PANNE to arrange accommodation for the Company.

Motor Driver RIMMINGTON. D.S.C. to his unit for leave.

Thursday

November 1st 1917.

Refilling

Court of Enquiry re Dr SHANNON 431 Coy ASC

Hd Qrs & Baggage Section move to LA PANNE

Supply Section under Lieut NEATS remain at NEW ZEALAND Camp.

Billets provided for only 60 men & few N.C.O's and four officers.

Stabling obtained for 50 horses only.

Weather wet and dull.

Friday November 2nd

Refilling

Visited Town Major re increased accommodation

/Sergt Saddler FORD. S.S. GAVES (supply)

/C.S.M. MORRIS join for duty.

2 Sections of D.A.C. attached 125 Bde supply officer

Saturday, November 3rd

Refilling

S.S. GAVES into Company office.

G.O.C visits Company lines.

Corporal LEES before O.C. Train and C.R.E. for a commission in R.E.
Company paid out.

Sunday. November 4th.
Refilling.
Report received that G.O.C was dissatisfied with the Company at his visit. Explained that Coy was in throes of moving & no camp available.
O.C. Train decided adviseable that whole company should reoccupy NEW ZEALAND Camp.
Move taken place in afternoon completed by 5 P.M.

Monday November 5th.
Refilling
Dr HENRY. M.R.V. to ENGLAND to join a Cadet unit. Pte WELLFOOT from detention.
Corpl TROUGHTON on leave to ENGLAND.
O.C. Train inspects camp & buildings.

Tuesday November 6th.
Refilling
Dr DAVIS. T.F. on leave to ENGLAND from 8th to 22nd Nov.
Corpl RAPSON under arrest charcoal fire in dug out.
Admonished.
2nd Corpl ROSSITER and 6 men join reinforcements from HAVRE.

Wednesday. November 7th.

Refilling

O.C. Train visits camp.

13 men D.S.C. charged with having dirty bivouacs

2 Forfeit 2 days pay each. Remainder admonished.

N.C.O's of D.S.C warned.

Sergt BARKER D.S.C. admonished for neglecting to put flags on supply train.

Rifles of D.S.C. detachment inspected. Not clean.

Thursday. November 8th

Refilling

Visited D.A.C Hd Qrs & 1 Section.

Remainder of Company paid out.

L.Cpl ROSSITER posted 430 Coy

Dr HINSON " 431 Coy

Friday. November 9th

Refilling

Inspection of all huts, bivouacs, stables occupied by Company & attached details.

Enlarging dining room for men.

Saturday. November 10

Refilling.

Inspection of Rifles det D.S.C.

Company paid out.

Strong wind and rain.

Lieut TAYLEUR & 12 wagons from Train to forward lines return midnight [illegible] shell fire

E.W. Alderson

MAJOR, A.S.C.

O.C. HD. QRS. COMPANY 42nd DIVL. TRAIN.

Sunday. November 11th
Refilling. One Remount received from 19 Mob. Vet.
One wagon replaced at D.H.Q.
All surplus Ordnance Stores to be collected & returned.

Monday. November. 12
Refilling twice & double delivery to units
One Water Cart received from Railhead
to replace one condemned.
G.S. Wagon C.210 condemned damaged by
shell fire. No 93399.
159419 Sergt WAGDIN. W. joins the company from HAVRE
Lieut TAYLEUR being granted leave to go to LA PANNE
for luncheon did not return to camp till 10 P.M.

Tuesday November 13
Use of DECAUVILLE Railway discontinued for bringing
supplies from St IDESBALD Railhead to dumps.
Horse Transport draws from railhead no issue
to units to-day.
Pte SERVICE joins from 430 Coy to complete establishment.

Wednesday. November. 14.
M.T. draws from Railhead with lorries
Notified at 9 P.M that Horse Transport will draw from
Railhead to-morrow morning
Horse transport refilling & delivering to units

Thursday November 15.
Horse Transport draws from Railhead. Units arrange transport for refilling.
Driver MEARS. H.A. to 1/2 E. LANCS. F.A.
Driver SMYTH. T. on leave 17·11·17 to 1·12·17.
4 Supply Wagons & Pairs detailed to 431 Coy.

Friday November 16.
Motor Transport draws from Railhead.
H.T. Refill at dump & deliver to units.
1 Wagon (D.210) & 2 wheelers to I.O.M. for repairs.
2 Officers 20 wagons to NIEUPORT removing ammunition to LLOYD siding in two parties parade at 6 & 8 P.M. return to camp 10·30 & 12·30 respectively.
Arrangements re detachment of Supply Wagons throughout Division for use as extra baggage wagons during pending move. Loaders Paid out

Saturday. November 17
Motor Transport draws from Railhead.
H.T. refilling.
Dr TURBITT withdrawn from Farm Work. COXYDE.
2 Wagons detached 430 Coy for Train H^d Qrs
1 on loan C. R.A. 210 Bde.
Company paid out.
French Ammunition Column arrive proposing to take over this camp on our departure.
Accommodation for officers & an office are provided.

handing over to 133 Div Amm Park. French Army.
Company proceeded via ADINKERKE to
GHYVELDE camping at St FRANCOIS Farm
on LES MOERES Road. Shelter for horses,
barns for men, outhouse & loft for N.C.O.s billet
for one officer, 2 officers & mess in GHYVELDE
Weather wet ground sodden. 1 horse slight Colic
during night. Farm owner unsatisfactory.

22nd November 1917.
Remained in Camp. Exercised horses. Company
Routine. Rations drawn in GHYVELDE Square
Reported G.O.C.R.A. concerning move.
Weather dull ground sodden.

23rd November.
Parade 11 a.m. Passed G.O.C. 42nd D.A. 11.59 to
12.3 at starting point place of encampment
GHYVELDE proceeded via LES MOERES
KROMIELHOEK. WEST CAPELLE. WYLDER
to camp on WORMHOUDT - CASSEL road at
RYSSEN's Farm arriving 6 P.M. Breakdown
on road due to meeting convoy French motor
lorries on a narrow road soft at sides, caused
½ hour delay. Good barns for men, good water,
accomodation 2 officers N.C.O.s one store room.
Farmer obliging. Weather fair & dry.
Rations drawn whilst passing through WORMHOUDT
Square.

HONDEGHEM

HONDEGHEM

24th November

Parade 2 P.M and marched ½ mile towards CASSEL camping at farm COCKENPOT.

Good barns for men, grass standing for horses, stabling for 5, mess & one room for officers. Mess for N.C.O's & barn.

Refilling on CASSEL Road, C.R.A. near ZERMEZEELE. Strong wind, Cold.

25th November. Sunday.

Marched 10.30 a.m via ZERMEZEELE – WEMAERS CAPPEL to starting point at ZUYTPEENE. 11.50 thence via BAVINCHOVE LONGUE CROIX to HONDEGHEM.

Ration dump HALLON CAPPEL. Accomodation at GRANDE FERME WESCHE poor for all ranks, officers in village. Arrive 2.30 P.M. Snow showers. Cold. Strong wind.

26th November.

Marched 10 a.m via LONGUE CROIX. HALLON CAPPEL. LA BELLE HOTESSE. BOESEGHEM. GUARLINGHEM to St MARTIN there halted watered fed & meal for men. O.C. Train cancels original instructions from G.O.C. R.A. at 2.30 P.M and the company must then move to ZAMBRES via AIRE horses & wagons in a sodden field barns for men. Offrs & N.C.O's messes.

Weather cold & rain later.

Capt TROUP. Lieuts YEATS & PAINE rejoin

ZOMBRES

27 November
~~Fourteen~~ supply wagons rejoin Company.
H.T. draws from Railhead with refill at ZOMBRES
Railhead at AIRE
Lieut PAINE goes to rejoin D.S.C
Capt SPRECKLEY joins company to replace Capt
TROUP for Infantry training in ENGLAND
to join on 1st December.

ZOMBRES

November 28
Additional stabling found for 40 horses.
Cpl GRIFFITHS. Dr McDAY. Dr St ELLIS before
O.C. Train for neglect of duty on Picquet case
dismissed Not Proven.
Horse transport to Railhead. Refilling by units.
Dr McDONAGH on leave 30.11 to 14.12.

ZOMBRES

November 29 Thursday
7 G.S. Supply Wagons detached to 210 Bde R.F.A
and 7 to 211 Bde by arrangement with S.C.R.A
Capt SPRECKLEY and Lieut YEATS detached
for supply duties with motor lorries to ROBECQ.
Railhead by motor transport, refilling by units.

November 30 Friday
Marched at 11 a.m. 13 G.S. Wagons 6 Limbers
2 Water. 1 Maltese Cart. 3 O.89 O.R. 52 Horses.
Inspected by G.O.C. 42 Div R.A 12 noon at
starting point Road Junction N.29.C.8.1. Again
inspected by G.O.C. 42nd Division at P.35.b.

Arrived RIEZ DU VINAGE 4 P.M. company in billets. One horse falls into a midden round which horses are standing in a burnt out Farm.
Fair accommodation for all ranks.

RIEZ DU VINAGE

December. 1st Saturday
Lieut MORPHY reported died of wounds in BETHUNE 29th inst. Funeral this day at CHOCQUES.
Company routine.
Weather cold, wet, windy.

RIEZ DU VINAGE

December 2nd Sunday
Marched 12 noon via LA BASSEE Canal Rd, PONT AVELETTE across Canal LAWE, LOCON Rd to GOUGH LINES LE HAMEL map reference BETHUNE X 20.D.1.7.
Shelters for horses, workshops, cookhouse, mens mess room, prepared barns for men, Sergts mess & Officers mess in billets 100 yds distant.
Mens billets mostly out of camp area.
Capt SPRECKLEY and Lieut YEATS returned to Coy HdQrs.
2 Supply wagons from 1/9 Lancaster Regt return to Camp.

LE HAMEL

December 3. Monday
Supply wagons to dump but not required, units making own arrangements.
O.C. Train inspects camp.
2 Wagons returned from 211 Bde R.F.A.

1 Wagon received to complete establishment.
10 Supply wagons returned from various units.
Water supply in camp runs out, temporary arrangements made. Frost at night

December. 4th Tuesday
Refilling
Supply wagons returned to Coy H^d Qrs

Dec 5th.

Dec. 6th. Thursday.
Major Alderman handed over the 428 Coy. A. S. C. to Capt. A [illegible]. Capt. A. F. ARIS. A.S.C. witnessed the handing over. The Coy. Cash book [illegible] were in rather a complicated state.
T Smyth returned off leave from England.
No/T4/156802 [illegible] W. transferred to 421 Coy. A.S.
No. T4/057914 [illegible] transferred from 421 Coy to 428 Coy A.S.C.

No. T4 160064 Cpl ~~[illegible]~~ Abell. W. H. promoted A/C.Q.M.S. with effect parade 18/10/17. with pay from 14/10/17.

Authy: P. 21/8734/4. 30-11-17.

"The following Units' Baggage or Supply Wagons reported to the Coy.

429 Coy R.E. 2 G.S.

Dec. 7th Friday.

All detached Baggage and Supply Vehicles returned to the Coy, except

1. A. P. M

2 Salvage. Coy.

1 Employment Coy

1 Reinforcement Coy

1. Train Hd Qrs.

1. 428 R.E. Coy.

Some Vehicles were in a very bad state of repair. Especially those of 210 Bgd. Arty.

1. H.D. Horse did not return from C.R.A. owing to sickness

1. H.D. Horse returned from ~~[illegible]~~ Employment Wing with bad Canker in fore foot.

Cpl LIMEINE attached to

429 Coy A.S.C.   L2394

Dec 8. Sat

428 Coy R.E. reported to Coy from 430 Coy A.S.C.
Coy paid out 6385 f.0

WL [initials]

Dec. 9th Sunday. Refilling.
Dr Smith evacuated C.C.S
Monday 10th Refilling. Dr Lewis placed under arrest for Absent off Stables, and stating a falsehood to a N.C.O.

Dec 11th Tuesday Dr Lewis given 7 days F.P. by O.C. for Absence off Stables and Stating a falsehood to a N.C.O.
Gd Bevill arrived with 5 H.D and 1 Rider from Boulogne.
Canteen closed for Stocktaking and Audit. Re opened at night.
A quantity of Ordnance Stores drawn including 79 pairs of H.S. Boots and nose bags.
~~5 HD~~ Dr Barton evacuated from C.C.S.

Dec 12th. S. Sgt. Gomes proceeded to coal dump for duty. Hd 25 Sect paid. S. S. Hodgson proceeded on leave.

Dec 13th. One H.D. Remount. sent to mobile Sect. with Opthalmia.

Dec 14th. To Hospital Pt Jackson. Dr Mill. Dr Walsley. Three Loaders attached to 431 Coy A.S.C. without Vehicles. Inspection of Rifles. Gas mask Rations etc.

Dec 15th. Sat. 1-H.D. sent to Mob Sect (Cellulitis). 1-H.D died.

Dec 16 Sunday. Nil

Dec 17 Monday. Dr Walsley evacuated to C.C.S. Pt Jackson evacuated to C.C.S.
T26913 Dr Sergant H. T4/262280 Dr Shaw E. joined Coy from Base. Dr Reams returned from leave. Dr McDonagh returned from leave

Dec 12th. S Sgt Gaves proceeded to coal dump for duty. Hd 2s⁻ Sect paid. S. S. Hodgson proceeded on leave.

Dec 13th. One H.D. Remount. sent to Mobile Sect: with Opthalmia.

Dec 14th. To Hospital Pt Jackson. Dr Mili. Dr Walsley. Three Loaders attached to 431 Coy A.S.C. without Vehicles. Inspection of Rifles Gas Mask Rations etc.

Dec 15th. Sat. 1-H.D sent to Mob Sect (Cellulitis). 1-H.D died.

Dec 16 Sunday. nil

Dec 17 Monday. Dr Walsley evacuated to C.C.S. Pt Jackson evacuated to C.C.S. T26913 Dr Sergant H. T4/262280 Dr Shaw E. joined Coy from Base. Dr Plane returned from leave. Dr McDonogh returned from leave

Dec 18th D Frankum admitted to Hospital.

Dec 19th D Reid under arrest. One H.D. 105 Admit Mob Vet. (Opthalmia)

Dec 20th D Reid. Awarded 21 days F.P. for disobeying A.R.O. and insolence to an N.C.O. C.R.A. visited

Dec 21st. Col. Slaughter round the camp. Complained of the Horses not being rough shod but accepted explanation of non-compliance.

Dec 22nd Dvr Pearce to Hospital. One H.D. to Mob Vet. ~~[illegible]~~. Opthalmia
Pt. ~~[illegible]~~ Collins Emp Coy proceeded on leave.
D Reid sent to A.P.M. who refused on medical grounds to take him in. &

[illegible]

December 23rd 1917.

T.4 S.R./01376. FRANKUM. W. Driver discharged from Hospital.

T/28194. TAYLOR F.H. Driver proceeded on leave.

December. 24. 1917 (Monday)

a/Cprl. BURVILL F.W. apptd. act./Sergeant.

a/Sergt. KING. T.H. transferred to 429 Coy.

a/Sergt. GULLY.P. transferred from 431 Coy.

a/L.Cpl. TURNER. F.G. appointed act/Corporal.

Driver JOBBINS. T. appointed. act./L. Cprl

Dec. 25th. Nil

Dec. 26th Dr Pearce evacuated to C.C.S. Lt Taylor proceeded with 9 G.S. Wagons etc to report to 12th Div Train at BOESEGHEM.

Decr. 27. Lieut. W. H. Taylor with 9 Wagons returned from 9th Divl. Train.

Decr. 28. Driver R. CRAIG. charged ~~with~~ with drunkenness i/c of a pair of horses, whilst on active service.

Lt Taylor promoted A/Capt.

Decr. 29. Driver. R. CRAIG. before C.O. Train and remanded for trial by F.G.C.M.

December 30. 1917.

BASTON G. Driver discharged from Hosp.
MANN A.
CROWTHER. E " admitted to ".

December 31. 1917.
FRANKUM. W. Dvr. proceeded on leave.

---

1 Jan. Pt Colbourn proceeded on leave.
Pt Jones " " "

Jan. 2nd:

Jan. 3rd Dr Wilson transferred
to 430 Coy A.S.C. Dr Smith
transferred from 430 Coy to
425 Coy.
Dr ~~[illegible]~~ Cumming proceeded
on leave.
Sgt Hayden and Dr Brown
proceeded to Boulogne
for the purpose of bringing up
remounts.
Dr Craig tried by F.G.C.M.

L/Cpl Fay appointed Cpl with pay with effect from 14/10/17.

Dr Tunbitt appointed L/Cpl vice Cpl Fay.

Jan 4th Capt Fazer. posted to 431 Coy A.S.C.

Dr Shaw proceeded on leave.

Jan 5th
Craig. A. Driver. sentence promulgated 90 days F.P. No 1.

Jan 6th nil

Jan 7th Coy paid out. Drivers Lee, Andrews, Hill, Lomas. joined as reinforcements.

Jan 8th Dr Reid released from 21 days F.P. Sgt Wayden arrived back from Boulogne with 7 Remounts. The weather was bad heavy snow having fallen. Dr Brown who accompanied Sgt Wayden lost a bit and remounts.

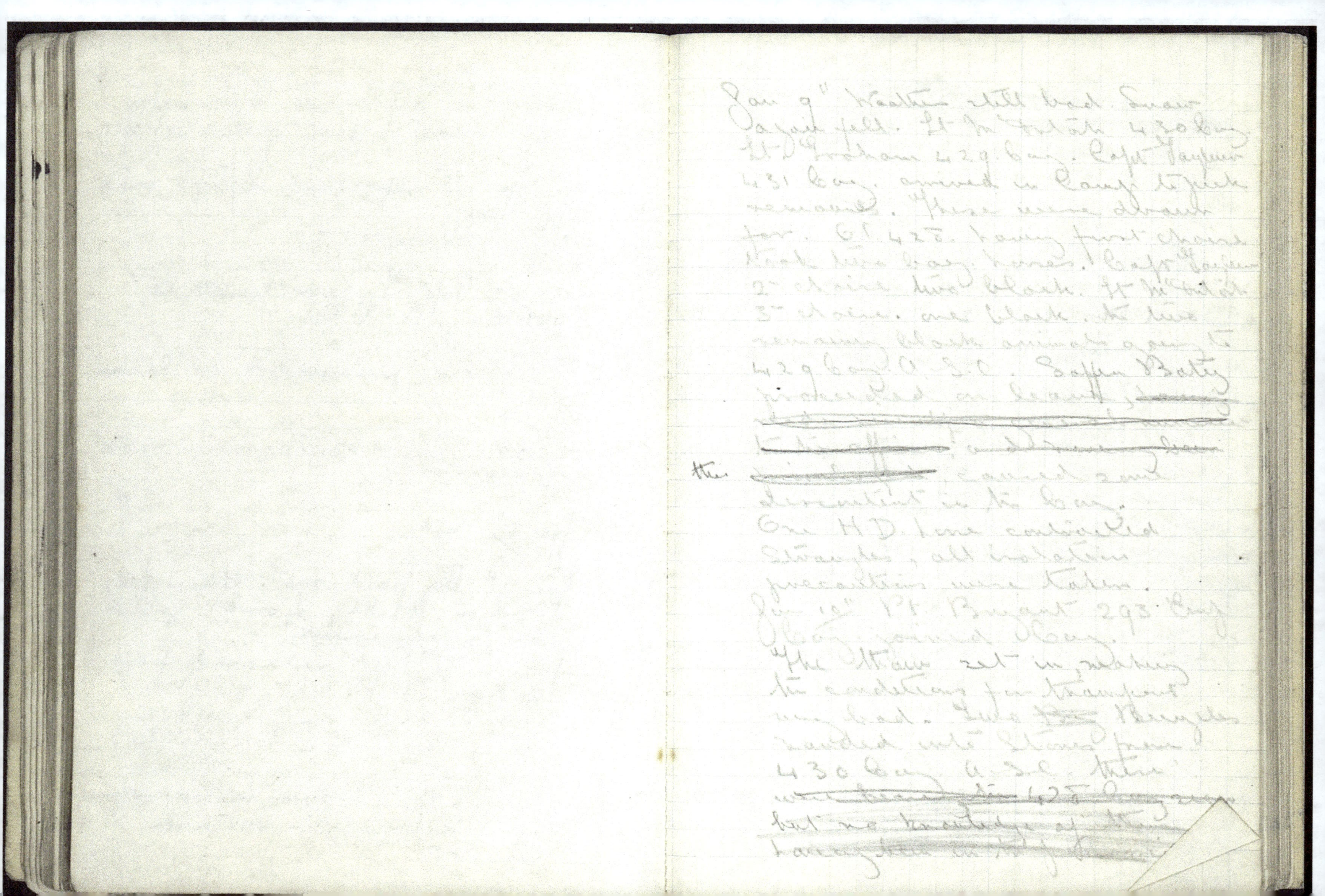

Jan 9th Weather still bad. Snow again fell. Lt McIntosh 430 Coy, Lt Graham 429 Coy, Capt Jaques 431 Coy, arrived in Camp to pick remounts. These were drawn for. O.C. 430 having first choice took two bay horses. Capt Jaques 2nd choice two black. Lt McIntosh 3rd choice, one black. The two remaining black animals going to 429 Coy A.S.C. Sapper Batty proceeded on leave, ~~[illegible]~~
~~[illegible]~~
~~[illegible]~~
~~[illegible]~~ caused some discontent in the Coy.
One H.D. horse contracted Strangles, all isolation precautions were taken.
Jan 10th Pte Bryant 293 Coy [illegible] joined Coy.
The thaw set in making the conditions for transport very bad. Two ~~[illegible]~~ Bangles handed into Stores from 430 Coy A.S.C. there ~~[illegible]~~
~~[illegible]~~
~~[illegible]~~

[illegible]. One was punished in both lyres, neither had lamps or jumps when returned.

Jan 11th. S.S.M. Harwood proceeded on leave. A short lecture on Economy was given by O.C. Coy.

Jan 12th Cpl Turner proceeded on leave also Pt Lang D. Cuf Coy proceeds on leave.
1 H.D. Horse sent to Mob Vet with Cellulitis.
Thaw precautions having come into force 4.30 am G.S. Wagon proceeded to Merville, under an Officer of 431 Coy. and returned at 4 p.m.

Jan 13th 9 G.S. Wagons to Merville on Thaw precaution duty; under an Officer of 429 Coy
S. Taylor F.H. returned from leave.

Jan 14th 9 G.S. Wagons to Merville on Thaw precaution duty. Under an Officer of 431 Coy. Roads very bad. H.D. 115 to Mobile Sect.

Jan 15 No Thaw Wagon. ordinary Standing detail was carried out.
Dr Gordon proceeded on leave.
~~Dr Brody " " "~~
A/Cpl Crompton transferred to 430 Coy
Dr Mc ~~[illegible]~~ Houl to 428 vice Cpl Crompton.

Jan 16 Thaw precautions again in force.
9 G.S. Wagon under an officer of 429 Coy. Sgt Gully arrested for Drunkenness with violence.
Dr Crowther evacuated 16 Dec. 1st C.R.S.
Road very bad indeed.
Dr Vickers replaced Dr Buckler at F.H.2

Jan 17. 20 G.S Wagon to Merville under Lt Blackman. Roads flooded. Sgt Burnville sent as escort to 54th C.C.S to fetch Sgt Gully who was suffering from an injury to his head.
Dr Bartlett proceeded on leave
Dr Mann reported to 42 Div Wing. to replace Dr Mann
Dr Franklin returned from leave.
Three Drivers and two loaders 6 HD with wagons of the 84th A.F.A reported to Coy, to be attached

Jan 18th Sgt Barder. 1/1st F.A. reported for test. Sgt Gully charged, and remanded for C.O.
22 Wagons under Lt Blackmore proceeded to Bethune to convey timber and coal to Div Dumps. Dr Vine proceeded on leave. Pt Colbourne Pt Jones returned from leave.
Three Drivers reported as reinforcements. Collection for St Dunstan's Home realised 450 frs.
Jan 19th 21 G.S. Wagon to Merville under Lt Yates. Roads still very bad. Sgt Gully to Train Hd Qrs, for trial by C.O. remanded for further evidence. Dr Waddington proceeded on leave. Five loaders reported to Coy for duty. Sgt Oldfield 1/2 F.A. reported for test as 2 M. Sgt. Had no knowledge of the work at all. 2-H D and Wagon reported for duty from 74th A F A. no drivers.

Jany 20 1918.

Jan. 21. 1918 7 Wagons sent to MERVILLE on thaw precautions.

C.H.T/272. Wor. HORNSBY. J. and C.H.T/588 Wor. HULLAH. W. transferred to 125th Brigade Hdqrs.

T/35959. Dvr. SHAW. W. reported back from leave.

Jany. 22. 1918. 2 Wagons sent to MERVILLE on thaw precautions.

T/24343. a/Cpl. HEARD. W. J. reverts at his own request to his permanent rank of driver.

T/33458. a/Sgt. CULLY. G. reverted to his permanent rank of driver by the C.O. for. (1) Drunkenness (2) Violently resisting the military police.

T/25732. a/Lce. Cpl. SPILLER. C. reverted to his permanent rank of driver by the C.O. for. (1) Neglect of duty. (2) Absent off Fire picquet parade.

TH/017689. Cpl. LEES. J. T. transferred to R.Es.

Jany. 23. 1918.

TH/249292 Dvr. ROBINSON. W. H. proceeded on leave.

T/254752. Pte. WEBLEY. W. H. proceeded on leave.

T4/2411320 Dvr. PAVEY. H. J. admitted to Corps. Rest Station.

127418. Pte. YOUNG. T. admitted to 1/2 East Lancs. Field Ambulance.

T/25189. Dvr. PORTER. E. rejoined from No 12 Stationary Hospital.

Jany. 24. 1918.

Ts/1135. Farr. Cpl. LLOYD C. transferred to 4th. Reserve Park.

T3/44479. HALL C. Driver. admitted to 1/2nd. East Lancs. F.A.

Jany. 25. 1918.

Ts/34458 Driver GULLY. P. transferred to 430 Company. A.S.C.

T4/088293. Driver HOLLIS. J. transferred from 430 Company A.S.C.

T/22343. Driver. CUNNING. F. reported back from leave.

Notified that. T4/071651. PEARCE Dvr. F. was evacuated to England on 14/1/18.

Jany. 26. 1918.

S/296654 Pte. EVANS. R.D. admitted to 1/2nd. East Lancs. F.A.

T2/10112. Dvr. HUMPHREYS. A.H. proceeded on leave.

10 Wagons G.S. detailed to report for duty at Kantara Dump returned to camp at 1 p.m. having done no work, owing to a muunderstanding at the Kantara and Bethune dumps

January. 27. 1918.

T/22843. GUNNING. F. Driver awarded 14 days F.P. No1 by the C.O. for being absent off leave from U.K.

T2/10121. HUMPHREYS. A.H. Driver proceeded on leave.

January. 28. 1917

Capt. A. FENNER. proceeded on leave to England. Capt. G. [illegible] takes command

T4/244310 PAVEY. H.J. Dvr. evacuated to 1st Corps Rest Station 25/1/18.

G.T.B.

T/22843. GUNNING. F. Dvr. sent to A.P.M. to undergo sentence awarded yesterday.

January. 29. 1917

T4/038321. TAYLOR G.W. proceeded on special leave to England.

T/16189 S.S.M. HARWOOD reported back from leave.

S/290654 EVANS. R.B. Pte. evacuated to No1. C.C.S. 27/1/18.

G.T.B.

January 30. 1918.

G.T.B.

January. 31. 1918.

T/14721. A/C.S.M. Morris J. transferred to 480 Coy. and appointed to the rank of A/S.S.M.

T/14307 A/C.S.M. Burdon. T.J. transferred from 43? Company. A.S.C.

G.T.B.

February. 1. 1918.

T/34376. TURNER. F. G. Cpl. reported back from leave.

T/12905. ROBSON. J. Dvr. proceeded on one months leave to England.

G.T.B.

February. 2. 1918.

1 Driver with 2. H. D. Horses and Wagon attached from 268 Machine Gun Coy.

T1/3296. JORDAN. W. Dvr. reported back from leave.

G.T.B.

February. 3. 1918.

T3/030657. BARTLETT. F. J. reported back from leave to U.K.

T4/125753. CROSBY. G. W. Driver reported back from leave to England on 31/1/18. G.T.B.

February. 4. 1918.

M.2./148167. TAIT. J. T. a/Cprl. reverted to his permanent rank of Private, on transfer to England. 10/1/18

G.T.B.

February. 5th 1918

T1/3822 TIMMS. W. Driver reported back from leave.

A. D. Q. S. T. visited the Camp. G.T.B.

February. 6. 1918.

Nil.

February. 7. 1918. Lance Cpl. GOUDGE with two drivers, proceeded to BOULOGNE for remounts.
T/34101. MORRIN. W. Dvr. admitted to 1/2nd. East Lancs. F.A.
350032 Cpl. HOWELL. W.H. (R.A.M.C.) returned to 1/1. E.L.F.A. All personnel attached for water duties having been recalled to their Units.

G. T. B.

February. 8. 1918.
T. 24492 WADDINGTON. H. Dvr. reported back from leave.

G. T. B.

February. 9. 1918.
T.1/317 HENRY. E.E. Dvr. transferred to 430 Coy.
T/22843. GUNNING. F. Dvr. returned to duty from undergoing term of F.P. No1. at A.P.M's compound.
T/24941. BURVILL. F.W. A/Sgt. awarded CROIX DE GUERRE, by His Majesty, King of the Belgians, in recognition of his services whilst the Division was employed in Belgium. Award published in 42nd D.R.O. 109 dated 8/2/1918.

G. T. B.

February. 13. 1918.

2 G.S. Wagons with H.D. Horses of 5th East Lancs attached from 430 Coy. A.S.C.

February. 14. 1918.

Driver Grosty with horses and wagon, attached to 3 Section D.A.C.

February. 15.

Baggage Wagons sent to the Batteries and Sections of the D.A.C. for move to the new area.

February. 16.

For Wkr. Day proceeded on leave to U.K.

Company moved to the BUSNES area, arriving at GONNEHAM at 12/30 p.m. An advance party under Lieut. J.P. BLACKMORE, left the camp at LE HAMEL, by motor lorry at 8.30 a.m. Remainder of the Company marched off at 9.30 a.m. Weather bright and frosty.

February 17. 1918.

8 Remounts which arrived on the 12nd distributed as follows. 1 H.D. and 1 Rider to 429 Coy. 1 H.D. to 430 Coy. 2 H.D. to 431 Coy. 3 H.D. remaining with this Company.

H.P.W.

February 18. 1918.

T/33032 S. GREEN T. (supply) and T4/045123 STANFORD A.M. Dvr, arrived as reinforcements from HAVRE.

H.P.W.

February 19. 1918.

T/Major. H.P. WILLIAMS. M.C. arrived for duty with the Train.

H.P.W.

February 20. 1918.

The baggage Pairs which had been with their Units for the move to the BUSNES area instructed to return to the Company. The Wagons to remain with their Units for a week from this date.

Captain C. THURLING BLACKWELL relinquished temporary command of the Company, Major H.P. WILLIAMS having arrived to assume command.

Captain A. FENNER M.C. returned from leave to U.K.

H.P.W.

February. 21. 1918.

Capt. A. FENNEL. M.C. handed over command of the Company to Major H. P. WILLIAMS. M.C., and certificate rendered to Train Headquarters.

H.P.W.

February. 22. 1918.

18 Horses sent to Corps Dep.
Capt. A. FENNEL. M.C. proceeded to join the 25th Divisional Train.

H.P.W.

February. 23. 1918.

Nil.

H.P.W.

February. 24th 1918.

No 25169

M/083361 AIRD. W. L. Pte. with Ford Car, taken on strength ~~from~~ with the Central Purchase Board.

H.P.W.

February. 25th 1918. 'War Savings campaign' explained to the Company.

H.P.W.

February 26. 1918.

2nd Lieut. S. S. James reported for duty with the Company.

£100 invested by Officers and O.R. in War Bonds and Certificates.

H.P.W.

February 27. 1918.

Divisional Commander paid a brief visit to the Horse Lines.
Total of Company's investments in the War Loan, during the 2 days campaign increased to £1.198. 19. 6.

H.P.D.

February 28. 1918.

Bathing parade

H.P.D.

March. 1. 1918.

Authority received from O/c A.S.C. Section Base, through Train Headquarters to appoint T.S/1227 THORPE. P. Dvr. Farr. to the vacancy for Farrier Cpl.
Thorpe refused to accept the rank, and his written statement to that effect forwarded to Train Headquarters.
T./12903 ROBSON. J. Driver on a months furlough, to remain in England for disposal and authority received to strike him off strength.

H.P.D.

March 2. 1918.
Baggage Units sent to the Units.

H.P.D.

March. 3. 1918.
Horses to Corps Dep.
K.P.C.

March. 4. 1918
Supply dump after refilling moved to BAS RIEUX. Dump established on [illegible]-[illegible] road.
K.P.C.

March. 5. 1918
Company moved to BAS RIEUX. Good stabling accommodation, and mens billets poor.
K.P.C.

March 6. 1918.
Supply vehicles on railhead park before refilling. Good weather. Beds and palliasses drawn for billets.
K.P.C.

March [illegible]
Nil
K.P.C.

March. 8. 1918
Bathing Parade. [illegible] Lonergan [illegible] attached to [illegible] Co. Temporarily.
K.P.C.

March. 9. 1918
Cpl. MARSH with 3 men to Bourecq for remounts.
K.P.C.

March. 9. 1918 (contd.)

... W.H. YEATS proceeded on leave. 2 Baggage Wagons returned from B.H.Q. Bathing parade.

<u>March 10th 1918.</u>

T/23728. a/Sdr. Cpl. Lipscombe A. posted to 2nd. Reserve Park in the rank of acting Sdr. Sergeant. T/24802 Sdr. Cpl. Severn W.H. posted to 3rd. Cavalry Res. Park, in the rank of acting Sdr. Sergeant. "Summer time" in force from 11 p.m. previous night.

<u>March. 11. 1918.</u>

Remainder of horses, not previously sent, to the Corps. Horse Dep.

<u>March. 12. 1918.</u>

A.A. & Q.M.G. visited the Horse Lines

<u>March. 13. 1918.</u>

One H.D. returned to Coy. lane from Div. Wing. Indent for Collar Chains submitted T3/022630 Dvr. Farr. Best. A. appltd. a/ Farr. Cpl. vice Cpl. Kidd, transferred.

<u>March. 14. 1918.</u>

12 Remounts (H.D.) for the Train arrived from Boulogne. Eliminary competition at BUSNETTES for Train vehicles taking part

in the Divisional competition. Two limbered wagons sent, one of them placed second.

H.P.

March 15. 1918.

The 12 remount which arrived yesterday, allotted, ~~to the boys.~~ & taken on strength. Lieut. A. James returned from leave. Company Parade.

H.P.

March. 16. 1918.

Bathing parade. 31 Collar Chains received from D.A.D.O.S.

Inspection of detached transport of D.H.Q. C.R.A. C.R.E. SALVAGE COY.

H.P.

March. 17. 1918.

Nil. Bathing parade

H.P.

March. 18. 1918. 3 H.D. Remounts for the train fetched from MARLES LES MINES. Driver. A.H. Humphreys awarded 7 days F.P. No1 by C.O. Company paid.

H.P.

March. 19. 1918. Dvr. Humphreys sent to A.P.M. Heavy rain.
1 Remount to 430 Coy, 1 to 431 Coy.

H.P.

March. 20 1918.
Auth. received to draw material from R.E's. for the construction of covered horse lines.
H.Pl.

March. 21. 1918.
1 Hotchkiss Gun. 303 No 11424 drawn from "Ordnance".
Transport at Divisional Wing inspected.
H.Pl.

March. 22. 1918.
Nil.
H.Pl.

March 23. 1918.
Baggage and Supply Wagons sent to Units.
Remainder of boys marched at 11-30 a.m to Mingoval. 3 H.D. to 1st Army Collecting station.
H.Pl.

March. 24. 1918.
Company moved to BIENVILLERS au BOIS. Supply dump at MONCHY au BOIS.
H.Pl.
March. 25 1918. Nil. Dump at ADINFER
H.Pl.
March. 26 1918.
Supply dump at ~~ADINFER~~ FONQUEVILLERS.
Company moved at 5 p.m. and camped on ~~At~~ "BIENVILLERS – ST. AMAND" road.
H.Pl.

March ~~27~~ 21. 1918

~~FONCQUEVILLERS~~ Camp Supply dump at ~~Company moved at 2 p.m. to ST. AMAND.~~

H.P.L.

March 28 1918.

Supply dump near to camp on BIENVILLERS - ST. AMAND. Rd Company moved at 8:30 a.m. to COUIN.

H.P.L.

March 29. 1918

At COUIN. Supply dump one kilometre outside village. Four horses attached to C.211 reported missing, owing to the Battery's wagon lines being shelled.

H.P.L.

March 30. 1918 Nil H.P.L.

March 31. 1918 Nil H.P.L.

April 1. 1918. Nil. H.P.L.

April 2. 1918 Company moved to SOUASTRE. Dump outside village on SOUASTRE - HENU Road. Horse lines in open, one barn for men H.P.L.

April 3. 1918
Nil.
H.P.L.

April 4. 1918
Supply vehicles returned to the Company. Heavy rain.
H.P.L.

April 5. 1918.
12 L mounts for the Train arrived. Supply dump moved nearer to HENU. Village shelled during the afternoon.
H.P.L.

April 6. 1918.
8 of the L mounts received yesterday taken on strength.
H.P.L.

April 7. 1918.
Nil.
H.P.L.

April 8. 1918.
Nil.
H.P.L.

April 9. 1918
Nil
H.P.L.

April 10. 1918.
Nil. 211 Bde moved back to SOUASTRE.
H.P.L.

April 11. 1918 Nil. 210 Bde moved to SOUASTRE.
H.P.L.

April 12 1918. Company moved to T.A.S. Horses on lines. No billets for the men. WPL

April 13. 1918. Stables and billets taken over from 37th Div Train. WPL

Sunday April 14. 1918: Company moved at 5.30 a.m to HENU. Weather cold. Horses in barns, Good barns as sleeping accommodation for the men. Four horses reported missing on 29/3/18 while with C/211 returned to Coy. WPL

Monday April 15. 1918. Company paid. General routine. 7 Tents received from D.H.Q. WPL?

Tuesday April 16 1918 General Routine. Estimate for material required for 12 frames on wagons submitted to T.H.Q. WPL

Wednesday April 17 1918. Refilling at 9 a.m and 4 p.m for the 18th and 19th, supplies for 18th delivered to Units. Supply wagons loaded and remained on dump overnight. Recommendation of 239 Lin. Coy that Pte. (a/cpl) GREEN G.T. N.C.O.'s roster be promoted Corporal, - receive pay of that rank. WPL

April 18. 1918:

Supply wagon + horses. 1/1 E.L.F.A. returned to Coy. Company routine.

April 19. 1918.

Slight fall of snow. Lecture on the Hotchkiss Gun, to all N.C.O's of the Company, by Corporal F.G. Turner.

April 20. 1918.

General routine. Company parade. Drs Lomas + Bennett (1st) tried by F.G.C.M.

April 21. 1918.

Company Routine

April 22. 1918

Company Routine

April 23. 1918 Dvr. W.H. Franklin sent to A.P.M. to undergo sentence of 28 days. F.P. No 1.

April 24. 1918 Court of Enquiry on loss of bicycle on charge of Dvr. Stanger.

Promulgation of sentence Drivers Lomas + Bennett.

April. 25. 1918.

Driver Whr. Lonergan/ proceeded on special leave to England.

W.P.L.

April 26. 1918.

Company Routine.

W.P.L.

April 27. 1918.

Company Parade, and General Routine.

Board assembled for the testing of cold shoes, in accordance with D.R.O. 344 of 25/4/18.

Lance. Cpl. Jobbins/ sent for Cookery Course, to 3rd. Army School.

W.P.L.

April 28. 1918.

Company Routine.

W.P.L.

April 29. 1918.

Bathing Parade

Company Routine.

W.P.L.

April 30. 1918.

4 Remounts arrived, and taken on strength. Board assembled for testing cold shoes.

W.P.L.

May 1 1918.

Company Routine. H.P.L.

May. 2. 1918

2/Lieut. J.A. James trans. to 430 Coy.
Lieut. W.W. Yeats " " 431 "
Capt. G.D.N. Wyatt " " 431 "
Lieut. J.L. Graham " from 429 " H.P.L.

May. 3. 1918

D.A.D.V.S. visited the Horse Lines.
Dvr Shaw W. returned from A.P.M.
Company Parade. H.P.L.

May. 4. 1918.

Application from Dvr. Jones for suspension of sentences forwarded to T.H.Q. Bicycle on charge of Dvr Stanyer, lost on 19/4/18 recovered from A.P.M. H.P.L.

May 5. 1918.

Baggage pairs with drivers returned from Hd. Qrs. and Sections of D.A.C.

Cpl. F.G. Turner returned from course of instruction on Hotchkiss Gun

G.S.A. H.P.L.

May. 6. 1918

S.S.M. Harwood returned from temporary duty at Divisional Rest Camp. Company paid.

H.P.L.

May. 7. 1918

Baggage Wagons & pairs retd to Coy. from Pioneer Batn.

H.P.L.

May. 8. 1918.

4 surplus wagons, 8 H.D. horses and drivers transferred to 3rd Army Aux. Horse Coy.

H.P.L.

May. 9. 1918

General Routine.

H.P.L.

May. 10. 1918.

Company parade and general routine.

H.P.L.

May. 11. 1918

Dor [illegible] sent to A.P.M. general routine

H.P.L.

May. 12. 1918. Company Routine.

May. 13. 1918. Canvas water trough with pump + hose handed over to No 2 Coy.
Board to test 2 men of 7/7th Northumberland Fuslrs. as shoeing smiths.

May. 14. 1918. Dvr Farrier RAYBOULD. W. T taken on strength from No 4 Coy
Inspection of all S.B. Respirators.
Application to T.H.Q. for all baggage pairs to return to Company.

May. 15. 1918. General Routine. Bombs dropped in vicinity of mens' billet about 11 p.m.

May. 16. 1918. Private SAVAGE. J. (Loader) sent to 55th Sanitary Section for course of instruction in Water duties.
Baggage pairs rejoin Coy.

May. 17. 1918. Company parade and equipment inspection.

May. 18. 1918. General Routine. H.P.

May. 19. 1918. Pte SAVAGE returned from Course of instruction in Water duties at 55th Sanitary Section, and takes charge of Company Water Cart.

General Routine H.P.

May. 20. 1918. Gunner TRUNKFIELD. W. (loader) returned to 2 Section D.A.C.

General Routine. H.P.

May. 21. 1918. Inspection of Horse Respirators. Board assembled to test shoeing smiths in accordance with G.R.O. 3668.

General Routine. H.P.

May. 22. 1918. Continuation of Board to test shoeing smiths.

Respirators worn at morning stables.

General Routine H.P.

May. 23. 1918.

Company paid.

Bell tent. for post office received from D.A.D.O.S.

Respirators worn at morning stables.

Sdr. Cprl. SCATES recommended to T.H.Q. for period at Third Army Rest Camp.

May. 24. 1918.

Dvr. TIMMS. W. admitted to 1/1st. E.L.F.A.

10 Loaders to PAS for medical inspection.

Lce. Cprl. JOBBINS returned from 3rd. Army School of Cookery.

General Routine

May. 25. 1918.

8 Loaders to PAS for medical inspection.

T.35959 SHAW. W. Dvr. sent to ETAPLES for posting to 1st. Btn. North. Fusbrs.

Company parade for inspection of arms and equipment.

Respirators worn from 8.45 p.m. to 9.45 p.m.

May. 26. 1918.

7 Loaders to PAS for medical inspection.

Sdr. Cpl. SCATES. to 3rd. Army Rest Camp for 14 days period.

Box Respirators Worn from 8/45 p.m. to 9/45 p.m.

WPL

May. 27. 1918.

General routine.

Driver STANLEY. W. charged with drunkenness and remanded for. C.O.

WPL

May. 28. 1918.

Material received from R.E. for construction of bivouacs.

Bathing parade.

Driver STANLEY. W. remanded by. C.O. for. F.G.C.M. and summary of evidence taken

WPL

May. 29. 1918.

Baggage Wagon from A/210 overhauled

General Routine

Box respirators worn from 9.0 p.m to 9.30 p.m

WPL

May. 30. 1918.

Baggage Wagon from B/210 overhauled.

Box respirators worn from 9.0 p.m. to 9.30 p.m.

WPL

May. 31. 1918. Dvr SPENCER. J. to Doulens for interview with Officer of R.A.F. re transfer

Company parade. Inspection of arms & equipment.

Box Respirators worn from 9.0 p.m. to 9.30 p.m.

W.P.L.

June. 1. 1918. Dvr STANLEY. W. tried by F.G.C.M. Baggage wagon, A/211 in for repairs, in very bad condition.

W.P.L.

June 2. 1918. Promulgation of sentence Driver W. STANLEY. - 56 days F.P. No 2.

2nd. Blankets returned to D.A.D.O.S.

W.P.L.

June. 3. 1918. Dvr STANLEY. to A.P.M.

Wagons & Horses at T.H.Q. Divl. Salvage and A.P.M. inspected.

W.P.L.

June. 4. 1918. Company Routine.

W.P.L.

June 5. 1918.
Kit inspection Supply Section
Company Routine.
H.M.

June. 6. 1918.
Company ~~parade~~ routine. Baggage
Wagon + horses to 3 Section D. A. C.
H.M.

June. 7. 1918
Company parade. Inspection
of arms + equipment. General routine
H.M.

June. 8. 1918.
Supply turnout (Limber) to C.R.A.
2 Supply turnouts to 3 Section D.A.C.
Company routine.
H.M.

June. 9. 1918.
Baggage Wagon 3 Section D.A.C.
to No 3 Company
L. Cpl. Turbitt and Dvr. Campbell to 3rd
Army Rest Camp.
H.M.

June. 10. 1918
General routine. Pay Parade.
H.M.

June 11. 1918. Driver Charlish W. A. evacuated. (accidental injuries)

Box Respirators worn from 9 p.m. to 9.30 p.m.

June 12. 1918. General routine.

June 13. 1918. Surplus spurs collected, and returned to D.A.D.O.S. in accordance with G.R.O.

June 14. 1918. Bathing parade at COUIN.

Inspection of Horses by D.A.D.V.S.

June 15. 1918. General routine.

Sunday. June 16. 1918.

Company parade - inspection of arms and equipment.
Box Respirator drill 9.0 p.m to 9.30 p.m.
Driver SPENCER. T. to England for duty with R.A.F.
H.P.W.

June. 17. 1918. Lieut. V. STEER posted to the Company. General routine.
H.P.W.

June 18. 1918. General routine.
H.P.W.

June 19. 1918. General routine.
H.P.W.

June. 20. 1918 General routine.
H.P.W.

June 21. 1918. Company parade. Inspection of arms & equipment.
H.P.W.

June 22. 1918. S.S.M. HARWOOD. A.H. evacuated to 56. C.C.S. Box respirator drill 9.0 p.m to 9.30 p.m
Material drawn from R.E's for construction of shed on Supply Dump.
H.P.W.

Sunday June 23rd 1918

L. Cpl. Turbitt & Dvr. Campbell returned from 3rd Army Rest Camp

General Routine

H.P.

June 24, 1918

Box Respirators worn from 9 p.m to 9.30 pm

General Routine

H.P.

June 25, 1918

General Routine

H.P.

June 26, 1918

General Routine

H.P.

June 27, 1918

General Routine

H.P.

June 28, 1918

Company Parade:- Inspection of Arms & equipment

Pay Parade

General Routine

H.P.

June 29, 1918

Box Respirators worn from 9 p.m to 9-30 p.m

General Routine

H.P.

Sunday June 30th 1918

General Routine

July 1st 1918

Ten N.C.O.s & men admitted to Hospital with Influenza
Box Respirators worn from 9 p.m to 9-30 p.m.
General Routine

July 2nd 1918

Four men to Hospital Influenza
Eight Drivers (reinforcements) arrive from A.S.C. Base Depot
General Routine

July 3rd 1918

Three men to Hospital Influenza
General Routine

July 4th 1918

Thirteen N.C.O.s & men to Hospital, Influenza
Four men (influenza cases) discharged Hospital
General Routine

Friday July 5th 1918

Company move from Henu to Louvencourt

Saturday July 6th 1918

Seven N.C.O.s & men (influenza cases) discharged Hospital

General Routine

Sunday July, 7th 1918.

General Routine

H.P.L.

July 8th 1918

Two Drivers (reinforcements) arrive from Base Depôt

Seven H.D. Remounts arrive from Gouy-en-Artois

General Routine

H.P.L.

July 9th 1918

General Routine

H.P.L.

July 10th 1918

General Routine

H.P.L.

July 11th 1918

General Routine

C.O.C. Visited Camp

H.P.L.

July 12th 1918

General Routine

1 H.D. to No 1 Coy.

H.P.L.

July. 13. 1918.

Company parade. Inspection of Arms & equipment. S.B. Respirator drill 8.45 p.m. – 9.45 p.m.

General Routine.

Inspection of Supply horses with Nos 3 & 4 Coys

H.P.W.

July. 14. 1918.

General Routine. Box Respirator drill for one hour at night.

H.P.W.

July. 15. 1918.

Auth. received for 14 days extension of leave in England Driver COWLARD. A.R.

General Routine.

Inspection Supply pairs No 2 Coy.

H.P.W.

July. 16. 1918.

3 Loaders detached to Divl. Baths. Company pay parade. General Routine

H.P.W.

July. 17. 1918.

Captain J.L.G. GRAHAM proceeded on leave to U.K. + Spratley

Dvr. LORD admitted to Hospital whilst on leave in England, and struck off strength.

General Routine.

H.P.W.

July. 18. 1918. H.D. 210 to 19th Mobile Vety. Section. General Routine.

July. 19. 1918. A.A. & Q.M.G. visited the Camp. General Routine.

July. 20. 1918. Company parade, Inspection of clothing, arms, and equipment. Draw for leave, for remainder of men who have not yet had leave to U.K.

General Routine.

D.A.G.
G.H.Q.
3rd Echelon

24

In accordance with para
Army Demobilization Regulations
I forward herewith original copy
of War Diary of 42nd Divnl
Train up to date of embarkation
of Cadres.

Oswestry
18/4/19.

G.F. Speckley Capt
for Lieut Colonel
O.C. 42nd Div Train

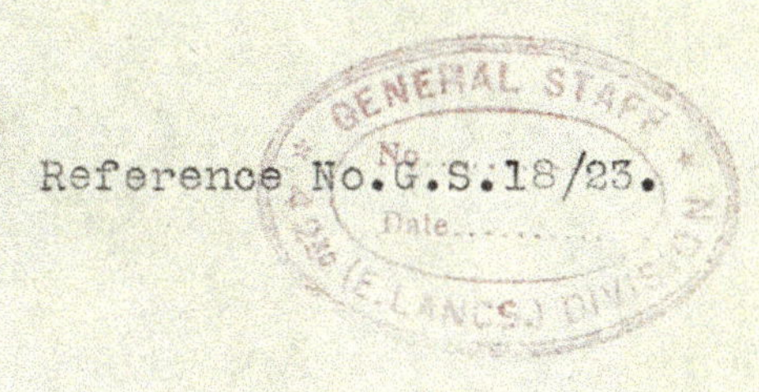

Reference No.G.S.18/23.

D.A.G.,

3rd. Echelon.

B.E.F.

Reference this Office G.SM 18/18 dated 9.4.17.

Herewith War Diary of 42nd. Divisional Train, A.S.C. for the month of March 1917.

Please acknowledge receipt.

A Crookenden Lt Col

~~Captain~~, for
Major General,
Commanding 42nd. Division.

10.4.17.

42 Div Train
Vol 1/42

Army Form C. 2118.

Instructions regarding War Diaries and Intelligence Summaries are contained in F. S. Regs., Part II. and the Staff Manual respectively. Title Pages will be prepared in manuscript.

WAR DIARY
~~or~~
~~INTELLIGENCE SUMMARY~~

(Erase heading not required.)

Place	Date	Hour	Summary of Events and Information	Remarks and references to Appendices
LARKHILL. SALISBURY PLAIN. and HAVRE.	25 2/17	10 a.m.	429 Coy: entrained at Amesbury. Embarked at Southampton on S.S. Siptah.	G.T.B.
	26 2/17	6 a.m.	430 " " " " " " " S.S. South West Miller.	G.T.B.
	27 2/17	7 a.m.	431 " " " " " " " S.S. Archimedes	G.T.B.
			429 Coy: disembarked at HAVRE, & proceeded to no: 1 rest camp SANVIC. HAVRE.	G.T.B.
"			430 Coy: " " " " " no: 1 " G.T.B.	
	28 2/17	8 a.m.	Half 428 (Hqrs:) Coy entrained at Amesbury. Embarked. Southampton under Major LAWSON W.D. (S.S.O. of Train) Ship. S.S. MANCHESTER. IMPORTER.	G.T.B.
			431 Coy disembarked at HAVRE, & Proceeded to no: 2 rest Camp SANVIC. HAVRE	
"	1 3/17	8 a.m.	Hdqrs. of TRAIN & remaining half of 428 Coy. entrained at Amesbury, & embarked at Southampton – ~~1st~~ G.T.B. in two ships. Personnel Ship. = S.S. LONDONDERRY. 9 Officers & 66 other ranks. Transport Ship. S.S. Volumnia 78 horses. 23 other ranks, & 2 Officers.	
			1st half disembarked at HAVRE & proceed no: 2 Camp SANVIC. HAVRE. 5 O.R's. 29. 4 wheeled Vehicles, & 2. two wheeled Vehicles left at Southampton to embark on S.S. HUNSGROVE.	G.T.B.

2449 Wt. W14957/M90 750,000 1/16 J.B.C. & A. Forms/C.2118/12.

Instructions regarding War Diaries and Intelligence Summaries are contained in F. S. Regs., Part II. and the Staff Manual respectively. Title Pages will be prepared in manuscript.

WAR DIARY

~~or~~

~~INTELLIGENCE SUMMARY~~

(Erase heading not required.)

Army Form C. 2118.

Place	Date	Hour	Summary of Events and Information	Remarks and references to Appendices
HAVRE.	2-3-17		Hqrs: of Train + second half Hqrs: Coy. disembarked HAVRE + proceed to no: 2 rest Camp. SANVIC HAVRE.	G.T.B.
			Discovered several horses had become casualties - (One case Rider pneumonia) the remainder 3 Riders + 6 H.D^s sent to Vet: Hospital with Catarrh - These were replaced by Remounts. Catarrh due to exposure after horses leaving stables in England	
"	3-3-17	10.0 a.m	Received orders to send S.S.O. + all supply officers at once by car to PONT RÉMY (Sheet 3. 1:250,000 FRANCE K.5:) to report to Hqrs: 42nd Div: Departed 1.10 p.m. Also received ~~[illegible]~~ orders from D.A.Q.M.G. HAVRE for Hqrs: of Train to proceed on 4th inst: by Road. G.T.B.	G.T.B.
HAVRE + HALLENCOURT (Sheet 3. Border Line J. K. 6.)	4-3-17.	9 a.m	C.O. + Adjut: with 2 O.R. left HAVRE for PONT REMY - Found nominally half the Division had arrived from Marseilles, + were being fed direct by R.S.O. by means of Motor Lorries. The R.S.O. issuing on A.B.55 (France). No Supply Column for the Division - Brigade Supply Officers proceeded to their Brigade areas - Found Billets for Hqrs: Train + Hqrs: Coy: through	G.T.B.
	5-3-17		Div: Hqrs: - 428 Coy: (Hqrs Coy) arrived in Two trains 1400 pm + 1700 p.m. (4 hours late) Marched into billets 1900 + 2100. General arrangements discussed for supplying Division with Supplies, Fuel, Coal etc; - G.T.B.	

2449 Wt. W14957/M90 750,000 1/16 J.B.C. & A. Forms/C.2118/12.

Instructions regarding War Diaries and Intelligence Summaries are contained in F. S. Regs., Part II. and the Staff Manual respectively. Title Pages will be prepared in manuscript.

WAR DIARY
or
~~INTELLIGENCE SUMMARY~~

(Erase heading not required.)

Army Form C. 2118.

Place	Date	Hour	Summary of Events and Information	Remarks and references to Appendices
HALLENCOURT	6.3/17		First A.F W 3317 rendered by S.S.O to ~~Railhead~~ S.O. – Great difficulty in distributing supplies owing to lack of Supply ~~Column~~ T.B., + Bde: Coys: not having arrived. –	Bad detraining arrangements at PONT REMY. G.T.B.
			No: 1 Brigade Coy: (429 Coy: A.S.C.) arrived PONTREMY 16.00. Billeted in Bde: area FONTAINE Sur SOMME. (K.5) (This Bde: is the 125th.)	
			No: 2 Brigade " (430 Coy: A.S.C.) arrived 19.00. Billeted in Bde: area at LIMERCOURT. (near Huppy Sheet 3. J.5.) This is the 127th: Brigade.	
"	7 3/17		Refilling commenced as follows:–	Ref: Map: North West Europe Sheet 3.
		09.30	125th: Bde:– from Railhead (PONT REMY) by Supply Sect: in wagons of 429 Coy:	
		09.30	126th .... } 127th: (One Battn:) } at a point 500 yds outside LIMEUX, on the LIMEUX – BAILLEUL – BELLIFONTAINE Road.	
		09.30	Divisional Troops quartered in + around HALLENCOURT. (Less Divl: Artillery) at SORREL.	
			Divisional Artillery drew direct from R.S.O. on A.B 55 (France)	
			Owing to great congestion of traffic, Motor Lorries were 2 hours late at Refilling Points, + a further delay was caused at all refilling points owing to inexperienced Issuers, (There being a large percentage of "loaders".) ~~[illegible]~~	G.T.B.

2449 Wt. W14957/M90 750,000 1/16 J.B.C. & A. Forms/C.2118/12.

Instructions regarding War Diaries and Intelligence Summaries are contained in F. S. Regs., Part II. and the Staff Manual respectively. Title Pages will be prepared in manuscript.

WAR DIARY

~~or~~

~~INTELLIGENCE SUMMARY~~

(Erase heading not required.)

Army Form C. 2118.

Place	Date	Hour	Summary of Events and Information	Remarks and references to Appendices
HALLENCOURT	7 3/17	14.30	431 Coy. (no. 127th Bde Transport Coy) arrived. Marched to FRUCOURT in 127th Bde area.	G.T.B.
			Most of the Baggage wagons which had arrived with 428-9-430 Coys: utilized for drawing Wood & Straw for troops –	
"	8 3/17	07.30	125th Bde: refilled at Sorel, & all refilling point hours changed to 07.30 a.m. Again late, but clerks & issuers getting more accustomed to their work – Loaders still no good – Great handicap. Have notified O.C. Coys: to help in every way –	
"	9 3/17		Unit Loaders beginning to report to O.C. Coys: in question.	G.T.B.
"	10 3/17		Nothing of particular note – Arranged with C.R.A + A.A + Q.M.G. to send over the Supply sectn wagons of the Divl Artillery to billet at L'HEURE (near ABBEVILLE)	G.T.B. G.T.B.
"	11 3/17		" " " " " " proceeded to L'HEURE –	G.T.B.
			Roads at Refilling points getting bad.	
"	12 3/17	08.30	Divl Troops (less Divl Artillery) attached 127th Bde for Supply purposes –	
			127th Bde, Divl Troops (less artillery), 126th Bde } Refilled at 8-30 a.m at the cross roads immediately South of the H in Huppy (on Map. N.W. Europe Sheet 3.)	G.T.B.

2449 Wt. W14957/M90 750,000 1/16 J.B.C. & A. Forms/C.2118/12.

Army Form C. 2118.

Instructions regarding War Diaries and Intelligence Summaries are contained in F. S. Regs., Part II. and the Staff Manual respectively. Title Pages will be prepared in manuscript.

WAR DIARY
~~or~~
~~INTELLIGENCE~~ SUMMARY

(Erase heading not required.)

Place	Date	Hour	Summary of Events and Information	Remarks and references to Appendices
HALLENCOURT	13/3/17		Divl. Artillery refilled for the 1st time. Refilling point. Immediately above second B in ABBEVILLE on ABBEVILLE - St. RIQUIER road (Ref. Map: ABBEVILLE No 14) Very late owing mistake Road Officer of Supply Column. 126th. Bde: issued with raw 50% flour in lieu of Bread. Error occurred at ABBEVILLE D.D.S.T 4th Army notified. + Instructions issued that no flour was to be sent up on Pack Trains unless asked for. 125th. Bde refilled a second time in preparation for move to HAMEL (J.10 Sheet 62.D) Most of Supply Column arrived. 430 Coy: moved Billets to LES CROISETTES	G.F.B.
"	14/3/17		125th. Bde (1st line + Train) moved to HAMEL under O.C. 429 Coy: A.S.C (Two day trek) + arrived there on 15th	G.F.B.
"	15/3/17		Rations drawn at WAFUSÉE Railhead by S.O. 125th. Bde, for this Bde. Other refilling pts: same as before.	G.F.B.
"	16/3/17		~~Nothing of note~~ G.F.B. Coal still being drawn from CORBIE. (O 5. on Sheet 62.D.) Stampede of Part of 428 Coy: A.S.C. at 22.30 17 H D. horses escaped + made off along HALLENCOURT CITERNE road	G.F.B.
"	17/3/17.		Informed by R.S.O. that no fresh meat to be issued until further notice, Otherwise nothing of note, except that Nine (9) of above mentioned horses recovered, + matter reported to A.A. + Q.M.G.	G.F.B.

2449 Wt. W14957/M90 750,000 1/16 J.B.C. & A. Forms/C.2118/12.

Army Form C. 2118.

WAR DIARY
or
INTELLIGENCE SUMMARY

(*Erase heading not required.*)

Instructions regarding War Diaries and Intelligence Summaries are contained in F. S. Regs., Part II. and the Staff Manual respectively. Title Pages will be prepared in manuscript.

Place	Date	Hour	Summary of Events and Information	Remarks and references to Appendices
HALLENCOURT	18/3/17		No traces of lost horses though every effort has been taken to recover them. Same Refilling points - Quicker issues now being performed -	S.T.B.
	19/3/17		No change.	S.T.B.
	20/3/17		No change	S.T.B.
	21/3/17		Board of Officers assembled (by D.H.Q on application) to Enquire into the circumstances of the stampede of Hqrs: Coy: horses - Board sat from 9 a.m to 6 pm. Supply Sect: horses at L'HEURE inspected - 6 prs: found poor - Reason - apparently too much work. Spare horses ordered from O.C. Hqrs. Coy: to relieve pressure.	S.T.B.
	22/3/17		Great difficulty still being experienced over inoculation of men - the Coys being so far scattered.	S.T.B.
	23/3/17		Inspections of 1st Line transport by O.C. Bde: Coys: still being carried out	S.T.B.
	24/3/17		No change -	

2449 Wt. W14957/M90 750,000 1/16 J.B.C. & A. Forms/C.2118/12.

Instructions regarding War Diaries and Intelligence Summaries are contained in F. S. Regs., Part II. and the Staff Manual respectively. Title Pages will be prepared in manuscript.

WAR DIARY
or
~~INTELLIGENCE SUMMARY~~
(Erase heading not required.)

Army Form C. 2118.

Place	Date	Hour	Summary of Events and Information	Remarks and references to Appendices
HALLENCOURT	25/3/17		No change.	
" "	26/3/17		125th Bde attached to 48th Division. Rationed at Railhead CHUIGNES	G.T.B.
			All supply section wagons (55 G.S. & 4 Limber) of Hqrs. Coy. & 430 & 431 Coys. left for ESTREES, by route march via LA CHAUSSEE, to join 59th Divisional Train & do supply column work.	
			As result of above, 1st Line transport draw rations from refilling points	
" "	27/3/17		Above mentioned supply sections filled at FOUILLOY by lorry.	G.T.B.
" "	28/3/17	9 am	431 Coy. A.S.C. & 1st Line transport of 127th Bde started for CHUIGNES by route march via St. SAUVEUR.	G.T.B.
			Supply sections mentioned above arrived at ESTREES.	
" "	29/3/17		127th Bde moved by rail (Tactical Trains) to neighbourhood CHUIGNES	G.T.B.
			"Paris Supplies" (Hay & Cauliflowers) received at Railhead PONT REMY.	

Instructions regarding War Diaries and Intelligence Summaries are contained in F. S. Regs., Part II. and the Staff Manual respectively. Title Pages will be prepared in manuscript.

WAR DIARY

or

~~INTELLIGENCE~~ SUMMARY

(Erase heading not required.)

Army Form C. 2118.

Place	Date	Hour	Summary of Events and Information	Remarks and references to Appendices
~~30-4-17~~ HALLENCOURT	30 4/17		Transport of Hqrs Coy of Divisional Troops less R.A. started move to neighbourhood of MERICOURT-SUR-SOMME. 127th Bde: drew iron rations from CORBIE	F.T.B.
	31 4/17		Rations for consumption 1st prox for above mentioned troops moving to MERICOURT sent by lorry to HAMEL.	F.T.B.

[illegible] Lt Col
O.C. 42 Div: Train

2449 Wt. W14957/M90 750,000 1/16 J.B.C. & A. Forms/C.2118/12.

Vol 3

CONFIDENTIAL

War Diary

of

42ND. Divisional Train

From 1/4/17 To 30/4/17

(Volume 2.)

Instructions regarding War Diaries and Intelligence Summaries are contained in F. S. Regs., Part II. and the Staff Manual respectively. Title Pages will be prepared in manuscript.

WAR DIARY
or
~~INTELLIGENCE SUMMARY~~
(Erase heading not required.)

Army Form C. 2118.

Place	Date	Hour	Summary of Events and Information	Remarks and references to Appendices
HALLENCOURT	1·4·17		No change.	S.T.B
MERICOURT SUR-SOMME	2·4·17	10 am	DIVISIONAL Hqrs: & Hqrs Train moved to MERICOURT-SUR-SOMME. Also balance of DIVISIONAL TROOPS. All Divisional Troops drew direct from R.S.O. CHUIGNES RAILHEAD on AFs B 55. BSO 125th Bde: drew from above mentioned Railhead making out his own A.F. W 3317. 125th Bde ceasing to be attached to 48th Division	S.T.B
" "	3·4·17		No Change.	
" "	4 4/17		S.S.O. & staff moved from PONT REMY to MERICOURT Sur SOMME. All artillery moved to St SAUVEUR. 125 Brigade refilled by H.T. from RAILHEAD with rations for consumption on 6th 47th	S.T.B
" "	5 4/17		Railhead for 42nd Division opened at CHUIGNES. (1st & 48th Divisions also using this Railhead.) Supply sections which had been attached to 59th Div: Train returned & were used as a Supply Column. 1st line Transport drawing from Dumps to Units. Supply Dumps as follows:- 125th Bde: G.25 b 88 (Sheet 62 C) Divl Artillery " " " " " under S.O. 125 Bde: 127 Bde Close to Sugar factory at Dompierre. Administration of Supplies for Divl Troops carried out by S.S.O. No S.O. being available.	S.T.B

2449 Wt. W14957/M90 750,000 1/16 J.B.C. & A. Forms/C.2118/12.

Army Form C. 2118.

Instructions regarding War Diaries and Intelligence Summaries are contained in F. S. Regs., Part II. and the Staff Manual respectively. Title Pages will be prepared in manuscript.

WAR DIARY
or
~~INTELLIGENCE SUMMARY~~

(Erase heading not required.)

Place	Date	Hour	Summary of Events and Information	Remarks and references to Appendices
MERICOURT Sur-SOMME	6/4/17		Divl: Artillery arrived at CAPPY & neighbourhood, & S.O. took over rations from dump there, & issued rations for consumption 7th inst: Supplies for 126th Bde: dumped at MORCOURT under guard to await arrival of this Bde: from HALLENCOURT area. 125th Bde: left CAPPY for BUIRE – Refilling point at BUSSU – Rations for consumption 8th for this Bde: were carried in Supply wagons from CHUIGNES RAILHEAD to BIACHES – From this point to R.P. at BUSSU where they were drawn by 1st line transport –	G.T.B
"	7/4/17		Nothing of note –	G.T.B
" "	8/4/17		" " " Supply Sections still being used as Supply Column	G.T.B.
" "	9/4/17		211th Bde: R.F.A. & one Sect: D.A.C. moved to DOINGT & were rationed commencing 10th by 48th Division –	G.T.B.
" "	10/4/17		Para Supplies viz: 3000 Kilos of carrots were received & issued as forage.	G.T.B

2449 Wt. W14957/M90 750,000 1/16 J.B.C. & A. Forms/C.2118/12.

Instructions regarding War Diaries and Intelligence Summaries are contained in F. S. Regs., Part II. and the Staff Manual respectively. Title Pages will be prepared in manuscript.

WAR DIARY
or
~~INTELLIGENCE SUMMARY~~
(Erase heading not required.)

Army Form C. 2118.

Place	Date	Hour	Summary of Events and Information	Remarks and references to Appendices
MERICOURT SUR-SOMME.	11 4/17		Lorries became available again for Supply Column work for 126th Bde, including Div: Troops & artillery & attached - Refilling was much more rapid owing to this fact. 127th Refilling point moved to HERBÉCOURT owing to Battns: of this Bde having been moved to FLAUCOURT & PERONNE. for road making etc.	G. T. B.
" "	12 4/17		No change. Inspection of 1st line Transport of 127th Bde: carried out.	G. T. B.
" "	13 4/17		S.S.O. handed over III Corps Coal Dump to 1st Division 93 tons 12 cwt: coal & 18 tons charcoal. He also received 100 tons coal by rail at MERICOURT. 4000 Kilos Linseed Cake received from LA FLAQUE Railhead & issued to Div'l Artillery, 126th Bde, 127th Bde. & Div'l Troops.	G. T. B.
" "	14 4/17		Divisional Hqrs: moved to PERONNE. Reinforcements (417 all Ranks) for 125th Bde: & 127th Bde. drew rations in detail from CHUIGNES Railhead. Inspection of 1st Line Transport of 126th Bde: carried out.	G. T. B.

2449 Wt. W14957/M90 750,000 1/16 J.B.C. & A. Forms/C.2118/12.

Army Form C. 2118.

Instructions regarding War Diaries and Intelligence Summaries are contained in F. S. Regs., Part II. and the Staff Manual respectively. Title Pages will be prepared in manuscript.

WAR DIARY
or
INTELLIGENCE SUMMARY
(Erase heading not required.)

Place	Date	Hour	Summary of Events and Information	Remarks and references to Appendices
MERICOURT SUR. SOMME.	15/4/17		Reinforcements 125th Bde: & 127th Bde: attached to 127th Bde: drew rations from 127th R.P at HERBECOURT. 2 Battns of 126th Bde: moving from PERONNE to LONGAVESNES drew two days rations.	G.T.B.
" "	16/4/17	10 p.m.	125th Infantry Brigade again under orders of 42nd Division. Rationed by 48th Division up to Midnight 17th inst. 125th B.S.O. established refilling point at HERBECOURT for this Bde moving to HERBECOURT area - Supplies taken by Horse Transport (Supply Sect of 429 Coy A.S.C.) to R.P.	G.T.B. Map references Sheet 62c.
" " & PERONNE	17/4/17		B.S.O. 126th Bde: moved from CAPPY to DRIENCOURT - R.P established for this Bde: here & supplies brought up from CHOIGNES Railhead by Lorry. B.S.O. 127th Bde: moved to LE MESNIL BRUNTEL & R.P for this Bde: established there. Train Hqrs: (including S.S.O & staff) moved to PERONNE	G.T.B.

Instructions regarding War Diaries and Intelligence Summaries are contained in F. S. Regs., Part II. and the Staff Manual respectively. Title Pages will be prepared in manuscript.

WAR DIARY
or
~~INTELLIGENCE SUMMARY~~

(Erase heading not required.)

Army Form C. 2118.

Place	Date	Hour	Summary of Events and Information	Remarks and references to Appendices
PERONNE.	18/4/17		R.P^s were as follows to-day:- DIVISIONAL ARTILLERY + attached troops. CAPPY. 125th Bde:- HERBECOURT also for part of 127th Bde: for to-day only. 126th Bde:- DRIENCOURT 127th Bde. LE MESNIL-BRONTEL. One Battn: only of 127th Bde. refilled here to-day. No: 2 Section D.A.C moved yesterday from CAPPY to LE MESNIL BRONTEL + have been attached to S.O. 127th Bde: from to-day inclusive.	Map Sheet 62^c S.T.B.
" "	19/4/17		R.P^s as above. Supplies delivered by Lorry. Railhead moved from CHUIGNES + opened at PERONNE. Great delay owing to Pack train having trouble on the line.	S.T.B.
" "	20/4/17		Supply train again very late + deficient of oat trucks. Oats obtained by lorry from LA FLAQUE. Railhead.	S.T.B.
" "	21/4/17		In preparation for moves of 125th + 127th Bdes: the B.S.O^s in question have exchanged R.P^ts (See Diary for 18th:).	S.T.B

Instructions regarding War Diaries and Intelligence Summaries are contained in F. S. Regs., Part II. and the Staff Manual respectively. Title Pages will be prepared in manuscript.

WAR DIARY

or

~~INTELLIGENCE SUMMARY~~

(Erase heading not required.)

Army Form C. 2118.

Place	Date	Hour	Summary of Events and Information	Remarks and references to Appendices
PERRONNE	22-4-17		Moves of 125th & 127th Bdes: completed - & rations drawn from their new R.Ps mentioned above. 210th Bdes: R.F.A. & remainder of Div: Amm Column & Div: Troops S.O. moving from CAPPY to PERONNE area with rations on their supply wagons for consumption 23rd.	G.T.B.
" "	23-4-17		Turn over commenced of 3 days dump at ROISEL. Supplies & forage (9 lbs: Oats per horse) Authority. III Corps Letter No A.Q. 15/3/17. dated 21/4/17. Balance of Hay & Oats came up on Pack train. Supply Column work from ROISEL Dump & Railhead to R.Ps carried out as follows:— 125th & 126th Bdes: by Train Supply Section Horse Transport. 127th Bdes: by 6 Lorries. All Divisional troops temporarily attached to B.S.Os for rations	G.T.B.
" "	24-4-17		Supplies same as for 23-4-17 Div: Troops R.P. selected at point I 24 c 70 on sheet 62c. & supplies for issue to-morrow dumped there.	

2449 Wt. W14957/M90 750,000 1/16 J.B.C. & A. Forms/C.2118/12.

Army Form C. 2118.

Instructions regarding War Diaries and Intelligence Summaries are contained in F. S. Regs., Part II. and the Staff Manual respectively. Title Pages will be prepared in manuscript.

WAR DIARY
or
~~INTELLIGENCE SUMMARY~~

(Erase heading not required.)

Place	Date	Hour	Summary of Events and Information	Remarks and references to Appendices
PERONNE.	25/4/17		R. P^s now as follows:–	
			Div^l Troops: Sheet 62^c. Point I 24 e 70.	
			125th Bde: LE MESNIL - BRUNTEL.	
			126th " DRIENCOURT.	
			127th " HERBÉCOURT	
			All Supplies drawn at Railhead by Tram Transport for consumption 24th.	
			The continual taking away of Lorries, greatly delays times selected for Refillings, & Tram transport having to be used for Supply Column work, ~~[illegible]~~ & the drawing of rations for units must be carried out by 1st Line Transport. Hence one of the causes for the poor condition of Horse transport throughout the Division. No horse transport being able to carry out ~~their~~ its normal duties.	S.T.B.
" "	26/4/17		Same as for 25/4/17	S.T.B.

2449 Wt. W14957/M90 750,000 1/16 J.B.C. & A. Forms/C.2118/12.

Army Form C. 2118.

Instructions regarding War Diaries and Intelligence Summaries are contained in F. S. Regs., Part II. and the Staff Manual respectively. Title Pages will be prepared in manuscript.

WAR DIARY

or

~~INTELLIGENCE SUMMARY~~

(Erase heading not required.)

Place	Date	Hour	Summary of Events and Information	Remarks and references to Appendices
PERONNE.	27/4/17		Owing to coming moves of 126th + 127th Bdes: (Div: order no: 9) the S.O.s of these Bdes: moved as follows:– 126th Bde: to I 24 c.8.7. 127th Bde: to TEMPLEUX LA FOSSE. Transport arrangements as for 25/4/17 + 26/4/17.–	G.T.B.
" "	28/4/17		R Ps to-day as follows:– Divl. Troops. I 24 c.7.8 Map 62c 125th Bde: LE MESNIL BRUNTEL. 126th " I 24 c.8.7 127th " TEMPLEUX LA FOSSE. } No change in transport arrangements.–	G.T.B.
" "	29/4/17		126th + 127th Bdes: moving. Supplies taken to units from R Pts by 1st line where possible + by motor Lorry in cases where 1st line could not be utilized.– Supplies drawn from Railhead by Train Transport.–	G.T.B.

2449 Wt. W14957/M90 750,000 1/16 J.B.C. & A. Forms/C.2118/12.

Instructions regarding War Diaries and Intelligence Summaries are contained in F. S. Regs., Part II. and the Staff Manual respectively. Title Pages will be prepared in manuscript.

WAR DIARY
or
~~INTELLIGENCE~~ SUMMARY
(Erase heading not required.)

Army Form C. 2118.

Place	Date	Hour	Summary of Events and Information	Remarks and references to Appendices
PERONNE	30/4/17		Owing to further moves of 126th & 127th Bdes: (42nd Division orders no. 9 dated 26th & 28th) also moves of 125th Bde: (42nd Divl order no. 10) a Divisional R.P. has to-day been established at J. 18. c. 38. Map: 62c from where all units of Division & attached troops will be issued with rations to-morrow for consumption 2nd inst: Transport arrangements as for 29/4/17.	
			Various Details stationed in HERBECOURT, & CAPPY areas struck off 42nd Division ration strength & attached to 1st Division	
			Three Infantry Battns: of 1st Division (1st S W Borderers, 2nd K.R.R. & 6th Welch Regt:) also 2 Batts: 48th Divl Artillery, 1 Sec: 48th D.A.C. & various small units stationed in 48th Div: Area, taken on our ration strength from 3rd May inclusive –	
			PERONNE. 30/4/17.	
			J. [illegible] OC 42 Div: Train	
			E. Thurling Blackwell. Capt: & Adjut: 42nd Divl: Train A.S.C.	

2449 Wt. W14957/M90 750,000 1/16 J.B.C. & A. Forms/C.2118/12.

Confidential

War Diary

of

42nd Divisional Train

From 1/5/17 to 31/5/17.

Volume 3

Instructions regarding War Diaries and Intelligence Summaries are contained in F. S. Regs., Part II. and the Staff Manual respectively. Title Pages will be prepared in manuscript.

WAR DIARY
or
~~INTELLIGENCE SUMMARY~~ S.T.B

(Erase heading not required.)

Army Form C. 2118.

Place	Date	Hour	Summary of Events and Information	Remarks and references to Appendices
PERONNE.	1/5/17		Refilling Point for all formations at J.18.c.38 (Sheet 62c. Train H.T. drew supplies from Railhead & units 1st line from R.P.	S.T.B
"	2/5/17		No change.	S.T.B
"	3/5/17		Supplies drawn from Railhead to R.P. by Supply Column Lorries. Authority III Corps letter no A.Q. 3/17 (Administration Instruction no. 27 dated 29/4/17). Turn over of the dump of supplies at ROISEL mentioned in above instructions postponed for 24 hours. All Coys: of the train now collected at TINCOURT Point J23 sheet 62c. Very good grazing adjacent to the horse lines, & it is hoped, that with the Train Transport resuming its normal duties, the condition of all horses will be shortly improved. The Supply Section horses, (with exception of 429 Coy: which were only at ESTREES for 2 days) particularly need care & attention – never having had a chance of recovering from the weather & heavy & long working hours while attached to the 59th Divl. Train at ESTREES.	S.T.B.
TINCOURT.	4/5/17		Train Hqrs: moved to TINCOURT. Pt. J.23.b55. Sheet 62c. No change R.Ps. Turn over of Dump of Supplies at ROISEL. Commenced	S.T.B

2449 Wt. W14957/M90 750,000 1/16 J.B.C. & A. Forms/C.2118/12.

Instructions regarding War Diaries and Intelligence Summaries are contained in F. S. Regs., Part II. and the Staff Manual respectively. Title Pages will be prepared in manuscript.

WAR DIARY

or

~~INTELLIGENCE SUMMARY~~ S.T.B.

(Erase heading not required.)

Army Form C. 2118.

Place	Date	Hour	Summary of Events and Information	Remarks and references to Appendices
TINCOURT	5/5/17		OC Supply Column received orders to discontinue turn over of reserve rations at ROISEL until further orders.	S.T.B
" "	6/5/17		No change.	S.T.B.
" "	7/5/17		No change	
" "	8/5/17		Railhead changed from PERONNE to ROISEL, & new R.P.[ts] for whole train established there, adjoining line on which Pack Train arrives. This will allow the Supply Sections H.T. to entirely resume their normal work. 10 Baggage wagons doing local work by carting bricks for road making.	
" "	9/5/17		No change.	
" "	10/5/17		ROISEL Railhead shelled by H.E. (21 cm.) during the afternoon. No damage to supplies.	
" "	11/5/17		No change.	
" "	12/5/17		Six high Explosive shells neighbourhood of J.18 C.&D (Sheet 62c) during the morning, & from 2-30 p.m. to 4 p.m. shelling continued. 13 H.E. (21 Cm) shells were dropped in J.23 a central. There was a few minutes interval between the 1st & 3 shells which enabled the men to get the horses clear. One riding horse very slightly wounded.	

2449 Wt. W14957/M90 750,000 1/16 J.B.C. & A. Forms/C.2118/12.

Army Form C. 2118.

Instructions regarding War Diaries and Intelligence Summaries are contained in F. S. Regs., Part II. and the Staff Manual respectively. Title Pages will be prepared in manuscript.

WAR DIARY
or
~~INTELLIGENCE SUMMARY~~

(Erase heading not required.)

Place	Date	Hour	Summary of Events and Information	Remarks and references to Appendices
TINCOURT	13.5.17		No change –	G.T.B.
" "	14.5.17		" –	G.T.B
" "	15.5.17		A marked improvement in the condition of the animals is noticeable.	
" "	16.5.17		No change.	
" "	17.5.17		127th Bde Group moved to YTRES area from ROISEL. Supplies drawn by motor lorry & sent to Pt. P.19b for issue 18. Supplies for issue to be taken by Supply Section.	Map Sheet 57c G.T.B.
" "	18.5.17		4th & 5th E LANCS. moved to DESSART area. Supplies for issue 19th sent by lorry to above mentioned R.P.	
" "	19.5.17		Railhead changed from ROISEL to PERONNE. 126th Group less 4th & 5th E LANCS moved to DESSART area. B.S.O. 127th Bde & staff moved to new R.P. i.e. P.19.b. (Sheet 57c) S.O's of 125th Bde & Div! Troops moved to R.P. at TINCOURT. All supplies for issue to-morrow drawn at PERONNE Railhead by motor lorries & delivered as follows – Div! Troops } TINCOURT 125th Bde } 126th Bde } 127th " " } P.19.b	G.T.B.

2449 Wt. W14957/M90 750,000 1/16 J.B.C. & A. Forms/C.2118/12.

Army Form C. 2118.

Instructions regarding War Diaries and Intelligence Summaries are contained in F. S. Regs., Part II. and the Staff Manual respectively. Title Pages will be prepared in manuscript.

WAR DIARY
or
~~INTELLIGENCE SUMMARY~~
(Erase heading not required.)

Place	Date	Hour	Summary of Events and Information	Remarks and references to Appendices
TINCOURT	20/5/17		125th Bde: Group moved to DESSART area. B.S.O. 125th Bde & staff to R.P. at P.19 b where supplies for issue 21 were sent by motor lorry from PERONNE RAILHEAD.	S.T.B.
" "	21/5/17		210th Bde R.F.A. and No 1 Section D.A.C. moved to YTRES. Supplies for issue 22nd sent by lorry from PERONNE Railhead to Pt. P 19 b.	Sheet 57c. S.T.B.
" "	22/5/17		211th Bde: R.F.A and D.A.C. less no 1 Sect also R.A. Hqrs: moved to YTRES Supplies for all groups for consumption 24th: Sent from PERONNE Railhead to Divl: R.P. at P.19 b. Sheet 57c by lorry. The 3 Bde: Groups had a double issue of rations to-day in order to release the Train Supply Sections for loading at Railhead ROCQUIGNY the 23rd. This now gives units two days rations in hand, & it is the system to be adopted pro tem.	S.T.B.

2449 Wt. W14957/M90 750,000 1/16 J.B.C. & A. Forms/C.2118/12.

Army Form C. 2118.

Instructions regarding War Diaries and Intelligence Summaries are contained in F. S. Regs., Part II. and the Staff Manual respectively. Title Pages will be prepared in manuscript.

WAR DIARY
or
~~INTELLIGENCE~~ SUMMARY
(Erase heading not required.)

Place	Date	Hour	Summary of Events and Information	Remarks and references to Appendices
~~23~~ 45 TINCOURT & BUS	23/5/17		Railhead Rocquigny instead of PERONNE. Supplies drawn by Train Supply Sections in Bulk - Split up at R.P^ts^ & handed to Units representatives on Supply Sect. wagons there. Div^l^ Troops had double refillings, thus giving all Units in Division two days supplies in hand. Train Hqrs moved to BUS. 4900 Kilos of cabbages arrived at Railhead - unfit for human consumption, & condemned by M.O.	S.T.B
" "	24/5/17		No change.	S.T.B
" "	25/5/17		R.P^s^ changed to Pt. O 23 e 7 d Sheet 57^c^ = Train Supply Section doing both Supply Column, & normal H.T. delivery of supplies.	S.T.B
" "	26		No change.	S.T.B
" "	27		No change	S.T.B
" "	28-31/5/17		" "	

J Carlton Lt. Colonel.
Commanding 42nd Div^l^ Train A.S.C.

1-6-17.

2449 Wt. W14957/M90 750,000 1/16 J.B.C. & A. Forms/C.2118/12.

Vol 5

Confidential.

War Diary

of

42ND Divisional Train A.S.C.

1ST. JUNE TO 30TH JUNE

1917.

VOLUME 4.

Instructions regarding War Diaries and Intelligence Summaries are contained in F. S. Regs., Part II. and the Staff Manual respectively. Title Pages will be prepared in manuscript.

WAR DIARY
or
~~INTELLIGENCE SUMMARY~~ ACh

(Erase heading not required.)

Army Form C. 2118.

Place	Date	Hour	Summary of Events and Information	Remarks and references to Appendices
BUS	1/6/17		Refilling Points for all Brigades & Div Troops on Bus, ~~Rocquigny~~ RUCQUIGNY road near ref Sheet 57C O23c4d. Horse Transport drawing from railhead ~~Rocquigny~~ RUCQUIGNY delivering to dumps & also to units. Infantry loaders stated to be replaced by men from Employment Coys	ACh
do	2/6/17		Sgt [illegible] returned from leave to ~~England~~ & again took up his duties as O/c Transport for R.E.s Infantry loaders continue to be replaced & returned to their units	ACh
do	3/6/17		325R/04223 Staff Sgt Osborne H. the S.S.O.s chief clerk admitted to Hospital Refilling as yesterday	ACh
do	4/6/17		Inspection of all Train animals by A.D.V.S. 42nd Div Lt Col [illegible] proceeded on 10 days leave to ~~England~~ ENGLAND. Major Reynolds took over temporary command of the Train.	ACh

2449 Wt. W14957/M90 750,000 1/16 J.B.C. & A. Forms/C.2118/12.

Army Form C. 2118.

WAR DIARY
or
INTELLIGENCE SUMMARY

(Erase heading not required.)

Instructions regarding War Diaries and Intelligence Summaries are contained in F. S. Regs., Part II. and the Staff Manual respectively. Title Pages will be prepared in manuscript.

Place	Date	Hour	Summary of Events and Information	Remarks and references to Appendices
BUS.	5/6/17		O.C. Train notified that a certain number of horses will be required for cutting & making hay in 3rd Corps area. Refilling as on 4th by Horse Transport from railhead etc.	ACh
—	6/6/17		12 pairs of H.D. horses 12 wagons 22 O.R.s under 2/Lt Chilton proceeded on haymaking in 3rd Corps area, and form a permanent camp, rationed & administered by 3rd Corps. Lecture on dressing, baking & cooking given by Captain McGregor at Train HQ Co.	ACh
—	7/6/17		Gas alarm from 1.30 am to 2 am. Refilling as usual. 2/Lt Hamilton proceeded to Amiens to purchase tea for Division.	ACh
—	8/6/17		Refilling as yesterday. Wagons detailed for R.E. work at 8.30 pm, did not return to Company until late at night.	ACh

2449 Wt. W14957/M90 750,000 1/16 J.B.C. & A. Forms/C.2118/12.

Instructions regarding War Diaries and Intelligence Summaries are contained in F. S. Regs., Part II. and the Staff Manual respectively. Title Pages will be prepared in manuscript.

WAR DIARY
or
~~INTELLIGENCE~~ SUMMARY

(Erase heading not required.)

Army Form C. 2118.

Place	Date	Hour	Summary of Events and Information	Remarks and references to Appendices
Bus	9/6/19		No. T/52419 Dr. Shannon 431 Coy ASC undergoing suspended sentence brought before CO. Wired to Base for information re this man's suspended sentence.	[illegible]
			Refilling as usual. H.T. doing supply column work as well as delivering supplies from dump to units.	
—	10/6/19		Very severe storm on night of 10th–11th. Camps all flooded. Horses remained quiet all through. 428 Coy's ration store flooded & rations rendered unfit for consumption.	[illegible]
—	11/6/19		Refilling as usual.	[illegible]
			428 Coy supplies destroyed by storm condemned by Lt. O'[illegible] on AF W.3333.	[illegible]
—	12/6/19		[illegible] men proceeded to [illegible] for dental treatment. Refilling as usual.	

2449 Wt. W14957/M90 750,000 1/16 J.B.C. & A. Forms/C.2118/12.

Army Form C. 2118.

WAR DIARY
or
INTELLIGENCE SUMMARY [initials]

(Erase heading not required.)

Instructions regarding War Diaries and Intelligence Summaries are contained in F. S. Regs., Part II. and the Staff Manual respectively. Title Pages will be prepared in manuscript.

Place	Date	Hour	Summary of Events and Information	Remarks and references to Appendices
BUS.	13/6/17		Refilling as usual. Horse Transport drawn from railhead delivered to dumps + units.	[initials]
			Wagon on detachment at Div Laundry to be refitted and returned	[initials]
—	14/6/17		Refilling as usual.	
—	15/6/17		Lt Col Carlson returned to duty on expiration of leave, & resumes Command of Train.	[initials]
			Capt Hayes S O Div Troops proceeded on 10 days leave to ENGLAND ~~England leave~~ [initials] granted on special grounds for private affairs.	
—	16/6/17		Capt J Harding Blackwell Adjutant off duty owing to sickness.	[initials]
—	17/6/17		Inspection of 1st Line Transport of 126th Inf. Brigade by O C Train, condition of animals & harness much improved on the whole.	[initials]
			Capt J Harding-Blackwell admitted to 1/3 Field Ambulance owing to debility	

2449 Wt. W14957/M90 750,000 1/16 J.B.C. & A. Forms/C.2118/12.

Instructions regarding War Diaries and Intelligence Summaries are contained in F. S. Regs., Part II. and the Staff Manual respectively. Title Pages will be prepared in manuscript.

WAR DIARY
or
~~INTELLIGENCE~~ SUMMARY

(Erase heading not required.)

Army Form C. 2118.

Place	Date	Hour	Summary of Events and Information	Remarks and references to Appendices
BUS	18/6/17		Capt V. Blackwell evacuated from 1/3rd F.A. to 34 C.C.S. PERONNE.	[illegible]
			2/Lt A.G. Murphy takes on the duties of Acting Adjutant	
			Very bad thunderstorm during the day, one [illegible] at ROCQUIGNY	
—	19/6/17		2/Lt H.V. Hamilton R.O. [illegible] proceeded on 3 days leave to HAVRE on [illegible] grounds	
			Inspection of 1st Line Transport of 124th Inf Bde by O.C. Train. Good general turnout & improvement on last inspection shown.	[illegible]
			6 H.D. Remounts arrive for Train and are allotted to Coys as follows	
			4 H.D. to 427 Coy. 1 HD to 430 Coy 1 HD to 431 Coy.	
			O.C. Train inspected camps of 431 Coy at ROCQUIGNY & 429 Coy at BARASTRE.	
—	20/6/17		O.C. Train inspected camps of 428 Coy & 430 Coy [illegible] at BUS	[illegible]
			D.D.S.&T. 2nd Army inspected horses & camps of 428 & 430 Coys and found them in good condition.	

Instructions regarding War Diaries and Intelligence Summaries are contained in F. S. Regs., Part II. and the Staff Manual respectively. Title Pages will be prepared in manuscript.

WAR DIARY
or
~~INTELLIGENCE~~ SUMMARY

(*Erase heading not required.*)

Army Form C. 2118.

Place	Date	Hour	Summary of Events and Information	Remarks and references to Appendices
Bus.	21/6/19		Inspection of 1st Line Transport of 1/3rd East Lancs Field Ambulance by O.C. Train at 7am. Animals in good condition with the exception of 6 H D which were poor, these needing special care & feeding. Harness required attention. [illegible] of 1 W.O.	[illegible]
—	22/6/19		2/Lt C. G. L. Bennett proceeded to Transport Lines of 127th Inf. Brigade to instruct transport officers of 1/9th Manchester [illegible] for the period of a fortnight. 2/Lt Graham attached to 420 Coy A.S.C. as O/c Supply Section for a fortnight in place of 2/Lt Bennett. Capt T. [illegible] S.O. 127th Inf Bde [illegible] preliminary [illegible] OC 42nd D.S. Column	[illegible]
—	23/6/19		2/Lt Graham takes charge of additional 12 pair of H.D., 1 wagon [illegible] R.E. [illegible] Regimental [illegible] in ~~[illegible]~~ Bus area	[illegible]

2449 Wt. W14957/M90 750,000 1/16 J.B.C. & A. Forms/C.2118/12.

Instructions regarding War Diaries and Intelligence Summaries are contained in F. S. Regs., Part II. and the Staff Manual respectively. Title Pages will be prepared in manuscript.

WAR DIARY
or
~~INTELLIGENCE SUMMARY~~

(Erase heading not required.)

Army Form C. 2118.

Place	Date	Hour	Summary of Events and Information	Remarks and references to Appendices
BUS	23/6/19		Return of officers born on & after May 12th 1887 called for re attachment to Infantry	[initials]
–	24/6/19		C.O. Inspected Horse lines & camp of 428 & 430 Coy at BUS also 429 Coy at BARASTRE. Inspection of 1st Line Transport of 125th Inf Bde at 5.30 pm, they presented a very good turn out, & are situated in a very good camp at YTRES with good brick standings.	[initials]
–	25/6/19		Inspection of 1st Line Transport of 1/1st & 1/2nd East Lancs Field Ambulances by C.O. Train at 10am & 10.30am at RUYAULCOURT. 1/1st F.A. has room for improvement. 1/2nd F.A. presented a very good turn out. Men of Train who refuse innoculation seen by C.O. & asked their reasons for refusing [illegible] considered [illegible].	[initials]

2449 Wt. W14957/M90 750,000 1/16 J.B.C. & A. Forms/C.2118/12.

Instructions regarding War Diaries and Intelligence Summaries are contained in F. S. Regs., Part II. and the Staff Manual respectively. Title Pages will be prepared in manuscript.

WAR DIARY
or
~~INTELLIGENCE~~ SUMMARY

(*Erase heading not required.*)

Army Form C. 2118.

Place	Date	Hour	Summary of Events and Information	Remarks and references to Appendices
BUS	26/[illegible]/19		2/Lt Hamilton returns from leave to ~~[illegible]~~ HAVRE	
			One leave place per week allotted to Division, to [illegible] Thursday	[illegible]
			2/Lt C. Hamilton 430 Bty [illegible] Supply Detach [illegible]	
			422nd [illegible] as a candidate for a Temporary Commission in the Artillery	
"	29/[illegible]/19		Capt J Sterling Blackwell Adjutant, returns to duty from Hospital	[illegible]
			Capt S Hays returns from 10 days leave in England	
			Capt S Hays takes over S.O. 126 Bde [illegible]	
			30 OR arrive as reinforcements attached to 430 Bty until distributed	
			Capt A Fenner departed on 10 days leave to England to 8/4/19	
"	[illegible]/19		30 OR Reinforcements distributed amongst the Company as follows	[illegible]
			432 Bty 1 Sgt 1 Cpl 3 Supply Privates 11 Drivers; 430 Bty 2 Drivers; 431 Bty 1 Sgt 1 Cpl.	

2449 Wt. W14957/M90 750,000 1/16 J.B.C. & A. Forms/C.2118/12.

Army Form C. 2118.

WAR DIARY
or
INTELLIGENCE SUMMARY

(*Erase heading not required.*)

Instructions regarding War Diaries and Intelligence Summaries are contained in F. S. Regs., Part II. and the Staff Manual respectively. Title Pages will be prepared in manuscript.

Place	Date	Hour	Summary of Events and Information	Remarks and references to Appendices
Bus	29/6/17		All officers of the Train under 30 years of age medically inspected as to whether fit for duty with Infantry or not	[illegible]
–	30/6/17		Capt. G. J. Stevenson interview by C.R.A. for transfer from A.S.C. to R.A. System of fuller filling of all cars on supply dumps instituted	[illegible]

J Carlton
Lt Col
Commanding 42nd Divisional Train A.S.C.

CONFIDENTIAL.

War Diary.

Period

1st July '17 To 31st July '17.

VOLUME V.

42ND DIVISIONAL TRAIN.

Army Service Corps.

Instructions regarding War Diaries and Intelligence Summaries are contained in F. S. Regs., Part II. and the Staff Manual respectively. Title Pages will be prepared in manuscript.

WAR DIARY
or
~~INTELLIGENCE~~ SUMMARY ~~aah~~

(Erase heading not required.)

Army Form C. 2118.

Place	Date	Hour	Summary of Events and Information	Remarks and references to Appendices
BUS	1/7/17		Turn over of Iron rations, 16000 Iron Rations drawn from 19 Reserve Park ROCQUIGNY	aah
			Advance from railhead ROCQUIGNY	
			P. Meat & Biscuits issued to troops in lieu of Fresh Meat & Bread by order of C.C. & Q.M.G.	
			Smoked bacon arrives in damp packed in sacks instead of boxes in poor condition a report to be submitted	
—	2/7/17		The C.O. & S.S.O. go to ACHIET LE GRAND to inspect billets & supply points prior to move to 3rd Army Reserve	aah
			Gas alarm 10.30 pm. Phone message S.O.S. Gas shell from 2 Guard School.	
			Gas off at 12.45 am	
—	3/7/17		Inspection of 1/3rd East Lancs Field Ambulance by O.C. Train at 2.30 pm.	aah
			Marked improvement all round in horses, harness & vehicles.	
			Orders for move come in by 9.30 D.R.L.S.	

2449 Wt. W14957/M90 750,000 1/16 J.B.C. & A. Forms/C.2118/12.

Instructions regarding War Diaries and Intelligence Summaries are contained in F. S. Regs., Part II. and the Staff Manual respectively. Title Pages will be prepared in manuscript.

WAR DIARY
or
~~INTELLIGENCE~~ SUMMARY

(*Erase heading not required.*)

Army Form C. 2118.

Place	Date	Hour	Summary of Events and Information	Remarks and references to Appendices
BUS	4/4/17		Gas alarm 1.30 am, till 2.15 am. Inspection of 1st Line Transport of 1/9th Bn Manchesters, marked improvement noticed all round. Orders for move to new area issued, & supply arrangements made.	[illegible]
—	5/4/17		S.O. 125th Infantry Brigade draws two issues of rations one in morning for consumption 6th & one in afternoon for consumption 7th. Move in afternoon to new supply point on BIHUCOURT — GOMIECOURT road West of 57C G12 a 0. Supplies remain on supply wagons overnight at BARASTRE with 429 Coy A.S.C. 42nd Division comes under administration of 5th Corps & 3rd Army.	[illegible]
—	6/4/17		429 Coy A.S.C. & 125 Inf. Brigade move to GOMIECOURT area, supply wagons left with Coy & deliver to units on arrival in new area. 429 Coy established in camp on South side of GOMIECOURT.	[illegible]

Army Form C. 2118.

Instructions regarding War Diaries and Intelligence Summaries are contained in F. S. Regs., Part II. and the Staff Manual respectively. Title Pages will be prepared in manuscript.

WAR DIARY
or
~~INTELLIGENCE~~ SUMMARY

(*Erase heading not required.*)

Place	Date	Hour	Summary of Events and Information	Remarks and references to Appendices
BOS	6 4/17		Supplies for issue 7th for 125th Brigade brought by lorries from ROCQUIGNY Railhead to new dump at G12 a o	AWh
—	7 4/17		Supplies for issue 8th for 125th Brigade brought by lorry from ROCQUIGNY railhead to new refilling point at G12 a o o. Supplies for 126 + 127 Bdes + Div. Troops delivered as usual. 42nd Division comes under Administration of 6th Corps and 3rd Army	AWh
—	8 4/16.		S.O. 126th Brigade issue rations direct in morning for consumption 9th in afternoon for consumption 10th. Issue in afternoon with Staff lorries refilling point at G12 a o. Map 57c. Divisional Supply Column moved to ACHIET LE PETIT. A.F. W.3317 rendered to R.S.O. at ACHIET LE GRAND. A.F. W 3316 for Div. Troops rendered to S.S.O. 58th Division	AWh

Instructions regarding War Diaries and Intelligence Summaries are contained in F. S. Regs., Part II. and the Staff Manual respectively. Title Pages will be prepared in manuscript.

Army Form C. 2118.

WAR DIARY
or
~~INTELLIGENCE SUMMARY~~ AWh

(Erase heading not required.)

Place	Date	Hour	Summary of Events and Information	Remarks and references to Appendices
BUS & ACHIET-LE-PETIT	9/4/16		Hd. Qrs of Train move to ACHIET-LE-PETIT and billet in old farm in HALIFAX ROAD. Railhead changes from ROCQUIGNY to ACHIET-LE-GRAND Supplies for 126th Brigade ~~[illegible]~~ for consumption 11th issue 10th drawn from new railhead by M.T. at about 3 am & brought to refilling point 6.12 am Supplies for 125th Brigade for consumption 11th issue 10th drawn from new railhead by M.T. at about 3 am & delivered to new refilling point 6.12 am Supplies for 127th Brigade for consumption 11th issue 10th drawn from new railhead by M.T. at about 3 am & delivered to old refilling point on BUS - ROCQUIGNY ROAD. Supplies for Div. Troops for consumption 11th issue 10th drawn by 51st Div with Horse Transport (H.D. Coy) at ROCQUIGNY railhead & delivered to refilling point on BUS - ROCQUIGNY ROAD.	AWh

2449 Wt. W14957/M90 750,000 1/16 J.B.C. & A. Forms/C.2118/12.

Army Form C. 2118.

Instructions regarding War Diaries and Intelligence Summaries are contained in F. S. Regs., Part II. and the Staff Manual respectively. Title Pages will be prepared in manuscript.

WAR DIARY
or
INTELLIGENCE SUMMARY [illegible]

(Erase heading not required.)

Place	Date	Hour	Summary of Events and Information	Remarks and references to Appendices
ACHIET-LE-PETIT	9/4/17		Div. H.Q. Coy. etc move from YTRES to ACHIET-LE-PETIT.	
			430 Coy. A.S.C. and 126th Infantry Brigade move to BIHUCOURT.	[illegible]
			Supply Officer 127th Brigade makes two issues, one in morning for consumption 10th & in afternoon for consumption 11th. Moves in afternoon to new refilling point near ACHIET-LE-PETIT Map ref. sheet 57 C G13 b59	
			Capt. A. Jenner returns from 10 days leave to England	
—	10/4/17		431 Coy. A.S.C. & 127th Inf. Bde. move to new area in ACHIET-LE-PETIT	[illegible]
			Supplies for 125 & 126th Inf. Brigades drawn by Horse Transport from railhead & delivered to dumps. 1st Line Transport take on to units.	
			Supplies for 127th Bde. drawn by Motor Transport from railhead & delivered to dumps. Supply section did not make any delivery.	
			All supplies drawn from railhead at 2.30 a.m.	

2449 Wt. W14957/M90 750,000 1/16 J.B.C. & A. Forms/C.2118/12.

Army Form C. 2118.

Instructions regarding War Diaries and Intelligence Summaries are contained in F. S. Regs., Part II. and the Staff Manual respectively. Title Pages will be prepared in manuscript.

WAR DIARY
or
INTELLIGENCE SUMMARY

(Erase heading not required.)

Place	Date	Hour	Summary of Events and Information	Remarks and references to Appendices
ACHIET-LE-PETIT	11/1/17		430 Coy A.S.C. & 126th Inf. Brigade move to COURCELLES. All supplies drawn from Railhead by Horse Transport & delivered to dumps. Refilling on previous days. Informed by R.S.O. that rice is now issued as a part of the ration at the rate of 1 oz per man & not as part or [illegible] of any component part of the ration. S.O. Div. Troops attached 58th Div. Bus hands over Div. R.A. & detachs [illegible] Corps Troops supply to [illegible]	AWh
–	13/1/17		S.O. 126th Infantry Brigade moves with staff of the refilling to new refilling point on ACHIET-LE-GRAND – COURCELLES road map ref 57c A22 C22. Supplies for issue 13th for 126th Brigade drawn from railhead by lorry & delivered to new dump at A22 C22. Capt. Mackay R.A.M.C. posted to Train as M.O. taken on strength of Train H.Qrs. O.C. & G.M. visits railhead during refilling with S.S.O.	AWh

2449 Wt. W14957/M90 750,000 1/16 J.B.C. & A. Forms/C.2118/12.

Instructions regarding War Diaries and Intelligence Summaries are contained in F. S. Regs., Part II. and the Staff Manual respectively. Title Pages will be prepared in manuscript.

WAR DIARY
or
~~INTELLIGENCE~~ SUMMARY Cdh

(Erase heading not required.)

Army Form C. 2118.

Place	Date	Hour	Summary of Events and Information	Remarks and references to Appendices
ACHIET-LE-PETIT	13/4/17		Capt Speckley ASC reports for duty, attached for duty with [illegible] Corp filling vacancy for Supply Officer. 1 Sgt + 50 ORs arrive as reinforcements. 58 Div Troops at BUS takes over 42nd Div RA [illegible] from 4th Corps Troops Supply Column & is attached to 58th Div for administration	Cdh
—	14/4/17		Refilling as yesterday for all Brigade. Three specialisation dumps as follows: 125 Bde Dump on BIHUCOURT–GOMIECOURT Road map ref 57C G12.a.0.0; 126 — — ACHIET-LE-GRAND – COURCELLES Rd — A22 a.2.4; 127 — — ACHIET-LE-PETIT — G8 a.9.7. 430 Coy ASC lines & camp inspected by Brigadier General [illegible]	Cdh
—	15/4/17		Refilling as yesterday for all Brigades. [illegible] ASC proceeds to BAPAUME to take charge of 42nd Div [illegible] to arrive at that railhead, 2 riders & 3 HD allotted to them	Cdh

2449 Wt. W14957/M90 750,000 1/16 J.B.C. & A. Forms/C.2118/12.

Instructions regarding War Diaries and Intelligence Summaries are contained in F. S. Regs., Part II. and the Staff Manual respectively. Title Pages will be prepared in manuscript.

WAR DIARY
or
~~INTELLIGENCE~~ SUMMARY CAWH

(Erase heading not required.)

Army Form C. 2118.

Place	Date	Hour	Summary of Events and Information	Remarks and references to Appendices
ACHIET LE PETIT	15/7/17		Daily proportion of iron rations ceases to come up on pack train by order of 3rd Army. R.S.O. refuses to issue iron rations from his detail stores without written authority from D.D.S.&T. 3rd Army.	CAWH
–	16/7/17		S.O. 125th Brigade ordered to move his refilling point to A28 b 9.4 57c. Consignment of sugar for the 125 & 126th Brigades unfit for consumption owing to being saturated with whale oil. Deficiency demanded on A.F.W. 3333, also several sacks of potatoes bad. O.C. Train visits 428 Coy. A.S.C. at BUS.	CAWH
–	17/7/17		S.O. 125th Bde after issue of supplies moves to new refilling point map ref. sheet 57c A28 b 9.4. Refilling for other Brigades as usual.	CAWH

Instructions regarding War Diaries and Intelligence Summaries are contained in F. S. Regs., Part II. and the Staff Manual respectively. Title Pages will be prepared in manuscript.

WAR DIARY
or
~~INTELLIGENCE SUMMARY~~ [initials]

(Erase heading not required.)

Army Form C. 2118.

Place	Date	Hour	Summary of Events and Information	Remarks and references to Appendices
ACHIET LE PETIT	18/4/17		Inspection of 1st Line Transport of 124th Infantry Brigade by O.C. Train. The turn out was on the whole very good, with the exception of Brigade Head Quarters who presented a very poor turn out.	[initials]
–	19/4/17		Inspection of 1st Line Transport of 126th Infantry Brigade by O.C. Train. 7th Bn Manchesters showed particular improvement, the 6th & 10th Manchesters did not present as good a parade, 2nd & 5th E.L. and 9th Manchesters. Inspection of 1st Line Transport of 1/1st East Lancs Field Ambulance by O.C. Train. Not a good a report could be rendered as previously as the horses and animals were not in as good condition.	[initials]
–	20/4/17		S.S.O. proceeded to ALBERT to see D.D.S.&T. 3rd Army, re queries raised on army subject. 2 men of H.Q. Coy. [illegible] for a [illegible] course with 1/4 East Lancashire Regiment	[initials]

Instructions regarding War Diaries and Intelligence Summaries are contained in F. S. Regs., Part II. and the Staff Manual respectively. Title Pages will be prepared in manuscript.

WAR DIARY

or

~~INTELLIGENCE~~ SUMMARY

(*Erase heading not required.*)

Army Form C. 2118.

Place	Date	Hour	Summary of Events and Information	Remarks and references to Appendices
ACHIET LE PETIT	21/7/17		Large percentage of consignment of potatoes drawn from railhead condemned & replacement demanded on A.F. W 333 & R.O.'s certificate S.S.M. Ralfe transferred on attachment from 431 Coy A.S.C. for duty with 1/3rd East Lancs Field Ambulance	[illegible]
—	22/7/17		Consignment of potatoes drawn from railhead yesterday replaced Refilling as usual. Telephone message from D.A.Q.M.G. saying that [illegible] places have been granted to the train comprising 22 [illegible] from BOULOGNE	[illegible]
"	23/7/17		Inspection of 1st Line Transport of 125th Bde. by O.C. Train. The general turn-out shows an improvement all through, but more attention to details is required, such as hogging manes, grooming horses' tails, & washing harness before dubbing is put on. Lieut. A.A. Murphy proceeded on leave to Ireland	[illegible]

2449 Wt. W14957/M90 750,000 1/16 J.B.C. & A. Forms/C.2118/12.

Army Form C. 2118.

Instructions regarding War Diaries and Intelligence Summaries are contained in F. S. Regs., Part II. and the Staff Manual respectively. Title Pages will be prepared in manuscript.

WAR DIARY
or
~~INTELLIGENCE SUMMARY~~ E.N.
(Erase heading not required.)

Place	Date	Hour	Summary of Events and Information	Remarks and references to Appendices
ACHIET LE PETIT	24.7/17		Major W.P. Reynolds proceeded on leave to England. Capt E.F. Sprackling assumed duties of S.S.O. temporarily. All Transport of Brigade Companies & Personnel inspected by O.C. Train: very good turn-out.	E.N.
			Capt. E.K. Scholtz A.S.C. reported for duty.	
	25.7/17		Refilling as usual.	E.N.
	26.7/17		No change.	E.N. E.N.
	27.7/17		No change	E.N.
	28.7/17		Refilling as usual.	
	29.7/17		No change	E.N.
	30.7/17		Refilling as usual. Divisional Sports held.	E.N.
	31.7/17		Refilling as usual. Lieut. H.V. Hemotin & 2/Lieut. C.C. Chittenden proceeded to England to join the Infantry to report No 2 School of Infantry Bedford	E.N.

1st Aug 1917 — J. [illegible] Lt. Col. O.C. 42 Div Train

2449 Wt. W14957/M90 750,000 1/16 J.B.C. & A. Forms/C.2118/12.

CONFIDENTIAL.

WAR DIARY.

42nd DIVISIONAL TRAIN., A.S.C.

VOLUME VI.

Period 1st August to 31st August 1917.

Army Form C. 2118.

Instructions regarding War Diaries and Intelligence Summaries are contained in F. S. Regs., Part II. and the Staff Manual respectively. Title Pages will be prepared in manuscript.

WAR DIARY
or
~~INTELLIGENCE~~ SUMMARY

(Erase heading not required.)

Place	Date	Hour	Summary of Events and Information	Remarks and references to Appendices
ACHIET LE PETIT	1 8/17		Capt. Macintosh proceeded to England on leave, his duties being taken over by Lieut. Somerville.	E.D.
	2 8/17		125 Bde Refilling Point moved on account of mud. Map reference the same.	E.D.
	3 8/17		No Change.	E.D.
	4 8/17		Major W.P. Reynolds returned from Leave. Lieut A.A. Murphy granted 4 days extension of Leave.	E.D.
	5 8/17		No Change	E.D.
	6 8/17		No Change	E.D.
	7 8/17		No Change	E.D.
	8 8/17		Lieut. A.A. Murphy returned from Leave.	E.D.

2449 Wt. W14957/M90 750,000 1/16 J.B.C. & A. Forms/C.2118/12.

Army Form C. 2118.

Instructions regarding War Diaries and Intelligence Summaries are contained in F. S. Regs., Part II. and the Staff Manual respectively. Title Pages will be prepared in manuscript.

WAR DIARY
or
~~INTELLIGENCE~~ SUMMARY

(Erase heading not required.)

Place	Date	Hour	Summary of Events and Information	Remarks and references to Appendices
ACHIET LE PETIT	9/8/17		Refilling as usual, Maxwell car returned from Army Purchase Board to duty for 2 days with 6th Corps. Preliminary judging for 6th Corps Horse Show to be held on 18th	[illegible]
—	10/8/17		Refilling as usual. No change.	[illegible]
—	11/8/17		Capt J Sterling-Blackwell Adjutant departs to England on 10 days leave. Capt Sholto takes over duties of Acting Adjutant. Divisional preliminary judging for 6th Corps Horse Show. 136th Inf. Brigade held sports at COURCELLES	[illegible]

2449 Wt. W14957/M90 750,000 1/16 J.B.C. & A. Forms/C.2118/12.

Instructions regarding War Diaries and Intelligence Summaries are contained in F. S. Regs., Part II. and the Staff Manual respectively. Title Pages will be prepared in manuscript.

WAR DIARY
or
~~INTELLIGENCE SUMMARY~~ AWh

(Erase heading not required.)

Army Form C. 2118.

Place	Date	Hour	Summary of Events and Information	Remarks and references to Appendices
ACHIET LE PETIT	12/8/17		All 1st Line Transport selected for Corps horse show is ordered to parade at 11 am daily for preliminary instruction in saluting etc.	AWh
	13/8/17		Major E. Alderson A.S.C. reports for duty with Train, posted to 428 Coy A.S.C.	AWh
—	14/8/17		Major E. Alderson A.S.C. departs for duty with 428 Coy A.S.C. at BOS & takes over from Capt G. L. Stevens A.S.C.	AWh
—			Capt McKay R.A.M.C. ordered to transfer to report for duty with 42nd D.A.C. at BOS	
—	15/8/17		Capt McKay R.A.M.C. departs to join 42nd D.A.C. for duty at BOS	AWh
			First Line Transport trained for Corps show, improvement shown. Owing to number of entries further eliminations have to be made on morning of sports	

2449 Wt. W14957/M90 750,000 1/16 J.B.C. & A. Forms/C.2118/12.

Army Form C. 2118.

Instructions regarding War Diaries and Intelligence Summaries are contained in F. S. Regs., Part II. and the Staff Manual respectively. Title Pages will be prepared in manuscript.

WAR DIARY
or
INTELLIGENCE SUMMARY

(Erase heading not required.)

Place	Date	Hour	Summary of Events and Information	Remarks and references to Appendices
ACHIET LE PETIT.	16/8/17		A.A & Q.M.G. requests that 2 oz. rum rations i.e. 63 galls. may be issued to the 125th Inf. Bde. Authority granted from 6th Corps & rum demanded from R.S.O. who obtains authority to issue from 3rd Army	[signature]
—	17/8/17		Lieut J. Macintosh reported from S.O. 125th Bde to O/C Baggage Section 430 Coy. Lieut Somerville reported from O/C Baggage Section 430 Coy. A.S.C. to S.O. 125th Bde. D.D.S.&T. 3rd Army inspects horses & camps of 429, 430 & 431 Coys A.S.C. & found everything very satisfactory	[signature]
—	18/8/17		6th Corps Horse Show takes place at BIHUCOURT. 429 Coy. A.S.C. win 1st place in pair of H.D. & limber wagon, & 4th place with pair of H.D. & G.S. wagon. Orders re move of Division expected	[signature]

Instructions regarding War Diaries and Intelligence Summaries are contained in F. S. Regs., Part II. and the Staff Manual respectively. Title Pages will be prepared in manuscript.

WAR DIARY
or
~~INTELLIGENCE SUMMARY~~ CWh

(Erase heading not required.)

Army Form C. 2118.

Place	Date	Hour	Summary of Events and Information	Remarks and references to Appendices
ACHIET LE PETIT	19/8/17		6 [illegible] of 42nd Division comes in. 125th Bde moves [illegible] to BOUZENCOURT etc.	CWh
			New refilling points selected, 125 & 127th Bdes at W13a4.9 Sheet 57D	
			126th Bde at P12c7.2 Sheet 57D	
			M.O. i/c R.E. takes over charge of Train	
			O.C. Train visits 428 Coy A.S.C. at BUS. Double issue of supplies to 125th Bde	
–	20/8/17		S.O. 125th Inf Bde moves with supplies on lorries to new refilling point at W13a4.9 Sheet 57D i.e. on West side of BOZENCOURT.	CWh
			429 Coy A.S.C. 125th Inf Bde group move to BOZENCOURT.	
–	21/8/17		S.O. 126th Bde moves with supplies on lorries from railhead to new refilling point at P12c7.2.	CWh
			431 Coy A.S.C. 126th Inf Bde group move to FORCEVILLE MAILLY-MAILLET & BERTRANCOURT.	

2449 Wt. W14957/M90 750,000 1/16 J.B.C. & A. Forms/C.2118/12.

Army Form C. 2118.

Instructions regarding War Diaries and Intelligence Summaries are contained in F. S. Regs., Part II. and the Staff Manual respectively. Title Pages will be prepared in manuscript.

WAR DIARY
or
~~INTELLIGENCE SUMMARY~~

(Erase heading not required.)

Place	Date	Hour	Summary of Events and Information	Remarks and references to Appendices
ACHIET LE PETIT	21/8/17		S.O. 124th Bde moves with supplies on lorries to new refilling point at at W13a49.	
			431 Coy A.S.C. & 124th Inf. Bde Group move to huts between AVELUY & BOZINCOURT	
			Train H.Q. Coy. D.H.Q. Signal Coy. etc move to ACHEUX	
			Complete double issue of supplies made	
ACHEUX	22/8/17		S.S.O. & 3 Brigade Supply Officers move with one day's supplies on lorries to new area between POPERINGE & WATOU	
			123rd Inf. Bde moves to new area	
			Supplies for troops moving on 23rd inst issued from dumps at BOUZENCOURT & MAILLY-MAILLET.	

Instructions regarding War Diaries and Intelligence Summaries are contained in F. S. Regs., Part II. and the Staff Manual respectively. Title Pages will be prepared in manuscript.

Army Form C. 2118.

WAR DIARY
or
~~INTELLIGENCE SUMMARY~~ [initials]

(Erase heading not required.)

Place	Date	Hour	Summary of Events and Information	Remarks and references to Appendices
ACHEUX.	23/8/17		127th Bde. Div Train & Remainder of Divisional less Artillery move to new area. Entraining station at [illegible] 6am	[initials]
			Railhead changes to WIPPENHOEK	
			Supplies for 23rd ~~[illegible]~~ issued on 22nd issued at various detraining points.	
			Supplies for issue 24th drawn by lorries from railhead & brought to new refilling points at L10B87.	
WATOU	24/8/17		Supplies for issue 25th drawn by lorries from railhead.	[initials]
			Supplies issued from new refilling points.	
			O.C. Train visits 3 Brigade Conferences.	
			~~Capt. G. W. B. Barnes posted to & attached for duty with 1/5th Lancashire Fusiliers of 125th Inf. Brigade~~	

2449 Wt. W14957/M90 750,000 1/16 J.B.C. & A. Forms/C.2118/12.

Instructions regarding War Diaries and Intelligence Summaries are contained in F. S. Regs., Part II. and the Staff Manual respectively. Title Pages will be prepared in manuscript.

WAR DIARY
or
~~INTELLIGENCE~~ SUMMARY

(*Erase heading not required.*)

Army Form C. 2118.

Place	Date	Hour	Summary of Events and Information	Remarks and references to Appendices
WATOU.	25/6/17		Supplies for issue 26th drawn by Horse Transport from railhead & delivered to dumps. 1st Line Transport draws supplies from dump. Capt G. Tharling-Blackwell Adjutant of Train returns from leave.	[initials]
—	26/6/17		Hd Qrs. Coy. A.S. & Div Artillery move from BOS to new Area. O.C. Train visits D.D.S.&T. 5th Army. Capt G. W. B. Bancroft. A.S. ordered to be attached to 1/5th Lancashire Fusiliers 125th Bde for duty.	[initials]

2449 Wt. W14957/M90 750,000 1/16 J.B.C. & A. Forms/C.2118/12.

Army Form C. 2118.

Instructions regarding War Diaries and Intelligence Summaries are contained in F. S. Regs., Part II. and the Staff Manual respectively. Title Pages will be prepared in manuscript.

WAR DIARY
or
~~INTELLIGENCE~~ SUMMARY [illegible]

(Erase heading not required.)

Place	Date	Hour	Summary of Events and Information	Remarks and references to Appendices
WATOU.	27/8/17		50 Div Train issues supplies to Artillery from same refilling point as 3 Infantry Brigades	[illegible]
			Refilling for Inf. Brigades as yesterday.	
—	28/8/17		Capt. G. W. B. Baines of K.A.S.C. reports to G.O.C. 1/5 Lancs Fusiliers for duty as an Infantry Officer	[illegible]
			Capt G Thursby-Blackwell late Adjutant takes over Command of 429 Coy A.S.C.	
			Capt E Scholtz takes over the duties of Adjutant	
			42nd Div R.A. take over line from 15th Div R.A.	
			50 125th Bde moves after a distribution to new refilling point at G.15.c.9.2.	
—	29/8/17		429 Coy A.S.C. moves to camp at G 15 c 9 2 in forward area	[illegible]
			125 Inf Bde moves into the line	

2449 Wt. W14957/M90 750,000 1/16 J.B.C. & A. Forms/C.2118/12.

Instructions regarding War Diaries and Intelligence Summaries are contained in F. S. Regs., Part II. and the Staff Manual respectively. Title Pages will be prepared in manuscript.

WAR DIARY
or
~~INTELLIGENCE SUMMARY~~ [initials]
(Erase heading not required.)

Army Form C. 2118.

Place	Date	Hour	Summary of Events and Information	Remarks and references to Appendices
WATOU	29/8/17	[illegible]	Supplies for 125 Bde drawn by lorry from railhead & delivered to new dump.	
			S O Div. Troops moves to new refilling point at G 9 c central and supplies are drawn from railhead by lorry.	[initials]
			1/1 [illegible] Coy. ASC moves to camp in new area, refilling [illegible] at G 9 c central	
—	30/8/17		430 Coy ASC moves to new camp at G15 b 2 0	[initials]
			S O 127th Bde after double issue moves to new dump at G15 b 2 0.	
			S O 126th Bde issues from new dump, supplies being drawn from railhead by lorry	
			127th Inf Bde moves into new area	

2449 Wt. W14957/M90 750,000 1/16 J.B.C. & A. Forms/C.2118/12.

Army Form C. 2118.

Instructions regarding War Diaries and Intelligence Summaries are contained in F. S. Regs., Part II. and the Staff Manual respectively. Title Pages will be prepared in manuscript.

WAR DIARY
or
~~INTELLIGENCE~~ SUMMARY

(Erase heading not required.)

Place	Date	Hour	Summary of Events and Information	Remarks and references to Appendices
WATOU & H7c92	31/8/17		127th Inf. Bde moves to new area 431 Coy. A.S.C. moves to new camp at G14 b92 D.H.Q. & Train H.Qrs move to new camp at H7c92 Div Troops 125/126th Bdes drawn by M.T. from railhead 127th Bde drawn by M.T. from railhead	

J. Carlton
LIEUT: COLONEL,
COMMANDING 42nd DIVISIONAL TRAIN, A.S.C.

2449 Wt. W14957/M90 750,000 1/16 J.B.C. & A. Forms/C.2118/12.

Confidential.

WAR DIARY.

42nd DIVISIONAL TRAIN

Army Service Corps.

Period

September 1917.

Volume No VII.

Instructions regarding War Diaries and Intelligence Summaries are contained in F. S. Regs., Part II. and the Staff Manual respectively. Title Pages will be prepared in manuscript.

Army Form C. 2118.

WAR DIARY
or
~~INTELLIGENCE SUMMARY~~ [illegible initials]

(Erase heading not required.)

Place	Date	Hour	Summary of Events and Information	Remarks and references to Appendices
Sheet 28 N.W. H.Q. C.9.8 BRANDHOEK	1/9/17		Complete double issue of supplies made to enable units to have one days supply in hand. Several shells were dropped during the afternoon & night in the vicinity of D.H.Q & T.H.Q, no casualities. Railhead was also shelled while supplies were being loaded one O.R. man injured, but two M.T. lorries struck.	[illegible]
—	2/9/17		Refilling as usual, part of 124th Brigades fill by pack transport. No shelling during the morning. 12 M.T. drivers from D.S. Column taken on ration strength of Train H.Q. Coy	[illegible]
—	3/9/17		O.C. Train visited D.D.S & T. 5th Army for the purpose of enquiry about issue of 3rd Day supply of Barrage rations to troops in the line. Hostile aircraft drop bombs in vicinity of D.H.Q & Park area around about 10.30 pm. 8 O.R. arrived as reinforcements for the Train	[illegible]

2449 Wt. W14957/M90 750,000 1/16 J.B.C. & A. Forms/C.2118/12.

Army Form C. 2118.

Instructions regarding War Diaries and Intelligence Summaries are contained in F. S. Regs., Part II. and the Staff Manual respectively. Title Pages will be prepared in manuscript.

WAR DIARY
or
~~INTELLIGENCE SUMMARY~~

(Erase heading not required.)

Place	Date	Hour	Summary of Events and Information	Remarks and references to Appendices
HQ. C9.8. BRANDHOEK	4/9/17		8. Reinforcements distributed amongst the Companies as under. 428 2 drivers 429 1 [illegible] 430 1 [illegible] 1 driver 431 2 drivers Refilling as usual Hostile aircraft again over camp at about 10.30 pm but no bombs were dropped in the vicinity	[illegible]
—	5/9/17		7. Remounts H.D. arrived for the Train distributed between the Companies as follows. 428 Coy. 2 429 – 3 430 – 1 431 – 1 7. Hostile aircraft over camp about 10.30 pm dropt bombs in close vicinity to D.H.Q.	[illegible]

2449 Wt. W14957/M90 750,000 1/16 J.B.C. & A. Forms/C.2118/12.

Instructions regarding War Diaries and Intelligence Summaries are contained in F. S. Regs., Part II. and the Staff Manual respectively. Title Pages will be prepared in manuscript.

WAR DIARY
or
~~INTELLIGENCE SUMMARY~~

(Erase heading not required.)

Army Form C. 2118.

Place	Date	Hour	Summary of Events and Information	Remarks and references to Appendices
H4.c.9.8. BRANDHOEK	6/9/17		Refilling as usual 59th Divisional Artillery brought to 125th Bde dump and issued by S O 125th Bde 1 Supply clerk arrives from HAVRE as reinforcement ~~[illegible]~~	[initials]
—	7/9/17		Refilling as usual 125th Inf Bde came out of line and are relieved by 127th Inf Bde Shoulder patches arrive for HQ Coy of Train and 428 Coy ASC of Train, same as HQ Coy with numeral 1 in centre Hostile aircraft drop bombs in vicinity of D.21.c about 11 pm New Supply clerk posted to S.O. 125th Bde and taken on strength of 429 Coy ASC Sandbag protection placed round officers sleeping quarters but not completed	[initials]

2449 Wt. W14957/M90 750,000 1/16 J.B.C. & A. Forms/C.2118/12.

Instructions regarding War Diaries and Intelligence Summaries are contained in F. S. Regs., Part II. and the Staff Manual respectively. Title Pages will be prepared in manuscript.

WAR DIARY
or
~~INTELLIGENCE SUMMARY~~

(Erase heading not required.)

Army Form C. 2118.

Place	Date	Hour	Summary of Events and Information	Remarks and references to Appendices
H.7.c.9.8 BRANDHOEK	8/9/17		Refilling as usual. S.O. Div. Troops 59th Div & HQ Coy of 59th Div. Train arrived in 42nd Div. area for the purpose of feeding 59th Div. Artillery who are with 42nd Div. Artillery Reserve of iron rations located in Cloth Hall YPRES inspected, checked and found correct, receipt obtained from Guard	ACW
—	9/9/17		Refilling as usual. O.C. 59th Div. Train visits O.C. Train with regard to taking over by 59th Div Train O.C. Train inspects camp & horse lines of 428 & 430 Coys. A.S.C. Boots dumped in 127th Bde. Transport Lines, north of D.H.Q. Letter to G.H.Q. Office re transfer of Bde. [illegible] O's clerk from D.S.C. to Train forwarded to O.C. D.S.C. for approval.	ACW

Army Form C. 2118.

Instructions regarding War Diaries and Intelligence Summaries are contained in F. S. Regs., Part II. and the Staff Manual respectively. Title Pages will be prepared in manuscript.

WAR DIARY
or
~~INTELLIGENCE~~ SUMMARY AWh

(Erase heading not required.)

Place	Date	Hour	Summary of Events and Information	Remarks and references to Appendices
H7c9.8 BRANDHOEK	10/9/17		Refilling as usual. O.C. Train inspects 1st Line Transport of 125th Inf Brigade Capt. G. W. B. Bruce of R.A.S.C. attached 1/5 L.F. and late O.C. 429 Coy A.S.C. takes over Brigade Transport Officer of 125th Bde	AWh
–	11/9/17		Refilling as usual. Full issue of sardines in place of meat issued to 127th Bde 42nd Division transferred from XIX Corps to V Corps H.Q. 6 Coy 9th Div. Train arrive in 42nd Divisional Area Saddler S. Sgt MEDLOCK W wounded by a Stray bullet - at 428 Coy A.S.C. Admitted to No 17 C.C.S.	AWh
–	12/9/17		Refilling as usual O.C. Train inspects Horse Lines & Camps of Train Coys	AWh

2449 Wt. W14957/M90 750,000 1/16 J.B.C. & A. Forms/C.2118/12.

Army Form C. 2118.

Instructions regarding War Diaries and Intelligence Summaries are contained in F. S. Regs., Part II. and the Staff Manual respectively. Title Pages will be prepared in manuscript.

WAR DIARY
or
~~INTELLIGENCE~~ SUMMARY ACW

(Erase heading not required.)

Place	Date	Hour	Summary of Events and Information	Remarks and references to Appendices
HQ C98. BRANDHOEK	13/9/17		Capt G J AKAS OC 430 Coy proceeds on 10 days leave to England. Lieut MACINTOSH takes over temporary command of the Company. 3000 Iron rations taken up to 13th Bde Advance Old Coy of Lt BONNETT. Lt was not able to get within ¾ mile of dump owing to hostile shell fire destroying wagons which completely blocked the road	ACW
–	14/9/17		Refilling as usual. Capt G FENNER & Lt R LATHAM succeed in getting 3000 Iron rations mentioned above to dump after being held up for several hours by enemy barrage	ACW
–	15/9/17		Capt E J Shuckley takes up 12000 Bivouac rations half to Cloth Hall YPRES & half to BAVARIA HOUSE	ACW

Army Form C. 2118.

Instructions regarding War Diaries and Intelligence Summaries are contained in F. S. Regs., Part II. and the Staff Manual respectively. Title Pages will be prepared in manuscript.

WAR DIARY
~~or~~
~~INTELLIGENCE SUMMARY~~ EKS

(Erase heading not required.)

Place	Date	Hour	Summary of Events and Information	Remarks and references to Appendices
BRANDHOEK	16/9/17	-	Captain L. G. TROUP EKS S.O. Div! Troops proceeds on leave for England Lt. A. A. MORPHY takes over S.O. DIV! Troops temporarily. E.A. very much in evidence during the day. Fifteen machines over D.H.Q. at about 10.45 AM flying very low. D.H.Q. shelled during the night, about 20 shells in the Camp, no casualties Shelling started at 10.20 pm and carried on at varying intervals till after midnight.	EKS
BRANDHOEK	17/9/17		The C.O. & S.S.O. motored to WATOU and other places reference EKS Refilling Points. ~~Railhead PROVEN from the 19th~~ EKS	EKS
BRANDHOEK	18/9/17		TRAIN HEADQUARTERS moved from BRANDHOEK AREA to 37 Rue CASSEL POPERINGHE during the morning. – Camp taken over by 9th DIVISION	EKS
POPERINGHE	19/9/17		Lieut. W. H. TAYLEUR o/c Headqtr. Section 428 Coy. proceeds on leave for England. No Refilling today. 430 Coy A.S.C. left their Camp at BRANDHOEK NO1 and moved to WINNEZEELE NO 1. Area 429 Coy A.S.C. left their Camp at BRANDHOEK and moved to ST. JAN TER BIEZEN. Area	

2449 Wt. W14957/M90 750,000 1/16 J.B.C. & A. Forms/C.2118/12.

Army Form C. 2118.

Instructions regarding War Diaries and Intelligence Summaries are contained in F. S. Regs., Part II. and the Staff Manual respectively. Title Pages will be prepared in manuscript.

WAR DIARY
~~or~~
~~INTELLIGENCE SUMMARY~~ EKL

(Erase heading not required.)

Place	Date	Hour	Summary of Events and Information	Remarks and references to Appendices
POPERINGHE	19/9/17	.	431 Coy ASC left their camp at BRANDHOEK and moved into WATOU NO 1 Area 428 Coy. Headqrs Coy remaining behind with Artillery.	EKL
POPERINGHE	20/9/17	-	Railhead PROVEN – Supplies by Lorries to Refilling Points, & by Train to Units NO T4/045295 DR HENRY. N.R.V. attached to 7th Bn Lancs Fusiliers on a month's probation – with a view to a commission. DR HENRY from 428 Coy ASC 431 Coy ASC move from WATOU area to WINNEZEELE Area.	EKL
POPERINGHE	21/9/17 EKL	.	430 Coy ASC from WINNEZEELE AREA to WORMHOUDT area. 431 Coy ASC from WINNEZEELE AREA to WORMHOUDT area. D.H.Q. Transport including four Wagons GS & 1 water Cart & 3 Riders of T.H.Q. proceed to WORMHOUDT area to be taken over by 126 Bde, on arrival there. Two remounts arrive for 428 Coy ASC.	EKL

2449 Wt. W14957/M90 750,000 1/16 J.B.C. & A. Forms/C.2118/12.

Army Form C. 2118.

Instructions regarding War Diaries and Intelligence Summaries are contained in F. S. Regs., Part II. and the Staff Manual respectively. Title Pages will be prepared in manuscript.

WAR DIARY
or
~~INTELLIGENCE SUMMARY~~ EKL

(Erase heading not required.)

Place	Date	Hour	Summary of Events and Information	Remarks and references to Appendices
LA PANNE	22 9/17		Headquarters of Train arrived at LA PANNE from POPERINGHE - billets in LA PANNE Headquarters 23 AVENUE BORTIER. 431 Coy ASC arrived in LA PANNE. FERNES PROVISIONAL ISSUE MAP W 17 d 9 2 429 Coy ASC arrived in ARNEKE by rail from ST JAN TER BIEZEN	EKL
LA PANNE	23 9/17		RAILHEAD ARNEKE 430 Coy arrived in LA PANNE, encamped off the RUE DE LA MER.	
LA PANNE	24 9/17		RAILHEAD ADINKERKE. 429 Coy ASC moved from ARNEKE to GHYVELDE 430 Coy ASC moved from LA PANNE to ST IDESBALD Rd FURNES PROVISIONAL ISSUE MAP W18 a 5.5 431 Coy ASC from LA PANNE to ST IDESBALD same map reference	EKL
LA PANNE	25 9/17		Headquarters of Train moved from LA PANNE to ST IDESBALD VILLA ALBATROSS. 429 Coy ASC moved from GHYVELDE to ST IDESBALD W18 c 5.9. EKL	EKL
ST IDESBALDE	26 9/17		Weather, cloudy & windy. 429 Coy ASC sent 2 G.S. wagons complete to Divisional Salvage Coy. ST IDESBALD wagons belonging to 428 Coy ASC	EKL

2449 Wt. W14957/M90 750,000 1/16 J.B.C. & A. Forms/C.2118/12.

Army Form C. 2118.

Instructions regarding War Diaries and Intelligence Summaries are contained in F. S. Regs., Part II. and the Staff Manual respectively. Title Pages will be prepared in manuscript.

WAR DIARY
~~or~~
~~INTELLIGENCE SUMMARY~~ EKL

(Erase heading not required.)

Place	Date	Hour	Summary of Events and Information	Remarks and references to Appendices
ST. IDESBALDE	27/9/17		All detailing of Train vehicles by XV Corps S.M.T.O	EKL
ST IDESBALDE	28/9/17		Railhead ST. IDESBALDE - DECAUVILLE railway from Railhead to Dumps - Train Supply wagons from Dumps to units Captain BANCROFT. G.W.B. reported after one month with 125 Infantry Brigade 1/5 Lancs Fusiliers MONS. CONRAD Belgian Interpreter reported for duty - attached Train Headquarters CAPTAIN ARIS OC 430 Coy ASC returned from leave from England. CAPTAIN TROUP Div Troops S.O. returned from leave from England.	EKL
ST. IDESBALDE	29/9/17		D.D.S.T. Fourth Army visits Train & inspects 429. 430 & 431 Coy ASC - everything very satisfactory 18 Wagons from 429 430 & 431 Coy take cement up to PELICAN BRIDGE at 5.30 P.M. CAPTAIN BANCROFT left for England today to report to No 2 School ELSTOW SCHOOL BEDFORD by the 6th October. S.S.M. WILKINS went on leave to England. 3 Lorries i/c of Cpl HEWSON reported for duty from 42 D.S.C. - Attached to 430 Coy A.S.C.	EKL
ST IDESBALDE	30/9/17		428 Coy A.S.C. moved to WORMHOUDT with Div. Art. from POPERINGHE. 15 Wagons from 430 & 431 Coys take cement up to PELICAN BRIDGE at 5.30 P.M.	EKL

[signature]
LIEUT: COLONEL,
COMMANDING 42nd DIVISIONAL TRAIN, A.S.C.

2449 Wt. W14957/M90 750,000 1/16 J.B.C. & A. Forms/C.2118/12.

4879

Confidential.

War Diary.

42nd Divisional Train.

Army Service Corps.

Volume XIII.

Period 1-X-1917 to 31-X-1917.

Army Form C. 2118.

Instructions regarding War Diaries and Intelligence Summaries are contained in F. S. Regs., Part II. and the Staff Manual respectively. Title Pages will be prepared in manuscript.

WAR DIARY
or
~~INTELLIGENCE SUMMARY~~ EKL

(Erase heading not required.)

Place	Date	Hour	Summary of Events and Information	Remarks and references to Appendices
ST IDESBALDE	1/10/17	.	A Course of instruction started at 429 Coy ASC, for drivers of Brigade Transport. 428 Coy ASC arrived in TETEGHEM.	EKL
ST. IDESBALDE	2/10/17	.	428 Coy ASC arrive in ST IDESBALDE encamped temporarily on Sand Dunes at W.17 b. central CAPTAIN. G.L. TROUP resumes duties of Div! Troops S.O. No T/33458 Dr (A/Cpl) PATRICK GULLY. 431 Coy ASC awarded the MILITARY MEDAL AUTHORITY D.R.O. 681. 2/10/17.	EKL
ST IDESBALDE	3/10/17	.	2/Lieut PAYNE J.A R.S.O, 42nd Divisional Supply Column and 52 details of DSC attached to 428 Coy ASC for discipline Captain F. HENSHAW. B.S.O 127 Bde proceeded on leave to ENGLAND. Lieut A.A. MORPHY. acting B.S.O 127 Bde. One H.D to 428 Coy from 19th Mobile Vet. Sec.	EKL
ST IDESBALDE	4/10/17		Blowing hard all day, & much rain. 1 Cpl & 2 privates with 3 Motor lorries transferred from 430 Coy to 428 Coy. Lieut. W.H. TAYLEUR. returns off leave from ENGLAND. No T 390004 Pte BUTLER. G! brought up before the C.O, & remanded for trial by F.G.C.M. from 42nd Div. Supply Column Charge - When on active service (I) Drunk II Kicking a N.C.O. III Striking a N.C.O. One H.D. to 428 Coy from 19th Mobile Vet Sec.	EKL

2449 Wt. W14957/M90 750,000 1/16 J.B.C. & A. Forms/C.2118/12.

Instructions regarding War Diaries and Intelligence Summaries are contained in F. S. Regs., Part II. and the Staff Manual respectively. Title Pages will be prepared in manuscript.

WAR DIARY

~~or~~

~~INTELLIGENCE SUMMARY~~ EKS

(Erase heading not required.)

Army Form C. 2118.

Place	Date	Hour	Summary of Events and Information	Remarks and references to Appendices
ST IDESBALDE	5/10/17		One H.D. horse of 431 Coy. died, suffering from Sand Colic. 428 Coy ASC moves into Camp vacated by No1 Coy 66th Divl. Train at St IDESBALDE. W18 a 1.1. 429 Coy ASC moves into Camp vacated by No 4 Coy 32 Divl. Train at LA PANNE. W. 15 b central. Summary of Evidence, of Private BUTLER G. taken down by the Adjutant, at 428 Coy. Camp. Supplies for 66th Divl. Artillery, consumption 7th were drawn from St IDESBALDE railhead by lorry and dumped at TETEGHEM.	EKS
St IDESBALDE	6/10/17		431 Coy ASC moves into Camp at LA PANNE. W15 b. 5. 3. Supplies for 66th Div Art. Consumption 8th drawn from railhead St IDESBALDE by lorry and taken to WORMHOUDT. Refilling points of 125, 126 & 127 Bdes changed to COXYDE. LA PANNE Road – 32nd Div. Dumps. Div. Troops refilling point as before	EKS
COXYDE BAINS	7/10/17		Much rain all day. Train Headquarters moved from ST. IDESBALDE to COXYDE BAINS W. 6 a 2.1 – took over from 32 Divl. Train 430 Coy ASC moved into new camp at LA PANNE W. 15 b. Central Time changed from Summer time at 1.0 am. 2/Lt EDWARDS C proceeds on leave to ENGLAND.	EKS
COXYDE BAINS	8/10/17		Daily issue of Rum authorized for all units. 1 H.D. Horse of 429 Coy ASC died – effects of Sand Colic, since diagnosed Congestion of lungs.	EKS

2449 Wt. W14957/M90 750,000 1/16 J.B.C. & A. Forms/C.2118/12.

Army Form C. 2118.

Instructions regarding War Diaries and Intelligence Summaries are contained in F. S. Regs., Part II. and the Staff Manual respectively. Title Pages will be prepared in manuscript.

WAR DIARY
~~or~~
~~INTELLIGENCE~~ SUMMARY EKL

(Erase heading not required.)

Place	Date	Hour	Summary of Events and Information	Remarks and references to Appendices
COXYDE BAINS	9/10/17		Audit Board assembled to audit Canteen Accounts. President Captain A. ARIS. Members Lieut. TAYLEUR and 2/Lieut LIVINGSTONE-LEARMONTH.	EKL
COXYDE BAINS	10/10/17		L/Cpl BROWN L.A. 428 Coy ASC deprived of appointment for neglect of duty. One H.D Horse of 429 Coy ASC wounded in the ear at OOST DUNKERKE. DR OLLIVE No T.12326 wounded slightly - (at duty) 429 Coy ASC LIEUT. R LATHAM proceeds on leave to ENGLAND. Captain A. FENNER and Lieut R. LATHAM awarded the Military Cross D.R.O. No 709 10/10/17	EKL
COXYDE BAINS	11/10/17		Nothing to report.	EKL
COXYDE BAINS	12/10/17		42 Div! Troops Dump changed to W. 18. C.6.6. 428 Coy ASC moved into new Camp NEW ZEALAND CAMP W. 18. C. 4.7. - taking over from Hdq Coy 32 Div! Train.	
COXYDE BAINS	13/10/17		Weather very bad - much rain.	EKL
COXYDE BAINS	14/10/17		CO. interviews, 76 Fld Coy RE. reference Hutments for Brigade Companies at LA PANNE. 10.000 Iron Rations drawn for issue in lieu of Meat Bread Tea & Salt.	EKL

2449 Wt. W14957/M90 750,000 1/16 J.B.C. & A. Forms/C.2118/12.

Instructions regarding War Diaries and Intelligence Summaries are contained in F. S. Regs., Part II. and the Staff Manual respectively. Title Pages will be prepared in manuscript.

WAR DIARY

~~or~~

~~INTELLIGENCE SUMMARY~~ EKS

(Erase heading not required.)

Army Form C. 2118.

Place	Date	Hour	Summary of Events and Information	Remarks and references to Appendices
COXYDE BAINS	15/10/17	.	Trial by F.G.C.M. of No T 290004 Pte BUTLER G at LA PANNE Adjutant – Prosecutor. S.S.M. WILKINS returns from leave.	EKS
COXYDE BAINS	16/10/17	.	The C.O inspects 429, 430 & 431 Companies at LA PANNE The C.O. inspects 1st Line Transport of 127 Brigade at LA PANNE & CANADA CAMP. Very satisfactory, except M.G.C. & 1/6 Manchester Regt. 2/Lt PAYNE o/c Det D.S.C., brought before the C.O. Mr CONRAD Belgian Interpreter left the Train.	EKS
COXYDE BAINS	17/10/17		S.S.O visits D.D.S.T. 4th Army reference candles etc. Lieut. YEATS proceeds on leave to ENGLAND. 428 Coy A.S.C. Camp shelled during the evening 3 killed 1 died of wounds 6 wounded. Pte MAYO died of wounds Sgt KING slightly wounded (at duty) the other men belonging to 42 Divisional Supply Column., 4 shells in the Camp area No S3/025156 St Sgt HARDY W.T. reverts to the rank of Sgt Lieut (T Capt) F. HENSHAW T.F. A.S.C. to be CAPTAIN with prec. from JUNE 1st 1916.	EKS
COXYDE BAINS	18/10/17.		2/Lieut BONNETT C.A.L. proceeds on leave to ENGLAND. 2/Lieut. McINTOSH J. McG. H. (T Lieut) T.F. to be Lieut with prec from JUNE 1st 1916	EKS

2449 Wt. W14957/M90 750,000 1/16 J.B.C. & A. Forms/C.2118/12.

Instructions regarding War Diaries and Intelligence Summaries are contained in F. S. Regs., Part II. and the Staff Manual respectively. Title Pages will be prepared in manuscript.

Army Form C. 2118.

WAR DIARY
~~or~~
~~INTELLIGENCE SUMMARY~~ EKS

(Erase heading not required.)

Place	Date	Hour	Summary of Events and Information	Remarks and references to Appendices
COXYDE BAINS	19/10/17	-	All clipping stopped until animals are properly stabled. The C.O. inspects Transport of 1/3 (E.L.) Field Ambulance & 1/2 (E.L.) Field Ambulance at COXYDE. 1/3 very poor turn out in all respects – 1/2 very creditable show altogether.	EKS
COXYDE BAINS	20/10/17	-	2/Lt EDWARDS C. reported from leave. 2/Lt. BLACKMORE J.P. reported for duty from HAVRE. "The following extract from List No 156 Appointments – Commission etc dated 6/10/17. A.S.C. The undermentioned to be Adjutant:– T/Capt E.K. SCHOLTZ 42 Div. Train vice T/Capt. THURLING-BLACKWELL (To. ENG) 27 Aug. 1917." as Capt BLACKWELL did not go to ENGLAND, this was taken up through 42 Division	EKS
COXYDE BAINS	21/10/17		CAPTAIN F HENSHAW arrives from leave – granted 5 days extension 2 days supplies to 127 Brigade – No TH/126535 Dr CRAIG R. before the C.O. charged with Drunkenness – Remanded for F.G.C.M. Promulgation of Sentence of Pte BUTLER by the Adjutant at 428 Coy ASC 1 Years Imprisonment with hard labour. 1 Sgt Farrier & 7 OR arrived from HAVRE – distributed among Companies 2/Lt J.P. BLACKMORE posted to 429 Coy ASC awaiting absorption Lieut. GRAHAM. J.L. proceeds on leave to ENGLAND. Lieut MORPHY A.A. rejoins T.H.Q.	EKS

2449 Wt. W14957/M90 750,000 1/16 J.B.C. & A. Forms/C.2118/12.

Army Form C. 2118.

Instructions regarding War Diaries and Intelligence Summaries are contained in F. S. Regs., Part II. and the Staff Manual respectively. Title Pages will be prepared in manuscript.

WAR DIARY

~~or~~

~~INTELLIGENCE SUMMARY~~ EKL

(Erase heading not required.)

Place	Date	Hour	Summary of Events and Information	Remarks and references to Appendices
COXYDE. BAINS	22.10.17		Lieut. R. LATHAM returns from leave —	EKL
			Summary of Evidence, reference DR CRAIG. R. taken at 478 Coy A.S.C, by the Adjutant.	
COXYDE BAINS	23.10.17		Authority given to 2/Lieut. H. LIVINGSTONE-LEARMOUTH. – 2/Lieut. C. EDWARDS – 2/Lieut. C.A.L. BONNETT to wear the badges of Lieutenant. – without payé, until Gazetted.	
			COXYDE BAINS shelled from 12 15 PM to about 2 30 PM.	
			5 Remounts arrived — distributed as follows 1 to 478. 2 to 479. 1 to 480 1 to 431.	EKL
COXYDE BAINS	24.10.17		Lieut. C.F. SOMERVILLE proceeds on leave to SCOTLAND.	
			Lieut. A.A. MORPHY. takes over B.S.O of 125 Brigade —	
			DR HENRY. N.V.R. 478 Coy A.S.C returns to duty, after months probation with 1/7 E. Lancs	
			F.G.C.M. – DR CRAIG. R. – Adjutant as prosecutor – held at. H.Q. 1/5 Lanc Fus. LA. PANNE.	
			Extract LONDON GAZETTE – To be Lieut from June 1. 1916 (July 1) Sec Lt (T. Lieut) C.F. SOMERVILLE (T.F).	EKL
COXYDE.BAINS	25.10.17		DR. WHLR. LONERGAN before the C.O. – drunkenness – 14 days F.P. No 1.	
			COURT of ENQUIRY held at 430 Coy Office re injuries to Dr FRAMPTON.	EKL
			Capt. ARIS. A.F. President. Lieut LATHAM R. and Lieut TAYLEUR. W.H. members.	
COXYDE. BAINS	26.10.17		The C.O. and S.S.O visit LA. PANNE re new DUMP for 178 Brigade	EKL
			The C.O. visits XV Corps re loads, & loading.	
COXYDE.BAINS	27.10.17		Promulgation of Sentence re Dr CRAIG. R. by Adjutant at 478 Coy. A.S.C – 28 days F.P. No 1.	EKL

2449 Wt. W14957/M90 750,000 1/16 J.B.C. & A. Forms/C.2118/12.

Army Form C. 2118.

Instructions regarding War Diaries and Intelligence Summaries are contained in F. S. Regs., Part II. and the Staff Manual respectively. Title Pages will be prepared in manuscript.

WAR DIARY
or
~~INTELLIGENCE SUMMARY~~ E.K.

(*Erase heading not required.*)

Place	Date	Hour	Summary of Events and Information	Remarks and references to Appendices
COXYDE BAINS	28/10/17		DUMPS shelled during the day - Very slight damage - no casualties. 14 MT lorries reported to 428 Coy ASC from 42 D.S.C. for duty. - Lieut PAYNE'S detachment. Lt YEATS arrived from leave - Capt. STEVENSON proceeds to No 2 Training School BEDFORD - struck off strength. 2/Lt. J.P. BLACKMORE posted to 428 Coy ASC vice Capt STEVENSON.	E.K.
COXYDE BAINS	29/10/17		Capt. E.F. SPRECKLEY proceeds on leave. A.D.V.S. 42nd Division inspected horse lines 429 Coy ASC. - proceed with clipping - Vet reasons.	E.K.
COXYDE BAINS	30/10/17		Raining all day — COXYDE BAINS & neighbourhood shelled from 9.30 AM. to 6.30 PM. Pte GIRDLER. J.W. and SUNBEAM CAR report to Fourth Army Troops Supply Column for duty - struck off strength. The C.O attends conference at 42 D.H.Q. at 3.0 PM. Lt BONNETT returns off leave. DR. SHANNON. W. No T/32419 died - 431 Coy A.S.C. Extracts from London Gazette Oct 30. 1917 A.S.C. To be Adjt.- Temp Capt E.K. SCHOLTZ vice Temp Capt G. THURLING. BLACKWELL (Aug 27.) ASC. T.F. To be Lt. 2/Lt. (T. Lieut) J.L. GRAHAM (July 1.)	E.K.
COXYDE BAINS	31/10/17		Capt. S.C.A. HAYS reported to 41. Div' Train for duty - struck off strength - Capt HENSHAW takes over 126 Bde DUMP temporarily - Summary of Evidence reference Drs FRAMPTON and GREEN - held at 429 Coy ASC by the Adjutant. 2/Lieut. H.H. PELLS reported for duty. vice Capt C.S.A. HAYS. [signature] LIEUT: COLONEL, COMMANDING 42nd DIVISIONAL TRAIN. A.S.C.	E.K.

2449 Wt. W14957/M90 750,000 1/16 J.B.C. & A. Forms/C.2118/12.

9 Vol 10

Confidential.

WAR DIARY.

42ND DIVISIONAL TRAIN

A.S.C.

Period- 1-XII-1917 — 30-XII-1917.

Volume IX.

Instructions regarding War Diaries and Intelligence Summaries are contained in F. S. Regs., Part II. and the Staff Manual respectively. Title pages will be prepared in manuscript.

WAR DIARY

or

~~INTELLIGENCE~~ SUMMARY. EKS

(Erase heading not required.)

Army Form C. 2118.

Place	Date	Hour	Summary of Events and Information	Remarks and references to Appendices
COXYDE BAINS.	1/11/17		Headquarters & Baggage Section of 428 Coy move into LA PANNE W.15.a Central – accommodation bad – Supply Section remain in old Camp. Court of Enquiry assembled at 431 Coy office, to investigate cause of death of T 32419 DR SHANNON. W President:- Major E.W. ALDERSON. ASC Members:- Captain G THURLING BLACKWELL ASC Lieut. C A L. BONNETT ASC Post MORTEM held today as well. S.Sgt. GAVES & a/S/Sgt Sdr FORD report for duty – taken on strength of 428 Coy A.S.C Dump 125 Bde to LA PANNE	EKS
COXYDE BAINS.	2/11/17		a/C.S.M. MORRIS transferred to 428 Coy from 429 Coy. Sgt GILLINGHAM to be a/CSM 429 Coy (Temp). The Divisional Commander inspects Companies of the Train.	EKS
COXYDE BAINS	3/11/17		Cpl. J.T. LEES 428 Coy before the C.O for a Temp Commission in the RE – interviewed by the C.R.E. S.S.M. WILKINS rejoins 429 Coy ASC from T.H.Q. The following alterations in postings of officers. Capt E F SPRECKLEY to be B.S.O 126 Bde vice Capt S C A HAYS to 41 Divisional Train. Lt A A MORPHY to be R.O.1 Vice Capt E F SPRECKLEY 2/Lt. H.H. PELLS to be R.O.2 Vice Lt. A A MORPHY. 2/Lt PELLS acting B.S.O 126 Bde temporarily-	EKS

A7092). Wt. W12839/M1298 750,000. 1/17. D. D & L., Ltd. Forms/C2118/14.

Instructions regarding War Diaries and Intelligence Summaries are contained in F. S. Regs., Part II. and the Staff Manual respectively. Title pages will be prepared in manuscript.

WAR DIARY

or

~~INTELLIGENCE SUMMARY.~~ EA

(Erase heading not required.)

Army Form C. 2118.

Place	Date	Hour	Summary of Events and Information	Remarks and references to Appendices
COXYDE BAINS	4/11/17		428 Coy ASC leave LA PANNE, & return to old Camp – NEW ZEALAND CAMP – owing to accommodation in LA PANNE	EA
COXYDE BAINS	5/11/17		Office of D.D.S.T. Fourth Army closes – Administration of Supplies and Transport taken over by S.M.T.O. XV Corps (Acting A.D.of S.&T. XV Corps) The CO attends Conference at D.H.Q. a/Sqt MOORE S.P. 430 Coy ASC before the C.O. Posting a letter in Belgian Civil Post office contrary to Censorship Orders Para 20. – Severely Reprimanded.	EA
COXYDE BAINS	6/11/17		LIEUT. C.F. SOMERVILLE returns from leave to ENGLAND LIEUT A.A. MORPHY rejoins T.H.Q. Neighbourhood of COXYDE BAINS shelled during the evening. 7 O.R. reported from Base H.T.&S. Depot HAVRE. 125 Bde Dump moved from LA PANNE to W17 a 5.2 127 Bde Dump from W.17 a 7 c to LA PANNE.	EA
COXYDE BAINS	7/11/17		Capt. G. THURLING BLACKWELL as representative of the Train – attends meeting re SPORTS at D.H.Q. 429 Coy ASC officers Mess and billets vacated in LA PANNE.	EA
COXYDE BAINS	8/11/17		Nothing to report	EA
COXYDE BAINS	9/11/17		The C.O. inspects the 1st Line Transport of 125 Inf Brigade at CANADA CAMP.	EA
COXYDE BAINS	10/11/17		Raining all day & blowing hard – DR FRAMPTON W.R.T. and DR GREEN. J.F. before the CO from 429 Coy ASC – reference the presence of a Petrol Tin containing petrol being left in the Cookhouse – DR FRAMPTON deprived of 7 days pay – DR GREEN. 21 days pay.	EA

A7092). Wt. W12839/M1297 750,000. 1/17. D. D & L., Ltd. Forms/C2118/14.

Army Form C. 2118.

WAR DIARY
or
~~INTELLIGENCE SUMMARY.~~ EH

(Erase heading not required.)

Instructions regarding War Diaries and Intelligence Summaries are contained in F. S. Regs., Part II. and the Staff Manual respectively. Title pages will be prepared in manuscript.

Place	Date	Hour	Summary of Events and Information	Remarks and references to Appendices
COXYDE BAINS	11/11/17		Wet. Cloudy 1 Remount from 19 Mobile Vet to 428 Coy ASC All surplus Ordnance Stores to be collected and Returned.	EH
COXYDE BAINS	12/11/17		No T4/159419 SERGT WAGDIN W reports from HAVRE for duty - 428 Coy ASC. Extract from London Gazette. Army Service Corps T F To be Lt. 2/Lieut. H. LIVINGSTONE LEARMOUTH (July 1st). Div! Troops make double issue of Supplies. COXYDE BAINS shelled between 1.0 pm & 1.30 pm. Light railway ceases from today	EH
COXYDE BAINS	13/11/17		Drawing from Railhead by H.T. Supply vehicles - and to Units by Baggage vehicles S.S.O attends Conference at XV Corps Hdqrs.	EH
COXYDE BAINS	14/11/17		No Pack Train. Lorries drawing Supplies from F.S.D. DUNKERQUE. S.S.O attends Court of Inquiry at PROVEN re Withdrawal of vegetables at EDWAARTSHOEK 2/Lieut J. J. SIMMS ASC reported for duty today - awaiting absorption.	EH
COXYDE BAINS	15/11/17		H.T. draws from Railhead Capt E F SPRECKLEY arrives from leave. Conference of Supply Officers at T H Q. to discuss move	EH
COXYDE BAINS	16/11/17		2/Lt H.H. PELLS RO2 reports for duty with Central Purchase Board ST POL - still retained on Strength. All Supply wagons to be used for Baggage on Move. 431 Coy ASC moved to LEFFRINCKHOUCKE Lt A.A. MORPHY to be B.S.O 126 Bde, with 2/Lt. J. J SIMMS as supernumary	EH

Army Form C. 2118.

WAR DIARY
~~or~~
~~INTELLIGENCE SUMMARY.~~ EKL

(*Erase heading not required.*)

Instructions regarding War Diaries and Intelligence Summaries are contained in F. S. Regs., Part II. and the Staff Manual respectively. Title pages will be prepared in manuscript.

Place	Date	Hour	Summary of Events and Information	Remarks and references to Appendices
COXYDE BAINS	EKL 16/11/17		Supplies for 127 Bde drawn by lorry from LEFFRINCK HOUCKE Supplies for 125. 126 Bdes & Div! Troops drawn from ST IDESBALDE by lorry.	EKL
COXYDE BAINS	17/11/17		Supplies for 127 Bde drawn at ARNEKE – no change for other Bdes & Div! Troops. No T4/091903 DR M WARDLE. 429 Coy ASC – shot himself through elbow – while cleaning rifle – apparently attempted suicide. 431 Coy ASC moved to WORMHOUDT.	EKL
COXYDE BAINS	18/11/17		430 Coy ASC move to COUDEKERQUE. BRANCHE. 431 Coy ASC move to L'ANGE. Supplies for 127 Bde drawn from ARNEKE – & for 126 Bde LEFFRINCKHOUCKE	EKL
AIRE	19/11/17		Train Headquarters move to 29 RUE DE BIENNES AIRE. 429 Coy ASC move to TETEGHEM AREA. 430 Coy ASC move to WORMHOUDT AREA 431 Coy ASC move to STAPLES. Supplies 126 Bde from ARNEKE Supplies 125 Bde from LEFFRINCKHOUCKE.	EKL

A7092). Wt. W12839/M1293 750,000. 1/17. D. D & L., Ltd. Forms/C2118/14.

Instructions regarding War Diaries and Intelligence Summaries are contained in F. S. Regs., Part II. and the Staff Manual respectively. Title pages will be prepared in manuscript.

WAR DIARY

~~or~~

~~INTELLIGENCE SUMMARY.~~ EKL

(Erase heading not required.)

Army Form C. 2118.

Place	Date	Hour	Summary of Events and Information	Remarks and references to Appendices
AIRE	20/11/17		429 Coy ASC move to WORMHOUDT A AREA. 430 Coy ASC move to ZERMEZEELE (WORMHOUDT B AREA) 431 Coy ASC move to LAMBRES AREA (AIRE) 125. 126. 127 Bdes drawn from ARNEKE. RAILHEAD.	EKL
AIRE	21/11/17		Div' Troops S.O. with Lt YEATS, 13 lorries, with loaders & issuing staff left STEENBECQUE and proceeded to GHYVELDE. 429 Coy ASC move to ZERMEZEELE (WORMHOUDT B. AREA) 430 Coy ASC move to STAPLES AREA 127 Bde Supplies from AIRE 126 Bde from EBLINGHEM. 125 Bde from ARNEKE	EKL
AIRE	22/11/17		429 Coy ASC move to STAPLES AREA 430 Coy ASC move to ST MARTIN (AIRE) 428 Coy ASC move to GHYVELDE. AREA 125 Bde Supplies from EBLINGHEM. DIV Troops Supplies from ARNEKE	EKL

Instructions regarding War Diaries and Intelligence Summaries are contained in F. S. Regs., Part II. and the Staff Manual respectively. Title Pages will be prepared in manuscript.

WAR DIARY
or
~~INTELLIGENCE~~ SUMMARY EKL

(*Erase heading not required.*)

Army Form C. 2118.

Place	Date	Hour	Summary of Events and Information	Remarks and references to Appendices
AIRE	23/11/17		428 Coy ASC move to WORMHOUDT AREA. 429 Coy ASC move to NEUFPRÉ (AIRE) 126 Bde Supplies from AIRE.	EKL
AIRE	24/11/17		428 Coy ASC move to HONDEGHEM. SADD CPL RYAN reported for duty from 1 Cav. Res. Park - posted to 429 Coy ASC 125 126 127 Bdes Supplies from AIRE - DIV! Troops from LUMBRES	EKL
AIRE	25/11/17		~~Div! Troops draw Supplies by H.T. - Refilling by first line.~~ EKL 3 drivers from the train, despatched to HAVRE as ploughmen	EKL
AIRE	26/11/17		Railhead AIRE. 428 Coy move to LAMBRES - Camp vacated by 431 Coy ASC 431 Coy moved to OBLINGHEM 2 drivers from the Train despatched to HAVRE as ploughmen.	EKL
AIRE	27/11/17		For Div! Troops H T draws from Railhead - refilling by first line. Lt. PAYNE with loaders & issuers rejoins 428 ASC 430 Coy ASC move to LA ROUPIE. 431 Coy ASC move to LOCON area.	

2449 Wt. W14957/M90 750,000 1/16 J.B.C. & A. Forms/C.2118/12.

Instructions regarding War Diaries and Intelligence Summaries are contained in F. S. Regs., Part II. and the Staff Manual respectively. Title Pages will be prepared in manuscript.

WAR DIARY
~~or~~
~~INTELLIGENCE SUMMARY~~ EKl

(Erase heading not required.)

Army Form C. 2118.

Place	Date	Hour	Summary of Events and Information	Remarks and references to Appendices
AIRE			429 Coy ASC move to OBLINGHEM. S.S.O. proceeds to new area	EKl
AIRE	28/11/17		125-126-127 Bdes Railhead LA GORGUE – Supplies from Railhead to Dumps by rail refilling by 1st Line – Div! Troops – H.T. from Railhead – refilling by 1st Line – 430 Coy ASC move to BETHUNE – area. 429 Coy ASC move to AVELETTE. – & take over from 25 Div! Train. CAPT. G. L. TROUP proceeds to ENGLAND for Infantry training. Capt. E. F. SPRECKLEY to be D.T.S.O. 2/Lt. J. J. SIMMS to be S.O. 126 Bde.	EKl
BETHUNE. LOCON	29/11/17		T.H.Q. move to new area BETHUNE LOCON. Lt A. A. MORPHY severely wounded by shell fire in BETHUNE – died of wounds same day in No 1. CCS.	EKl
BETHUNE. LOCON	30/11/17		Div! Troops draw from LA GORGUE. 428 move to RIEZ DU VINAGE. ~~[illegible]~~ EKl 1 Rider & 3 HD from Remounts.	EKl

J. Carlton
LIEUT: COLONEL
COMMANDING 42nd DIVISIONAL TRAIN, A.S.C.

2449 Wt. W14957/M90 750,000 1/16 J.B.C. & A. Forms/C.2118/12.

Vol 11

CONFIDENTIAL.

WAR DIARY.

42ND Divisional Train,

A. S. C.

Period - 1-XII-1917 to 31-XII-1917.

VOLUME X.

Instructions regarding War Diaries and Intelligence Summaries are contained in F. S. Regs., Part II. and the Staff Manual respectively. Title Pages will be prepared in manuscript.

WAR DIARY
or
~~INTELLIGENCE SUMMARY~~ EKS

(Erase heading not required.)

Army Form C. 2118.

Place	Date	Hour	Summary of Events and Information	Remarks and references to Appendices
BETHUNE·LOCON	1 12/17		Railhead for all Groups LA GORGUE. Position of Refilling points Div! Troops X 13 a 0.0. 125 126 Bde W.30 c 3.0 127 Bde X 1 d 2.3. S.S.O visited D.D.S.T. 1st Army. CO. attends lecture on Staff duties at HOUDAIN. Lt. A.A. MORPHY buried at CHOCQUES CEMETERY. The three Bde Coy Officers attend T.H.Q for a conference.	EKS
BETHUNE·LOCON	2 12/17		428 Coy ASC move to LE HAMEL X 20 d 1.7. 430 Coy ASC move to BELZAGE FARM. W 22 d Central.	EKS
BETHUNE·LOCON	3 12/17		T.Captain G.O.N. WYATT reported for duty. CO attends conference at D.H.Q.	EKS
BETHUNE·LOCON	4 12/17		T.Capt G.O.N. WYATT posted to 431 Coy ASC T.Major E.W. ALDERSON before the Div! Commander.	EKS
BETHUNE·LOCON	5 12/17		No T4/160006 Cpl ABELL W.H. to be A/CQMS. from 13/10/17.	EKS
BETHUNE·LOCON	6 12/17		Major E.W. ALDERSON proceeds to Base H.T.&S. Depot HAVRE Authority AC/79 4/12/17 Captain A. FENNER takes over Command of 428 Coy ASC. vice Major E.W. ALDERSON Captain G.O.N. WYATT takes over Command of 431 Coy ASC. vice Capt. A FENNER.	

2449 Wt. W14957/M90 750,000 1/16 J.B.C. & A. Forms/C.2118/12.

Army Form C. 2118.

Instructions regarding War Diaries and Intelligence Summaries are contained in F. S. Regs., Part II. and the Staff Manual respectively. Title Pages will be prepared in manuscript.

WAR DIARY
~~or~~
~~INTELLIGENCE SUMMARY~~ E.K.

(Erase heading not required.)

Place	Date	Hour	Summary of Events and Information	Remarks and references to Appendices
	6/12/17		Captain G. THURLING-BLACKWELL attends SPORTS MEETING at G.H.Q.	E.K.
BETHUNE. LOCON	7/12/17		Baggage Wagons of 478 Coy ASC returned from units, with the exception of those permanently detached.	E.K.
BETHUNE LOCON	8/12/17		Instructions given to 479 Coy ASC to vacate their camp.	E.K.
BETHUNE. LOCON	9/12/17		3000 Kilos Linseed Cake - part Extra forage drawn from No 4 F.S.D.	E.K.
BETHUNE. LOCON.	10/12/17		479 Coy moved into new Camp. X21. C 4 5. LE HAMEL Baggage wagons sent to 125 Bde for relief in the line. 1 Rider 15 HD Horses arrive from Remounts R to 430 Coy 5 HD to 478 Coy.	E.K.
BETHUNE LOCON	11/12/17		Loading practice put into operation for Brigade Transport, supervised by OC Coys. Court of Enquiry assembled at 430 Coy Office re 2 bicycles lost at ST. MARTIN on move President Capt. G.D.N. WYATT. 431 Coy Members Lt. C.EDWARDS 479 Coy 2/Lt. BLACKMORE 478 Coy ASC	E.K. E.K.
BETHUNE LOCON	12/12/17		The CO. attends lecture at HOUDAIN. St. Sgt. GAVES takes charge of Coal Dump vice St Sgt HODGSON — leave	E.K.
BETHUNE. LOCON	13/12/17		Nothing to report.	E.K.
BETHUNE LOCON	14/12/17		The CO. inspects 1st Line Transport 126 Bde — very unsatisfactory in every respect Capt. A. FENNER boarded & pronounced unfit for Infantry -	E.K.
BETHUNE. LOCON	15/12/17		Major. E.W. ALDERSON reported - posted to T.H.Q pending decision as to ~~employment~~ employment. No T4/242953 Sgt WYNN G.D joins 1/8 Man. 1 months attachment - for commission in the Tank Corps.	E.K.

2449 Wt. W14957/M90 750,000 1/16 J.B.C. & A. Forms/C.2118/12.

Instructions regarding War Diaries and Intelligence Summaries are contained in F. S. Regs., Part II. and the Staff Manual respectively. Title Pages will be prepared in manuscript.

WAR DIARY

~~or~~

~~INTELLIGENCE SUMMARY~~ EKJ

(Erase heading not required.)

Army Form C. 2118.

Place	Date	Hour	Summary of Events and Information	Remarks and references to Appendices
BETHUNE LOCON.	16/12/17		1 NCO & 5 OR with horses & vehicles report from 176 Bde to 430 Coy for instruction - from 176 M.G.C	EKJ
"	17/12/17		Snow all day -	EKJ
"	18/12/17		Freezing hard. Lt Col. J. COULSON OC Train proceeds on leave to ENGLAND. Major W.P. REYNOLDS assumes command. Capt E.F SPRECKLEY to be a/S.S.O. Capt. G.D.N. WYATT. to be O.T.S.O. temporarily.	EKJ
"	19/12/17		Major W.P. REYNOLDS attends conference at D.H.Q. - still freezing hard.	EKJ
"	20/12/17		Still freezing -	
"	21/12/17		Still freezing - Baggage Wagons of 125 Bde sent to units. AA & QMG visited 428 Coy ASC	EKJ
"	22/12/17	-	Still freezing - Baggage & Supply vehicles required by 125 & 127 Brigades - for relief. a/cpl P GULLY. 431 Coy. to be a/Sgt. and transferred to 428 Coy ASC. a/cpl F.W BURVILL 428 Coy to be a/Sgt.	EKJ
"	23/12/17	-	5 Reinforcements report from HAVRE 3 to 431 Coy 2 to 429 Coy. Freezing.	EKJ
"	24/12/17	-	Raining during the day. a/L/cpl TURNER F.G 428 Coy ASC to be a/CPL. a/Sgt KING T.H transferred from 428 Coy to 429 Coy. DR J. JOBBINS to be a/L/cpl. a/L/cpl S.B FRANKLIN 431 Coy to be a/CPL	

Instructions regarding War Diaries and Intelligence Summaries are contained in F. S. Regs., Part II. and the Staff Manual respectively. Title Pages will be prepared in manuscript.

WAR DIARY
or
~~INTELLIGENCE SUMMARY~~ EKL

(Erase heading not required.)

Army Form C. 2118.

Place	Date	Hour	Summary of Events and Information	Remarks and references to Appendices
"	24/12/17		Extract from London Gazette 24/12/17 Army Service Corps Temp Lieuts to be Temp Capts – H. W. TAYLEUR (DEC 25th) 478 Coy ASC	EKL
BETHUNE Locl	25/12/17		Thawing slightly. No T4/091903 DR WARDLE M. died at LA PANNE on the 20/12/17 Snowing hard in evening & through the night — Take Thaw precaution order received at 10.0 PM Instructions sent out to all companies	EKL
"	26/12/17		Slight Thaw — 24 GS wagons under LIEUT TAYLEUR sent to 12 DW Train at BOESEGHEM reference Thaw precautions. Supply vehicles to be half loaded No lorries allowed on road Thaw Precautions Cancelled at 12.0 Noon. Wagons wired for. Instructions received that in the event of Thaw precautions coming into force again the 24 wagons will report to 15 Corps Troops Supply Column. MERVILLE. DR ROBINSON T 431 Coy to be a/L/Cpl	EKL
"	27/12/17		Snowing all day. 1 Rider and 3 HD arrive from Remounts 1R to 479 Coy 2 HD to 430, 1 to 478. 24 Wagons report back from BOESEGHEM. 14 000 iron rations drawn from Railhead to turn over. Orders received that no HD are to go out without frost cogs. – difficulty in obtaining them.	EKL
"	28/12/17		Fine but still frosty 3 Trucks of coke received from R.H.	EKL

Army Form C. 2118.

Instructions regarding War Diaries and Intelligence Summaries are contained in F. S. Regs., Part II. and the Staff Manual respectively. Title Pages will be prepared in manuscript.

WAR DIARY
or
INTELLIGENCE SUMMARY
(Erase heading not required.)

Place	Date	Hour	Summary of Events and Information	Remarks and references to Appendices
BETHUNE LOCON	29/12/17	.	Fine but still frosty Instructions reference Thaw precautions cancelled again. In the event of it coming into force again 24 Wagons to proceed to 12 Divl Train BOESEGHEM DR CRAIG R 478 Coy, charged with DRUNKENNESS, on duty, remanded for F.G.C.M. Summary of Evidence taken by Adjutant or 478 Coy. New leave allotment from Jan 1st 1 daily, plus 1 every alternate day commencing 3rd, excluding 27th	EKL
"	30/12/17	.	Frosty - four reinforcements report from HAVRE - posted to 430 Coy ASC	EKL
"	31/12/17		Frosty - Major E.W. ALDERSON proceeds to ENGLAND via BOULOGNE Auth. DDST 1st Army C/520 28/12/17	EKL

W.P. Reynolds Major
a/O.C. 42nd Divnl Train.

2449 Wt. W14957/M90 750,000 1/16 J.B.C. & A. Forms/C.2118/12.

Vol 12

CONFIDENTIAL.

WAR DIARY.

42ND DIVISIONAL TRAIN., A.S.C.

Period.

1-1-1918 to 31-1-1918.

Volume XI.

Instructions regarding War Diaries and Intelligence Summaries are contained in F. S. Regs., Part II. and the Staff Manual respectively. Title pages will be prepared in manuscript.

Army Form C. 2118.

WAR DIARY

or

~~INTELLIGENCE SUMMARY.~~ EKL

(Erase heading not required.)

1918

Place	Date	Hour	Summary of Events and Information	Remarks and references to Appendices
BETHUNE LOCON	1/1/18		Frosty. Nothing to report.	EKL
"	2/1/18		Frosty. No T/213481 Sgt SPIBY reported - posted to 430 Coy as a/CQMS	EKL
"	3/1/18		Frosty Baggage wagons required by 126 Bde & 127 Bde - 127 to line FGCM re T4/126535 DR CRAIG R. 428 Coy ASC at the Chateau LE QUESNOY Lt Col J. COULSON returns off leave from ENGLAND. L/Cpl FOY J. 428 Coy ASC appointed a/Cpl with pay (from the 14th) DR TURBITT R. appointed a/L/Cpl with pay vice a/Cpl FOY.	EKL
"	4/1/18		Frosty. Capt H.W. TAYLEUR to be OC 431 Coy ASC vice Capt G D N WYATT Capt G D N WYATT to be RO I vice Lieut A.A. MORPHY (deceased) Capt E F SPRECKLEY resumes duties of SO DT.	EKL
"	5/1/18		Frosty Promulgation of Sentence of DR CRAIG R by the Adjutant at 428 Coy ASC 90 days FP No I	EKL
"	6/1/18		Fine, but still frosty. Nothing to report.	EKL
"	7/1/18		Thawing slightly - raining. Inspection of 1st Line Transport of 127 Inf Brigade by the CO. at LE QUESNOY - good Major W.P.K. REYNOLDS proceeds on leave - as from the 8th	

A7092). Wt. W12839/M1293 750,000. 1/17. D. D & L., Ltd. Forms/C2118/14.

Instructions regarding War Diaries and Intelligence Summaries are contained in F. S. Regs., Part II. and the Staff Manual respectively. Title pages will be prepared in manuscript.

WAR DIARY

~~or~~

~~INTELLIGENCE SUMMARY.~~ EKL

(Erase heading not required.)

Army Form C. 2118.

Place	Date	Hour	Summary of Events and Information	Remarks and references to Appendices
BETHUNE LOCON	–		Captain E.F. SPRECKLEY acting S.S.O. — four reinforcements arrive, posted to 428 Coy A.S.C. 2 Snow ploughs drawn from R.E. – one to be horsed by 431 Coy A.S.C., & the other by 430 Coy A.S.C. 2 HD horses from 431 Coy A.S.C. sent to Vet Section – Opthalmia.	EKL
"	8/1/18		Snowing hard. – Seven (7) remounts arrive from BOULOGNE. Capt A.F. FARIS & CAPT G. THURLING-BLACKWELL proceed on leave to ENGLAND (as from the 9th) 84 A.F.A. Bde attached to 42 DIVISION – Transport to be taken over by Divisional Train	EKL
"	9/1/18		Fine, but still frosty – snowing during the afternoon – raining during the evening. Remounts posted as follows 2 to 428, 1 to 430, 2 to 431, & 2 to 429 Coys A.S.C. Lieut H. LIVINGSTONE LEARMOUTH proceeds on leave to ENGLAND. Daily issue of Rum to all Troops.	EKL
"	10/1/18		Slight thaw during night & part of the day – fine – roads bad. Inspection of 1st Line Transport – 126 Inf Brigade – very good – great improvement. At 5.30 am a fire broke out on 126 Bde Supply Dump 666 lbs Sugar 124 lbs tea destroyed – all the rest saved – origin of fire unknown at present. 1 HD horse to Mobile Vet Sec from 431 Coy A.S.C. – Opthalmia.	EKL
"	11/1/18		Raining – thawing hard – roads very bad – Received Wire R20/342 from D.H.Q. adopt Thaw precautions from midnight.	EKL

A7092). Wt. W12839/M1293 750,000 1/17. D. D & L., Ltd. Forms/C2118/14.

Army Form C. 2118.

WAR DIARY
or
~~INTELLIGENCE SUMMARY.~~ EKL

(*Erase heading not required.*)

Instructions regarding War Diaries and Intelligence Summaries are contained in F. S. Regs., Part II. and the Staff Manual respectively. Title pages will be prepared in manuscript.

Place	Date	Hour	Summary of Events and Information	Remarks and references to Appendices
BETHUNE LOCON	12/1/18		Cloudy – roads bad – Thawing – Thaw Precautions in force Supply vehicles carrying half loads. 24 Wagons dispatched to MERVILLE RAILHEAD to XV Corps Troops Supply Column, under Lieut R. LATHAM 9 wagons from 428 Coy, & 5 from each brigade Coy. – 1 wagon from 429 Coy to 251 Tunnelling Coy R.E. All standing detail ceases. owing to uncertainty of Pack Train, which did come up short, but supplies were obtained from Portuguese Pack	EKL
"	13/1/18		Thaw precautions in force – Fine – standing detail resumed except in one or two cases 24 Wagons to MERVILLE RLD. i/c Lt EDWARDS. for XV Corps	EKL
"	14/1/18		Thaw precautions in force – snowing all day – 24 Wagons to MERVILLE i/c Lt BONNETT 50 Wagons drawing fuel wood from BETHUNE. All standing detail cancelled. Court of Enquiry – Board of Officers assembled at THQ as under, re fire at 126 Bde Dump on the 10/1/1918. President Capt G.D.N. WYATT RDI Members { Lt R. LATHAM. 431 Coy ASC Lt W.W. YEATS 428 Coy ASC Inspection of Transport 1/1 E.L FIELD AMBULANCE, BETHUNE – Very good turnout. Thaw precautions off – resume normal traffic – wire from DHQ Instructions to send Baggage & Supply Vehicles to 125 & 126 Bdes tomorrow – Cancelled	EKL

A7092). Wt. W12839/M1293 750,000. 1/17. D. D & L., Ltd. Forms/C2118/14.

Army Form C. 2118.

Instructions regarding War Diaries and Intelligence Summaries are contained in F. S. Regs., Part II. and the Staff Manual respectively. Title pages will be prepared in manuscript.

WAR DIARY
or
~~INTELLIGENCE SUMMARY~~ EKS
(Erase heading not required.)

Place	Date	Hour	Summary of Events and Information	Remarks and references to Appendices
BETHUNE-LOCON	15/1/18		Thaw Precautions in force Slight thaw – Raining all afternoon – increase in RE wagons Inspection of Transport 1/2 & 1/3 E.L. FIELD AMBULANCES. – Very good show. Adopt Thaw Precautions from 6.0 am 16th. Q 20/342 15th Rations drawn from Railhead for 84 A.F.A. Bde for issue 16th a/Sgt MOORE 430 Coy to be a/CQMS 430 Coy. a/Cpl MONAGHAN 430 Coy to be a/Sgt 430 Coy DR TROUGHTON 428 Coy to be a/L/Cpl & transferred to 430 Coy.	EKS
"	16/1/18		Raining & very windy – Thaw precautions in force – 24 Wagons to MERVILLE i/c Lt EDWARDS. Instructions received to send Baggage & Supply vehicles to 125 & 126 Bdes Transport Lines on the 17th also 3 wagons to 126 MGC on the 18th & Thaw precautions still in force Q 20/371	EKS
"	17/1/18		Raining – Thaw precautions in force Re. G.R.O 3091 4-1-1918 the 1st Line Transport of 84 A.F.A. Bde, attached to the Train – instructions dispatched to send wagons into Companies 8 to 430, 4 to 428, 2 to 429 & 431. 24 Wagons to MERVILLE – 34 to two Brigades – All wagons detailed First issue of Rations at the reduced scale –	EKS

A7092). Wt. W12839/M1293 750,000. 1/17. D. D & L., Ltd. Forms/C2118/14.

Army Form C. 2118.

Instructions regarding War Diaries and Intelligence Summaries are contained in F. S. Regs., Part II, and the Staff Manual respectively. Title pages will be prepared in manuscript.

WAR DIARY
or
~~INTELLIGENCE SUMMARY~~. EKS

(Erase heading not required.)

Place	Date	Hour	Summary of Events and Information	Remarks and references to Appendices
BETHUNE. LOCON.	18/1/18		Thaw precautions in force - Dull & Cloudy - all Transport detailed - 7 Reinforcements report from HAVRE. 316478 - 316479 - 116431.	EKS
"	19/1/18		Thaw precautions in force - Cloudy - all wagons detailed -	EKS
"	20/1/18		Thaw precautions in force. Cloudy. All wagons detailed. 268 M. G. Coy draw rations from 127 Bde for 1st time for consumption 21st.	G. W.
"	21/1/18		" " " " . Rain. " " "	G. W.
"	22/1/18		" " " " . Fine. 24 wagons to [illegible] not required.	
			Capt. E. K. Scholtz proceeds on leave to England. Capt G. D. W. Wyatt to be A/Adjt.	
			A/Corpl Heard 428 Coy reverts to Driver, own request.	
			A/Sergt Gatty " " " " " " . Drunk.	
			A/L/Cpl Spiller " " " " " " . Neglect of duty	G. W.
"	23/1/18		Thaw precautions in force. Fine. All wagons detailed. Major Reynolds returns from leave. Capt. Spreckley resumes duty of S.O. to Divl Troops.	G. W.

A7092). Wt. W12839/M1293 750,000. 1/17. D. D & L., Ltd. Forms/C2118/14.

Army Form C. 2118.

WAR DIARY
or
INTELLIGENCE SUMMARY.
(Erase heading not required.)

Instructions regarding War Diaries and Intelligence Summaries are contained in F. S. Regs., Part II. and the Staff Manual respectively. Title pages will be prepared in manuscript.

Place	Date	Hour	Summary of Events and Information	Remarks and references to Appendices
BETHUNE. LOCON	24/1/18		Thaw precautions off from 6.30 am. Roads still v. bad. Motor traffic largely forbidden. Fine. Capts ARIS & BLACKWELL return off leave.	G. W.
	25/1/18		Fine. Nothing to report.	G. W.
	26/1/18		Fine. LIEUT Mc G. H. Mc INTOSH is posted to 55th DIVl TRAIN. 2/LIEUT. R. H. KEEVIL (on leave to ENGLAND) is posted to 42nd DIVl TRAIN.	G. W.
	27/1/18		Fine. No T/21875 Dr. E. GOSDEN, 431 Coy before F.G.C.M. Drunk on duty. LIEUT. LIVINGSTONE LEARMONTH reports off leave. All wagons detailed. 1 H.D. Horse evacuated to 19th Mob: Vet: Section from 431 Coy.	G. W.
	28/1/18		Fine & frosty. Restrictions on use of Bethune Lestrem road by lorries removed. Capt. FENNER goes on leave. Capt. BLACKWELL takes over temporary command of 428 Coy & LIEUT. GRAHAM of 429 Coy. All wagons detailed	G. W.
	29/1/18		Fine & frosty. All wagons detailed.	G. W.

A7092). Wt. W12839/M1293 750,000. 1/17. D. D & L., Ltd. Forms/C2118/14.

Army Form C. 2118.

Instructions regarding War Diaries and Intelligence Summaries are contained in F. S. Regs., Part II. and the Staff Manual respectively. Title pages will be prepared in manuscript.

WAR DIARY
or
INTELLIGENCE SUMMARY.
(Erase heading not required.)

Place	Date	Hour	Summary of Events and Information	Remarks and references to Appendices
BETHUNE. LOCON	30/1/18		~~Wet~~ Wet Mist. All wagons detailed	G.W
	31/1/18		Wet mist. All wagons detailed.	
			Sentence promulgated on Dr. GOSDEN, 431 Coy. 1 Year Imprisonment with H.L. DRUNK on duty.	G.W.
			No. T/14721 A/C.S.M. MORRIS J. 428 Coy is transferred to 430 Coy & appointed to the rank of A/S.S.M.	G.W.
			No. T/14307 A/C.S.M. BURDON T.J. 431 Coy is transferred to 428 Coy	

[signature]
LIEUT: COLONEL,
COMMANDING 42nd DIVISIONAL TRAIN, A.S.C.

A7092). Wt. W12839/M1293 750,000. 1/17. D. D & L., Ltd. Forms/C2118/14.

WO 95/4672 [marginal pencil mark, rotated]

CONFIDENTIAL.

WAR DIARY.

42nd Divisional Train.

A. S. C.

Period:- 1-2-1918 to 28-2-1918

Volume - XII

Instructions regarding War Diaries and Intelligence Summaries are contained in F. S. Regs., Part II. and the Staff Manual respectively. Title pages will be prepared in manuscript.

WAR DIARY

or

~~INTELLIGENCE SUMMARY.~~ EKS

(Erase heading not required.)

Army Form C. 2118.

Place	Date	Hour	Summary of Events and Information	Remarks and references to Appendices
BETHUNE LOCON	1/2/18		Wet Summary of Evidence in the Case of DR MILLS taken by A/Adjutant. Rum issue ceases.	EKS
"	2/2/18		Fine — 1/c SSM H.G ROLFE rejoined 431 Coy ASC from attachment to 1/3 E.L Field Ambulance 268 M.G Coy joins DIVISION — 1 driver with 2 HD horses 1 wagon joins 428 Coy ASC	EKS
"	3/2/18		Wagon & pair return to 431 Coy ASC from Town Major LA GORGUE Fine	EKS
"	4/2/18		Fine —	EKS
"	5/2/18		Fine — D.D.S.T 1st Army inspects 428 & 429 Coys ASC	EKS
"	6/2/18		Fine — 3 Reinforcements arrive RAMC personnel returned to their units from Train Coys.	EKS
"	7/2/18		Wet — F.G.C.M. of DR MILLS at LE QUESNOY. — A/Adjutant prosecutor. 1 NCO & 4 men to BOULOGNE for remounts Captain E.K SCHOLTZ returns off leave from U.K — resumes duties of Adjutant — Captain G.D.N. WYATT resumes duties of R.O I	
"	8/2/18		Wet — CO and Adjutant visit new area.— 5 men before an interviewing Committee regarding their trades in Civil life — none eligible.	EKS
"	9/2/18		Wet — promulgation of Sentence re DR MILLS 90 days F.P No I — remit 28 days. The following awarded the BELGIAN CROIX de GUERRE T 24941 a/Sgt BURVILL 428 Coy ASC. DR OLLIVE 429 Coy ASC DR WAREHAM. 430 Coy ASC	EKS

A7092). Wt. W12839/M1293. 750,000. 1/17. D. D & L., Ltd. Forms/C2118/14.

Instructions regarding War Diaries and Intelligence Summaries are contained in F. S. Regs., Part II. and the Staff Manual respectively. Title pages will be prepared in manuscript.

WAR DIARY
or
~~INTELLIGENCE SUMMARY~~ EKS

(Erase heading not required.)

Army Form C. 2118.

Place	Date	Hour	Summary of Events and Information	Remarks and references to Appendices
BETHUNE LOCON	10/2/18		Wet – nothing to report	EKS
"	11/2/18		Dull & Cloudy – Wagons for RE work cease – only standing detail carried on by 428 Coy ASC. Baggage wagons of 127 Bde sent to their units.	EKS
"	12/2/18		Dull & Cloudy – Supplies for 127 Bde Group drawn by lorry from LA GORGUE Railhead and delivered to new R.P. at HAUTRIEUX V.23 a 9.6 Sheet 36A. Refilling by 1st Line. 431 Coy ASC move from LOCON to HURIONVILLE V.21 C. Central. Sheet 36A. Reinforcements arrive 1 Saddler Corporal posted to 430 Coy, 3 Corporals, 2 posted to 428 Coy & 1 to 429 Coy 1 Sergeant posted to 428 Coy. 7 H.D. & 1 Rider arrive – retained by 428 Coy pending instructions – poor type of horse. Instructions issued to Coys to return Wagons to 84 A.F.A. Bde, before moving.	EKS EKS
"	13/2/18		Dull & Cloudy. Baggage wagons of 125 Bde sent to units.	
"	14/2/18		Dull & Cloudy Railhead LILLERS. Supplies of 125. 126. Bde Groups & DW Troops by lorry, & 127 Bde Group by Horse Transport. R.P. 125 Bde ANNEZIN E.8 a 5.5 Sheet 36B. – R.P. 126 Bde BUSNES P. 25 d 8.3 Sheet 36A 429 Coy ASC move from LE HAMEL to ANNEZIN AREA. 430 Coy ASC move from BELZAGE FME to BUSNES.	EKS
GONNEHAM	15/2/18		Cold & frosty – freezing during night. T.H.Q. move to GONNEHAM Baggage wagons of DW Troops sent to units	EKS
"	16/2/18		Fine – 428 Coy ASC move from LE HAMEL to GONNEHAM. R.P. GONNEHAM CHURCH V.18 a 7.7 36A Supplies of 126 & 127 Bdes drawn from Railhead by Horse Transport, 125 & DW Troops by lorry. Move of Division complete.	EKS

A7092). Wt. W12839/M1293 750,000. 1/17. D. D & L., Ltd. Forms/C2118/14.

Army Form C. 2118.

Instructions regarding War Diaries and Intelligence Summaries are contained in F. S. Regs., Part II. and the Staff Manual respectively. Title pages will be prepared in manuscript.

WAR DIARY
or
~~INTELLIGENCE SUMMARY~~ EKS

(Erase heading not required.)

Place	Date	Hour	Summary of Events and Information	Remarks and references to Appendices
GONNEHAM	17/2/18		Frosty – Court of Enquiry re the loss of Bicycle from 431 Coy ASC, held at 431 Coy Office. President Captain G.D.N. WYATT Members Lieut C.A.L. BONNETT, 2/Lieut J.P. BLACKMORE. Remounts distributed 429 Coy. 1R & 1 H.D. 430 Coy 1 HD 431 Coy 2 H.D. 428 Coy 3 H.D.	EKS
"	18/2/18		Fine. – Reinforcements arrive 1 CSM to 431 Coy ASC 2 Drivers to 429 Coy – 1 driver to 428 Coy 1 Pte to 431 Coy. Details of Div Bombing School – attached to 431 Coy	EKS
"	19/2/18		Fine – Three Bns leave Division for 66th Division 1/6 Lancs Fusiliers, 1/4 East Lancs Regt. and 1/9 Manchester Regt. T Major H.P. WILLIAMS MC reported for duty from 39 Div! Train	EKS
"	20/2/18		Dull & Cloudy – Rain during the day – T Major H.P. WILLIAMS MC takes over Command of 428 Coy ASC vice T Capt A. FENNER MC. T Capt. G. THURLING BLACKWELL assumes command of 429 Coy ASC. T Capt A. FENNER MC returns off leave (7 days extension).	EKS
"	21/2/18		Fine.	EKS
"	22/2/18		Windy – The CO attends conference at S&T Office 1st Army. T Capt. W.H. TAYLEUR proceeds on leave. T Capt A FENNER MC proceeds to join 25th Div! Train for duty.	EKS
"	23/2/18		Dull in morning – but Fine all day – 5 OR posted to Field Ambulances.	EKS

Army Form C. 2118.

Instructions regarding War Diaries and Intelligence Summaries are contained in F. S. Regs., Part II. and the Staff Manual respectively. Title pages will be prepared in manuscript.

WAR DIARY

~~or~~

~~INTELLIGENCE SUMMARY.~~ EKL

(*Erase heading not required.*)

Place	Date	Hour	Summary of Events and Information	Remarks and references to Appendices
GONNEHAM	24/2/18		Cloudy - rain - Car No. M25169 FORD - Driver No M1/08361 Pte AIRD. W. R reported at Purchase Board. taken on strength.	EKL
"	25/2/18		Rain - 2/Lieut. J. A. JAMES ASC reported from 4th Cavalry DW. for duty, & posted to 428 Coy ASC. 2/Lieut S. S. SMITH ASC reported from HAVRE for duty & posted to 430 Coy ASC. Inspection of 1st Line Transport 125 Bde by OC Train.	EKL
"	26/2/18		Windy. cloudy - Surplus wagon of 428 Coy. transferred to 73 Bty R.F.A. Auth S & T. 229. 18th.	EKL
"	27/2/18		Cloudy - 2/Lt J. A. JAMES proceeds on leave on special grounds. Inspection of 1st Line Transport 127 Bde, by OC. Train. The Divisional Commander visits 428 Coy ASC. War Savings Campaign - amount subscribed by Train £2100.	EKL
"	28/2/18		Raining - Sgt. WYNN 431 Coy ASC proceeds to U.K. to join Cadet School with a view to a commission.	EKL

[signature]

LIEUT: COLONEL,
COMMANDING 42nd DIVISIONAL TRAIN, A.S.C.

A7092). Wt. W12839/M1293 750,000. 1/17. D. D & L., Ltd. Forms/C2118/14.

WO 95/4714

CONFIDENTIAL.

WAR DIARY.

42ND DIVISIONAL TRAIN.

A.S.C.

Period:- 1-3-1918 to 31-3-1918.

Vol. XIII.

Instructions regarding War Diaries and Intelligence Summaries are contained in F. S. Regs., Part II. and the Staff Manual respectively. Title pages will be prepared in manuscript.

WAR DIARY
or
~~INTELLIGENCE SUMMARY.~~ EKS

(Erase heading not required.)

Army Form C. 2118.

Place	Date	Hour	Summary of Events and Information	Remarks and references to Appendices
GONNEHAM.	1/3/18		Cloudy – Conference of Company Commanders at T.H.Q. reference Sports.	EKS
"	2/3/18		Windy & Cloudy – snowing hard during the day – leave allotment increased to 4 daily from March 3rd. Baggage wagons of 210 & 211 Bdes R.F.A. sent to units for move	EKS
"	3/3/18		Wet – Inspection of M. Gun Battalion by O.C. Train – 1st Line Transport. Horses of 428 & 429 Coy put through the Dip –	EKS
"	4/3/18		Cloudy – 431 Coy moved from HURIONVILLE to BUSNES, and 430 Coy from BUSNES to HURIONVILLE Refilling points now = D.W. Troops BAS RIEUX U24 a6.8. 36A 125 Bde ANNEZIN E8.d5.5 36B Railhead LILLERS 126 Bde HAUT RIEUX U23 d9.6 36A 127 Bde BUSNES P25 a7.3 36A	EKS
"	5/3/18		Windy & rain – 428 Coy moves from GONNEHAM to BAS RIEUX – horses in the open – Supplies drawn by H.T. from railhead – for D.W. Troops Captain J HENSHAW and Lieut C EDWARDS proceeded on leave to U.K.	EKS
"	6/3/18		Fine – Divisional Fuel Dump moved from GONNEHAM to ANNEZIN Supplies for 126 & 127 Bde groups & D.W. Troops drawn from Railhead by Train Transport Supplies of 125 Bde drawn by lorry.	EKS
"	7/3/18		Fine – 429 Coy A.S.C. on "Working isolation" on account of Case of Epizootic lymphangitis instructions sent out to 429 Coy A.S.C. re horses, lines, harness, rugs etc.	EKS
"	8/3/18		Fine –	
"	9/3/18		Fine – Lieut W.W. YEATS proceeds on leave to U.K. 1 NCO & 5 men to BOULOGNE for remounts – Summer Time comes into force – at 11. PM clocks put on 1 hour.	EKS

A7092). Wt. W12839/M1293 750,000. 1/17. D. D & L., Ltd. Forms/C2118/14.

Instructions regarding War Diaries and Intelligence Summaries are contained in F. S. Regs., Part II. and the Staff Manual respectively. Title pages will be prepared in manuscript.

WAR DIARY

~~or~~

~~INTELLIGENCE SUMMARY.~~ EKL

(*Erase heading not required.*)

Army Form C. 2118.

Place	Date	Hour	Summary of Events and Information	Remarks and references to Appendices
GONNEHAM.	10 3/18		Fine — Two Sadd Cpls left the Train for 3rd Cav. Res. Park, in rank of Sadd Sgts C S M MORGAN H. lent to the 42 Bn. M.G Coy for temporary duty from 431 Coy ASC	EKL
"	11 3/18		Fine — Inspection of 1st Line Transport 126 Inf. Bde by OC Train Division to be held in readiness to move at 12 hours notice	EKL
"	12 3/18		Fine — A.A & QMG inspects 428 Coy ASC Captain G. D N WYATT with Ford Car proceeds to Central Purchase Board St POL for duty Lt C.A.L BONNETT to be B.S.O 127 Bde temporarily	EKL
"	13 3/18		Fine — DR Farr BEST A. appointed A/Farr Cpl vice Cpl KIDD — 428 Coy ASC	EKL
"	14 3/18		Raining in morning — dull all day Captain W.H TAYLEUR ASC returns from leave — 431 Coy horses put through dip. 12 Remounts from BOULOGNE — 6 for 428 — 4 for 431 — 1 for 429 — 1 for 430	EKL
"	15 3/18		Fine — 2 Sgts & 4 Drivers reported for duty — 1 Sgt & 2 Drs to 431 Coy 1 Sgt & 1 Dr. to 430 " 1 Dr to 429 " Lt J.A. JAMES ASC returns from leave	EKL
"	16 3/18		Fine — nothing to report.	EKL

A7092). Wt. W12839/M1293 750,000. 1/17. D. D & L., Ltd. Forms/C2118/14.

Army Form C. 2118.

Instructions regarding War Diaries and Intelligence Summaries are contained in F. S. Regs., Part II. and the Staff Manual respectively. Title pages will be prepared in manuscript.

WAR DIARY

~~or~~

~~INTELLIGENCE SUMMARY.~~ EKS

(*Erase heading not required.*)

Place	Date	Hour	Summary of Events and Information	Remarks and references to Appendices
GONNEHAM.	17/3/18		Fine. nothing to report	EKS
"	18/3/18		Fine. Lieut R. LATHAM M.C. proceeds on leave to U.K. – 3 Remounts drawn from No 1 Remount Section MARLES-LES-MINES – posted 1 to 478 Coy 1 to 430 Coy 1 to 431 Coy	EKS
"	19/3/18		Raining – nothing to report.	EKS
"	20/3/18		Raining in morning – fine during the day – Lecture by A.A. & QMG. on Economy, at FOQUIERES.	EKS
"	21/3/18		Fine – LILLERS railhead bombed during the night Lieut C.F. SOMERVILLE proceeds on leave to U.K. – Lieut C. EDWARDS returned from leave. 4 Hotchkiss Guns .303 drawn from D.A.D.O.S. – one to each Company.	EKS
HAUT RIEUX	22/3/18		Fine – T.H.Q. move from GONNEHAM to HAUT RIEUX – 431 Coy A.S.C. moved to CANTRAINNES and Refilling Point at V7 b.3.3 same place – Supplies for 125 Bde & 127 Bde by M.T. 126 Bde & Dw' troops by H.T. from Railhead. Captain J. HENSHAW returns from leave. Instructions received to move to new area South of ARRAS	EKS
MONCHY-AU-BOIS	23/3/18		Fine – EKS THQ moves to MONCHY AU BOIS Railhead CHOCQUES – Refilling Point at MONCHY-AU-BOIS – ADINFER Road. Supplies carried by M.T. & dumped at new R.P. Baggage & Supply vehicles sent to units. 478 Coy ASC moved to MINGOVAL 479 Coy ASC moved to MAGNICOURT. 430 Coy ASC moved to MINGOVAL 431 Coy ASC moved to MINGOVAL	EKS

A7092). Wt. W12839/M1293 750,000. 1/17. D. D & L., Ltd. Forms/C2118/14.

Instructions regarding War Diaries and Intelligence Summaries are contained in F. S. Regs., Part II. and the Staff Manual respectively. Title pages will be prepared in manuscript.

Army Form C. 2118.

WAR DIARY
or
~~INTELLIGENCE SUMMARY.~~ EKS
(Erase heading not required.)

Place	Date	Hour	Summary of Events and Information	Remarks and references to Appendices
MONCHY-AU-BOIS	24/3/18		June – Captain G.D.N. WYATT and Ford Car report from Central Purchase Board. Railhead changed to SAULTY. – supplies drawn by M.T. Orders received from 42 D.H.Q. to adopt normal system of supplies i.e. lorries to park loaded until just before Refilling Time, then dump & proceed direct to Railhead for supplies for issue next day. Supply lorries i/c 2/Lt WELCH with S.C.S.O and staff attached to Train to enable normal system to be carried out. Refilling Point moved after issue to BIENVILLERS-AU-BOIS – FONQUEVILLERS Road. All Companies of the Train move to BIENVILLERS-AU-BOIS & were held in readiness to move at a moment's notice – All leave Cancelled.	EKS
BIENVILLERS-AU-BOIS	25/3/18	June –	T.H.Q. moved to BIENVILLERS-AU-BOIS – Wire received from VI Corps that railhead was BEAUSSART. – this was wrong, as Pack Train had arrived at SAULTY. Lorries had proceeded to BEAUSSART in the meanwhile. Congestion of traffic owing to false rumours. Lt SOMERVILLE returns from Base – leave stopped. Companies still standing by. – water scarce	EKS
ST. AMAND	26/3/18		June – T.H.Q. moved to ST. AMAND – Refilling Point moved to BIENVILLERS-AU-BOIS – ST AMAND Road. All Companies move to ST AMAND, still standing by.	EKS
"	27/3/18		June – order received from IV Corps that Refilling is to be done before dawn. Second refilling carried out at 10.0 p.m. Men rejoining Companies – leave being Cancelled.	EKS

A7092). Wt. W12839/M1293. 750,000. 1/17. D. D & L., Ltd. Forms/C2118/14.

Instructions regarding War Diaries and Intelligence Summaries are contained in F. S. Regs., Part II. and the Staff Manual respectively. Title pages will be prepared in manuscript.

WAR DIARY

~~or~~

~~INTELLIGENCE SUMMARY.~~ EKS

(*Erase heading not required.*)

Army Form C. 2118.

Place	Date	Hour	Summary of Events and Information	Remarks and references to Appendices
COUIN.	28/3/18		Dull & Cloudy – T.H.Q.s & all Companies moved to COUIN. – raining during the day. Refilling Points on the PAS – COUIN Road. 2/Lt. J. H. LUXTON reported for duty – posted to 428 Coy A.S.C. Supernumary.	EKS
"	29/3/18		Cloudy – refilling at 4.0 am – report received that 4 H.D horses attached to C/211 Bty kitting on the 28th. Division relieved in the line by the 41st DIVISION	EKS
"	30/3/18		Fine – but cloudy. rain during the day. Summary of Evidence taken by the Adjutant Pte HECTOR 429 Coy A.S.C. DRUNKENNESS.	EKS
"	31/3/18		Fine – but cloudy. Summary of Evidence taken by the Adjutant. DR LOMAS Disobeying orders. Rainy during the day. New Sunbeam Car arrives from D Corps M.T. Column to replace Ford. ~~Division relieve 41st Division in the line~~ EKS	EKS

31. 3. 1918.

J. [signature]
Lieut. Colonel
Commanding 42nd Divisional Train ASC

A7092). Wt. W12839/M1295. 750,000. 1/17. D. D & L., Ltd. Forms/C2118/14.

Vol 15

CONFIDENTIAL.

WAR DIARY.

42ND. DIVISIONAL TRAIN

A.S.C.

Period - 1 - 4 - 1918 to 30 - 4 - '18.

Volume XIV.

Instructions regarding War Diaries and Intelligence Summaries are contained in F. S. Regs., Part II. and the Staff Manual respectively. Title pages will be prepared in manuscript.

WAR DIARY
~~or~~
~~INTELLIGENCE SUMMARY.~~ EKS

(Erase heading not required.)

Army Form C. 2118.

Place	Date	Hour	Summary of Events and Information	Remarks and references to Appendices
COUIN.	1/4/18	.	Fine – Railhead SAULTY. – refilling at 4.0 am 42nd Division relieve 41st in the line. Instructions received for Train to move out of present area. C.S.M MORGAN rejoined 431 Coy from M.G. Corps.	EKS
"	2/4/18	.	Cloudy. fine during the day – all Train Companies move to SOUASTRE – Camped in open. Refilling points on HENU – SOUASTRE road at Windmill.	EKS
HENU	3/4/18		Rain – Train H. Qrs move to HENU. Summary of evidence re L/Cpl ROSSITER 430 Coy ASC taken at T.H.Q. – Drunkenness Lieut R. LATHAM. M.C. returns from leave.	EKS
"	4/4/18		Rain – Sgt Parkinson 428 Coy. reports from Base – was evacuated. Lieut. W.W. YEATS returns from leave. 126 – 127 Bde Dumps & Div! Troops dump. to D 20 a Cent. on the HENU side of the HENU – SOUASTRE Road owing to former spot being too exposed. 1 officer & 6 OR proceed to PUCHEVILLERS Railhead to draw 12 H.D. remounts.	EKS
"	5/4/18		Rain – Sgt PARKINSON returns to Base – surplus to Est. Remounts alloted as follows 8 to 428 Coy 2 to 429 " 2 to 430 " Refilling 7.0 am.	EKS

A7092). Wt. W12839/M1293. 750,000. 1/17. D. D & L., Ltd. Forms/C2118/14.

Instructions regarding War Diaries and Intelligence Summaries are contained in F. S. Regs., Part II. and the Staff Manual respectively. Title pages will be prepared in manuscript.

WAR DIARY

~~or~~

~~INTELLIGENCE SUMMARY.~~ EKS

(Erase heading not required.)

Army Form C. 2118.

Place	Date	Hour	Summary of Events and Information	Remarks and references to Appendices
HENU.	6/4/18		Fine - 42nd DW - began coming out of the line - relieved by 62nd DW.	EKS
PAS	7/4/18		Rain - 42nd DW. relieved by 62 DW in line. (less artillery) T.H.Q move to PAS. 428 Coy ASC remain at SOUASTRE - 429 Coy ASC move to AUTHIE 430 Coy ASC to HENU - 431 Coy ASC to AUTHIE. DW. Troops Dump no change - 125 Bde I 15 b 2.8 - 126 Bde C 24 a 9.3. 127 Bde I 15 b 2.8	EKS
"	8/4/18		Dull - cloudy - 125 Bde Dump to I 33 b 8.8 127 Bde Dump I 34 a 5.2	EKS
"	9/4/18		Rain - Baggage wagons of Bde Groups withdrawn from units.	EKS
"	10/4/18		Fine but cloudy - Lieut C.A.L BONNETT to Hospital. 429 Coy move to VAUCHELLES CQMS H.J. DOBINSON reported from 1st Cavalry Reserve Park - posted to 429 Coy ASC as A/S.S.M. Four NCOs to 42 DW. M.T Coy for instruction in Hotchkiss Gun.	EKS
"	11/4/18		Cloudy & rain. 2/Lieut. J.H LUXTON (Supernumy) posted to 430 Coy vice Lt BONNETT to Hospital Baggage wagons of Bdes returned to Units.	EKS
"	12/4/18		Fine - 10 GS wagons & 1 pair surplus to Establishment despatched to A.H.T. Depot ABBEVILLE by road i/c Capt G. WYATT. (12 surplus - 1 destroyed by shell fire - 1 with 79 C.L.C.). 428 Coy move to PAS. 429 & 431 Coy to AUTHIE - BUS-LES-ARTOIS Rd I 17 a 2.2. Dumps I 17 c 8.3	EKS

A7092). Wt. W12839/M1293. 750,000. 1/17. D. D & L., Ltd. Forms/C2118/14.

Instructions regarding War Diaries and Intelligence Summaries are contained in F. S. Regs., Part II. and the Staff Manual respectively. Title pages will be prepared in manuscript.

WAR DIARY

or

~~INTELLIGENCE SUMMARY~~ EK

(*Erase heading not required.*)

Army Form C. 2118.

Place	Date	Hour	Summary of Events and Information	Remarks and references to Appendices
PAS	13/4/18		Fine: F.G.C.M. re Pte HOCTOR - Not Guilty. held at LOUVENCOURT.	EK
"	14/4/18		Cloudy & Windy - THQ moved into CHATEAU grounds - 428 Coy ASC moved to HENU D 19. Central sheet 57d. 4 H.D. horses of 428 Coy ASC lost on the 29 March recovered.	EK
"	15/4/18		Cloudy. 3 Reinforcements report from HAVRE, posted 1 to each Bde Coy - 1 G.S. wagon drawn by 430 Coy to replace one destroyed by shell fire, sent to No 1 Sec. DAC	EK
COUIN.	16/4/18		Fine - cloudy - 42nd Div relieve 37 Div. in line. THQ move to COUIN. 430 Coy ASC move to COUIN. Dump of 126 & 127 Bde move to I 17 c 9.5 sheet 57d. on the AUTHIE - BUS - LES - ARTOIS Road. Fuel Dump same place I 17 c 9.5.	EK
"	17/4/18		Rain during day - Double Refilling at 9.0 am & 4.0 pm. all groups - wagons loaded overnight. 59 Div Arty handed over to 62 Div.	EK
"	18/4/18		Rain - Railhead changes to WARLINCOURT - LES - PAS HALTE - Refilling 4.0 P.M. 4 NCOs from Train return from Hotchkiss Training at M.T. Coy.	EK
"	19/4/18		Rain & Snow - 41. & 47 Div Artys & 4 Aust. Bde taken over from 37 Division. Railhead for 47 Div Arty. AUTHIEULE. Refilling Points as under. 42 Div Arty D 20. a 5.7 ; 41 " C 30 a 2 8 ; 47 " C 27 b. 1. 8 ; 125. 126. 127 Inf Bdes I 17 c 9. 5 } Sheet 57 d. Summary of Evidence re Drvr BRAZIER 430 Coy (Drunk) taken. 431 Coy moved their Camp across the Road.	EK EK

A7092). Wt. W12839/M1293 750,000. 1/17. D. D & L., Ltd. Forms/C2118/14.

Instructions regarding War Diaries and Intelligence Summaries are contained in F. S. Regs., Part II. and the Staff Manual respectively. Title pages will be prepared in manuscript.

WAR DIARY
or
~~INTELLIGENCE SUMMARY.~~ EKL

(Erase heading not required.)

Army Form C. 2118.

Place	Date	Hour	Summary of Events and Information	Remarks and references to Appendices
COUIN	20/4/18		Rain. – F.G.C.M. held at 1/8 Manchester Rear Hdq. COIGNEUX Cpl ROSSITER 430 Coy ASC Drunkenness DR BENNETT 428 " absent without leave " LOMAS 428 " Refusing to obey an order.	EKL
"	21/4/18		Fine – Baggage Wagons with Bdes used for fatigues from now onwards – detailed from this office. Court of Enquiry re lost Bicycle from T.H.Q. President. Capt. G WYATT. ASC RO.1 Members { 2 Lt. C. EDWARDS 429 Coy ASC; 2/Lt S.S. SMITH 430 Coy ASC Board assembled at T.H.Q.	EKL
"	22/4/18.		Fine. nothing to report.	EKL
"	23/4/18.		Cloudy – but fine – Conference at IV Corps O.C. Trains re sites for Camps & R.P. 2/Lt S.S SMITH to Hospital.	EKL
"	24/4/18		Rain. Court of Enquiry re lost Bicycle 428 Coy ASC President. Capt G. WYATT RO. I Members. Lt C EDWARDS 429 Coy ASC; Lt H. LIVINGSTONE LEARMOUTH 431 Coy ASC. 47 Div Arty off feeding strength. 4 Aust Inf Bde off feeding strength. Promulgation of Sentence DR LOMAS 428 Coy ASC 2 years I.H.L DR BENNETT 428 Coy ASC 90 days F.P. No 1. Cpl ROSSITER 430 Coy ASC 90 days F.P. No 1.	EKL
"	25/4/18		Fine – Rain in evening. – nothing to report.	EKL
"	26/4/18.		Cloudy – S.S.M HARWOOD 428 Coy. for duty (Temp) to Rest Camp MARIEUX. 2/Lt J.A JAMES 428 Coy posted to 430 Coy temporarily – Capt G. WYATT RO.1 to 428 Coy temporarily.	EKL
"	27/4/18.		Fine. – rain in evening. F.G.C.M. at COUIN of DR W.L. BRAZIER 430 Coy ASC – Drunkenness. Board of officers assembled at 428 Coy ASC to test cold shoers. Major H.P. WILLIAMS MC 428 Coy ASC Capt. O'NEIL A.V.C Lt LIVINGSTONE-LEARMOUTH 431 Coy ASC 31 men tested.	EKL

A7092). Wt. W12839/M1298. 750,000. 1/17. D. D & L., Ltd. Forms/C2118/14.

Instructions regarding War Diaries and Intelligence Summaries are contained in F. S. Regs., Part II. and the Staff Manual respectively. Title pages will be prepared in manuscript.

WAR DIARY
or
~~INTELLIGENCE SUMMARY.~~ EKS

(Erase heading not required.)

Army Form C. 2118.

Place	Date	Hour	Summary of Events and Information	Remarks and references to Appendices
COUIN.	28/4/18		Cloudy. – Promulgation of Sentence re DR WHR BRAZIER 430 Coy ASC 21 days F.P. No 1.	EKS
"	29/4/18		Cloudy – Rain in evening. Remounts sent for to PUCHEVILLERS. 1 Rider + 9 H.D. Posted 4 to 428 Coy 2 to 429 Coy 3 + 1 Rider to 430 Coy.	EKS
"	30/4/18		Dull – Cloudy – rain during the day. Board of officers reassembled re Cold Shoers to test men who were unable to attend on the 27th. – Board held at 428 Coy ASC	EKS

[signature]
Lieut. Colonel
Comndg 42nd Divisional Train ASC

2. 5. 1918.

A7092). Wt. W12839/M1293. 750,000. 1/17. D. D & L., Ltd. Forms/C2118/14.

Vol 16

CONFIDENTIAL.

WAR DIARY.

42ND. Divisional Train.

A.S.C.

Period - 1-5-1918 to 31-5-'18.

Volume XV.

Instructions regarding War Diaries and Intelligence Summaries are contained in F. S. Regs., Part II. and the Staff Manual respectively. Title pages will be prepared in manuscript.

WAR DIARY
~~or~~
~~INTELLIGENCE~~ SUMMARY. EKL

(Erase heading not required.)

Army Form C. 2118.

Place	Date	Hour	Summary of Events and Information	Remarks and references to Appendices
COUIN	1 5/18		Cloudy - Cpl DYKES 431 Coy ASC appointed A/Sgt issuer - Pte HUISH 428 Coy ASC appointed A/cpl issuer with 431 Coy ASC. 2nd Blankets returned to D.A.D.O.S.	EKL
"	2 5/18		Fine - CAPTAIN F HENSHAW proceeds to Base. Auth. DGMS-GHQ. 445/1 19/1/17. CAPTAIN G D N WYATT RO.1 to be BSO 127 Bde. LIEUT. J L GRAHAM from 429 Coy to 428 Coy - LIEUT. R. LATHAM. M.C. from 431 Coy to 429 Coy i/c Supply Section - LIEUT. W W YEATS from 428 Coy to 431 Coy i/c Supply Section - 2/LIEUT. J A JAMES from 428 Coy to 430 Coy i/c Supply Section. 4 NCO proceed to MARIEUX - instruction in AA. Sights - two days course.	EKL
"	3 5/18		Fine - Rain at night.	EKL
"	4 5/18		Cloudy - but fine - rain at night. Bicycle stolen from 428 Coy recovered in forward area. 41st DW. Art transferred to 57 DW. after drawing at Railhead today.	EKL
"	5 5/18		Dull & wet. Baggage pairs & drivers returned from D.A.C.	EKL
PAS-EN-ARTOIS	6 5/18		Fine - 42nd Division relieved in the line by the 57 Division. No 1. Coy 41 DW Train handed over to 57 T.H.Q. Authority to strike 2/Lt S.S. SMITH off strength (To ENGLAND sick) and to take 2/Lt. J.H. LUXTON (Super) on strength. T.H.Q move to PAS. EN. ARTOIS. 429 Coy to COUIN J1. a.8.3; 430 Coy to PAS C17.c.9.2; 431 Coy to HENU D13.c.9.0 } Sheet 57 d. Refilling Points. 126 Bde to C23 d 8.1. COUIN-PAS ROAD 127 Bde to D19. a.9.9 HENU. 128 Bde to C30 d.9.0 COUIN-PAS ROAD. Fuel Dump C16 a.3.3. PAS. GRINCOURT ROAD.	

A7092). Wt. W12839/M1293. 750,000. 1/17. D. D & L., Ltd. Forms/C2118/14.

Instructions regarding War Diaries and Intelligence Summaries are contained in F. S. Regs., Part II. and the Staff Manual respectively. Title pages will be prepared in manuscript.

Army Form C. 2118.

WAR DIARY

~~or~~

~~INTELLIGENCE SUMMARY.~~ EKS

(Erase heading not required.)

Place	Date	Hour	Summary of Events and Information	Remarks and references to Appendices
PAS-EN-ARTOIS			2 Sgts 1 Driver & 1 Pte issue, reported from HAVRE. Posted 1 Sgt to 430 Coy. 1 Sgt to 431 Coy. Driver & issuer to 429 Coy. Cpl Farrier reported for 1/1 Field Ambulance from HAVRE. S.S.M. HARWOOD reported back from MARIEUX	EKS
"	7/5/18		Rain - Fine during the day - rain at night	EKS
"	8/5/18		Fine. - Four complete G.S. wagons dispatched to Third Army Aux (H) Coy - Authority Third Army T. NCO i/c was instructed to report at GEZAINCOURT, but found unit near HESDIN.	EKS
			Baggage wagons ~~pairs~~ & drivers of Brigades withdrawn from units.	EKS
"	9/5/18		Fine - The C.O. and S.S.O visit Third Army. Companies of Train designated No 1. 2. 3. 4 Coys for Divisional purposes only.	EKS
"	10/5/18		Fine - cold at night. 2/Lieut J.H. LUXTON slightly wounded (at duty) by shell fire.	EKS
"	11/5/18		Cloudy - DR LOMAS' sentence of 2 years IHL put into execution - sent to APM today.	EKS
"	12/5/18		Cloudy. Fine - little rain.	EKS
"	13/5/18		Rain during day & night - Board re shoeing smiths reassembled at No 1. Coy to test two men from 1/7 N.F.	
"	14/5/18		Fine - 307 Inf. U.S.A joined 42nd Division - attached to 3 Brigades - transport affiliated to Bde Coys concerned. - Refilling Point next to 125 Bde Dump.	EKS
"	15/5/18		Fine - At midnight bombs dropped by E.A on No 4 Coy Camp - Said St. Sgt WITHAM. B. killed - a/Cpl HUISH. E.J. wounded.	EKS
"	16/5/18		Fine - Purchasing of vegetables locally - CAPT G. WYATT to THQ (Temp) as R.O. I. LIEUT W.W. YEATS to be S.S.O 127 Bde (Temp). Lecture by Corps C.M officer for Staff Captains and Adjutants at theatre PAS. 4 horses from Train sent to 55 San Sec. FAMECHON for instruction in water duties. Baggage wagon horses & drivers from Artillery Bdes withdrawn.	EKS

A7092). Wt. W12839/M1297. 750,000. 1/17. D. D & L., Ltd. Forms/C2118/14.

Instructions regarding War Diaries and Intelligence Summaries are contained in F. S. Regs., Part II. and the Staff Manual respectively. Title pages will be prepared in manuscript.

WAR DIARY
or
~~INTELLIGENCE SUMMARY.~~ EKS

(*Erase heading not required.*)

Army Form C. 2118.

Place	Date	Hour	Summary of Events and Information	Remarks and references to Appendices
PAS-EN-ARTOIS	17/5/18		Fine – Five reinforcements reported from HAVRE. Posted 1 Dr & 1 Farrier to No 1 Coy. 1 Dr to No 2 Coy. 1 Dr & 1 L/cpl to No 3 Coy.	EKS
"	18/5/18		Fine – Inspection of 1st Line Transport 126 INF BDE by OC Train.	EKS
"	19/5/18		Fine. –	EKS
"	20/5/18		Fine – 6 HD remounts arrive from GEZAINCOURT. LIEUT E.H. MANNERS ASC reported for duty from HAVRE posted temporarily as B.S.O 127 Bde. CAPT G.O.N WYATT resumes duties of R.O. 1 (Temp) LIEUT YEATS resumes duties of O/c Supply Section No 4 Coy. Four Reinforcements arrive – posted 2 to No 2 Coy – 2 to No 3 Coy	EKS
	EKS			
"	21/5/18.		Fine – Remounts posted 4 to No 3 Coy, 1 to No 4 Coy, 1 to No 1 Coy. Board re Shoeing Smiths reassembled same time & place	EKS
"	22/5/18.		Fine. – Box Respirators worn by all ranks for 1 hour during the day & on two days for one hour at night from the 22nd to the 26th both days inclusive	EKS
"	23/5/18		Fine – Inspection of 1st Line Transport 125 Inf Bde at COUIN at 11.0 am by OC Train.	EKS
"	24/5/18		Rain – Inspection of 1st Line Transport 127 Inf Bde at HENU at 11 am by OC Train. Four loaders to 55 San Sec for training in Water duties. Loaders sent to A.D.M.S for medical inspection – taking three days for inspection	EKS
"	25/5/18		Fine –	EKS
"	26/5/18		Cloudy but fine – Lt. H. LIVINGSTONE-LEARMOUTH supervises transport of 427 Fld Coy RE. Four OR. dispatched to Rest Camp ST. VALERY – One from each Company.	EKS

A7092). Wt. W12839/M1293. 750,000. 1/17. D. D & L., Ltd. Forms/C2118/14.

Instructions regarding War Diaries and Intelligence Summaries are contained in F. S. Regs., Part II. and the Staff Manual respectively. Title pages will be prepared in manuscript.

WAR DIARY

~~or~~

~~INTELLIGENCE SUMMARY.~~ EKS

(Erase heading not required.)

Army Form C. 2118.

Place	Date	Hour	Summary of Events and Information	Remarks and references to Appendices
PAS EN ARTOIS	27/5/18		Fine – Inspection of 1st Line Transport of 1/1, 1/2, & 1/3 Field Ambulances by O.C. Train. LIEUT C.F. SOMERVILLE to be A/Adjutant from today till the 30th inst. CAPT. E.K. SCHOLTZ on two days leave in FRANCE.	EKS
"	28/5/18		Fine – 3 drivers & 1 issuer report from HAVRE. Posted 1 driver & 1 issuer to No 1 Coy – 1 driver to No 3 Coy, 1 driver to No 4 Coy. Summary of Evidence taken re DR STANLEY W. drunkenness No 1 Coy	EKS
"	29/5/18		Fine –	EKS
"	30/5/18		Fine – Owing to shelling of WARLINCOURT railhead changes to ORVILLE. CAPT E.K. SCHOLTZ returns – LIEUT C.F. SOMERVILLE returns to No 2 Coy.	EKS
"	31/5/18		Fine – LIEUTS. C.F. SOMERVILLE and J.L. GRAHAM to be Acting Captains, while so employed with Divisional Train. – dated 16 May 1918 Auth. G.H.Q. List No 189. 26.5.1918	EKS

[signature]

LIEUT: COLONEL,
COMMANDING 42nd DIVISIONAL TRAIN, A.S.C.

A7092). Wt. W12839/M1298 750,000. 1/17. D. D & L., Ltd. Forms/C2118/14.

8017

CONFIDENTIAL.

WAR DIARY.

42nd DIVISIONAL TRAIN

A.S.C.

Period:-

1-6-1918 to 30-6-1918.

Volume XVI.

Army Form C. 2118.

Instructions regarding War Diaries and Intelligence Summaries are contained in F. S. Regs., Part II. and the Staff Manual respectively. Title pages will be prepared in manuscript.

WAR DIARY
~~or~~
~~INTELLIGENCE SUMMARY.~~ EKS

(Erase heading not required.)

Place	Date	Hour	Summary of Events and Information	Remarks and references to Appendices
PAS. EN ARTOIS	1/6/18		June. FGCM assembled at 1/7 Man. H.Q. HENU - re DR STANLEY No 1 Coy for DRUNKENNESS Time of Refilling changed from 4.0 PM. to 8.0 P.M.	EKS
"	2/6/18		June - Promulgation of Sentence re Dr STANLEY by the Adjutant 56 days F.P. No 2 Ins Blankets returned to D.A.D.O.S. DR JAMES J No 4 Coy to 3rd Army School of Cookery	EKS
"	3/6/18		June - 1 Sadd. S Sgt - 1 Cpl issuer and 1 driver report from HAVRE - posted to No 4 Coy.	EKS
"	4/6/18		June - DR DADE No 4 Coy appointed a/L/Cpl with pay Colonel J COULSON receives the Distinguished Service Order in Birthday Honours Gazette 3/6/18	EKS
"	5/6/18		June -	EKS
"	6/6/18		June -	EKS
BUS. LES ARTOIS	7/6/18		June - 42nd Division (less Artillery) relieve N Z Division (less Artillery) in right Sector - IV Corps Front. 6/7. 7/8 T.H.Q. move to BUS LES ARTOIS No 2 Coy moves to J13 c 19 on the BUS - ST. LEGER ROAD R.P. J 19 a Cent BUS - AUTHIE ROAD No 4 Coy moves to I29 Cent near LOUVENCOURT R.P. I29 a 2 5 LOUVENCOURT - AUTHIE ROAD FUEL DUMP to I 36 Central (Sheet 57 d)	EKS
"	8/6/18		June. No 3 Coy move to I 22 Cent on the LOUVENCOURT - AUTHIE ROAD R.P. I 36 Cent 307 Inf Regt U.S.A. left 42nd Division - drew Supplies for Consumption 9th CAPTAIN G.D.N. WYATT resumes duties of B.S.O 127 Inf Bde. CAPTAIN. C.F. SOMERVILLE to be R.O. I LIEUT. E H MANNERS to be B.S.O 125 Inf Bde.	EKS
"	9/6/18		June - slight rain at night 1 Sgt 1 L/Cpl report from HAVRE from Hospital - surplus to Establishment, retained at No 4 Coy.	EKS

A7092). Wt. W12839/M1293 750,000. 1/17. D. D & L., Ltd. Forms/C2118/14.

Instructions regarding War Diaries and Intelligence Summaries are contained in F. S. Regs., Part II. and the Staff Manual respectively. Title pages will be prepared in manuscript.

WAR DIARY
or
~~INTELLIGENCE SUMMARY.~~ EKS

(Erase heading not required.)

Army Form C. 2118.

Place	Date	Hour	Summary of Events and Information	Remarks and references to Appendices
BUS-LES-ARTOIS	10/6/18		Cloudy - little rain during the day. Authority to strike LIEUT C A L BONNETT off strength A.S.C 20332/18 dated 6/6/18. 1 Sadd Cpl & 2 Cpls report from HAVRE, posted 1 Sadd Cpl & 1 Cpl to No 2 Coy, 1 Cpl to No 3 Coy.	EKS
"	11/6/18		Fine - Nil to report.	EKS
"	12/6/18		Fine - Reduction of Spurs GRO 4232 - Spurs allowed, 1 pair per saddle, 1 pair per set of harness Rides Drive 1 pair per groom. Surplus returned to D.A.D.O.S. Board of officers re lost bicycle belonging to Staff Sgt Gaves. President. Capt A.F. ARIS. Members. Lieut. E H MANNERS, Lieut C. EDWARDS	EKS
"	13/6/18		Fine - Refilling at 12 Noon, all Groups — Refilling Point 126 Inf Bde move to I34a7.1 LOUVENCOURT - VAUCHELLES ROAD. The CO visits D.D.S.T Third Army.	EKS
"	14/6/18		Cloudy - but fine - Nil to report.	EKS
"	15/6/18		Fine - Inspection of 42 Bn M.G. Corps 1st Line Transport by O.C. Train. T. LIEUT. V STEER ASC reported for duty from HAVRE. Posted to No 1 Coy.	EKS
"	16/6/18		Cloudy - little rain. Restricted leave opens from the 20th A/222/23 13 places for the train for JUNE.	EKS
"	17/6/18		Fine cloudy, slight rain at night. 1 Sgt transferred to Base - surplus - L/Cpl DADE reverts on arrival of L/Cpl ROBINSON from HOSPITAL No 4 Coy	EKS
"	18/6/18		Fine - rain in evening and at night.	EKS
"	19/6/18		Rain in morning. The C.O. away from today till the 22nd. A/CQMS BARRY No 4 Coy to 1/7 MANCHESTER REGT for 1 Month on probation for commission	EKS

A7092). Wt. W12839/M1293. 750,000. 1/17. D. D & L., Ltd. Forms/C2118/14.

Instructions regarding War Diaries and Intelligence Summaries are contained in F. S. Regs., Part II. and the Staff Manual respectively. Title pages will be prepared in manuscript.

Army Form C. 2118.

WAR DIARY

~~or~~

~~INTELLIGENCE SUMMARY~~ EKL

(Erase heading not required.)

Place	Date	Hour	Summary of Events and Information	Remarks and references to Appendices
BUS-LES-ARTOIS	20/6/18		Cloudy – rain in evening 2 men from each Brigade attached to Brigade Company for instruction in shoeing.	EKL
"	21/6/18		Cloudy –	EKL
"	22/6/18		Cloudy – 6 remounts arrived drawn by No 4 Coy from GEZAINCOURT on the 21st Posted 2 to No 1 Coy, 1 to No 2, 2 to No 3, 1 to No 4. S.S.M. HARWOOD No 1 Coy evacuated – poisoned finger.	EKL EKL
"	23/6/18		Cloudy – 1 Sqt Clerk reports from HAVRE, posted to No 3 Coy.	EKL
"	24/6/18		Cloudy – rain during the day.	EKL
"	25/6/18		Fine.	
"	26/6/18		Cloudy – Inspection of 1st Line Transport 1/7 Northumberland Fusiliers (Pioneers) by OC Train. Influenza breaks out – many cases in No 4 Coy.	EKL
"	27/6/18		Fine – O.C. Train & S.S.O. visit Third Army. Country between BUS-LES-ARTOIS and SARTON reconnoitred for tracks by three Brigade Companies.	EKL
"	28/6/18		Fine –	EKL
"	29/6/18		Fine – Major W. P. REYNOLDS proceeds on leave – Capt. E. F. SPRECKLEY from D W Tps S.O. to be a/S.S.O. Lieut. V. STEER to be a/D W Tps S.O.	EKL
"	30/6/18		Fine – 1 L.D. Horse drawn from GEZAINCOURT, posted to No 2 Coy. Three Bombs dropped in BUS-LES-ARTOIS at about 11.30 P.M.	EKL

J. Emerson
LIEUT: COLONEL,
COMMANDING 42nd DIVISIONAL TRAIN, A.S.C.

A7092). Wt. W12839/M1298. 750,000. 1/17. D. D & L., Ltd. Forms/C2118/14.

WO 95/4718

Confidential.

War Diary.

42nd Divisional Train.

A.S.C.

Period 1-VII-'18 to 31-VII-1918.

Volume XVII.

Army Form C. 2118.

Instructions regarding War Diaries and Intelligence Summaries are contained in F. S. Regs., Part II. and the Staff Manual respectively. Title pages will be prepared in manuscript.

WAR DIARY
or
~~INTELLIGENCE SUMMARY~~ EKS

(Erase heading not required.)

Place	Date	Hour	Summary of Events and Information	Remarks and references to Appendices
BUS-LES-ARTOIS	1/7/18	.	Fine:- 11 Reinforcements report from HAVRE, all drivers.	EKS
"	2/7/18	.	Fine:- Reinforcements posted as follows 8 to No 1 Coy, 3 to No 2 Coy. 4 Sick horses in Train, the lowest for many months, 2 Kicks, 1 Colic, 1 P.U.N.	EKS
"	3/7/18	.	Cloudy but fine: 1 Pte Clerk reports from HAVRE for T.HQ – posted to Fuel Dump. The Divisional Commander visited No 3 Coy Camp.	EKS
"	4/7/18	.	Cloudy, but fine: 42 Div Arty begin moving to new area. 5th & 6th	EKS
"	5/7/18	.	Cloudy, but fine: H.Q Coy move from HENU to LOUVENCOURT O 5 a 7.8 sheet 57d, taking over Camp from N.Z. Train. Refilling Point in Camp. S.S.M. HARWOOD returns from Hospital – taken on strength again. P.U.O still bad in the Train, especially H.Q Coy & No 4 Coy. Leave allotment 50 places to Aug 3rd 1918. L.D. Horse which was posted to No 2 Coy on the 30th June, taken on strength as a Rider.	EKS
"	6/7/18	.	Fine. – nil to report.	EKS
"	7/7/18		Fine. 1 Pte Clerk reported from HAVRE – posted to No 3 Coy. 1 Staff Sgt Farrier & 2 drivers reported – posted to No 2 Coy & No 1 Coy. – drivers to No 1 Coy. 1 Sgt from HAVRE posted to No 2 Coy vice Sgt CLEMENTS (to ENGLAND)	EKS
"	8/7/18		Fine – rain in the morning. LIEUT R. LATHAM M.C. to Hospital P.U.O. 7 Remounts H.D. drawn by No 1 Coy from GOUY EN ARTOIS retained by them.	EKS
SARTON.	9/7/18		Fine. Captains. C.F. SOMERVILLE and G.D.N. WYATT proceed on leave to ENGLAND. D.H.Q divided into 2 portions. ADMS, DADMS, DAD.O.S. APM, DADVS, Div GAS officer. Div Salvage Officer, Senior Chaplains, French Mission & Train HQ to SARTON. DHQ remains at BUS LES ARTOIS	EKS

A7092). Wt. W12839/M1293 750,000. 1/17. D. D & L., Ltd. Forms/C2118/14.

Instructions regarding War Diaries and Intelligence Summaries are contained in F. S. Regs., Part II. and the Staff Manual respectively. Title pages will be prepared in manuscript.

WAR DIARY
~~or~~
~~INTELLIGENCE SUMMARY.~~ EKL
(*Erase heading not required.*)

Army Form C. 2118.

Place	Date	Hour	Summary of Events and Information	Remarks and references to Appendices
SARTON	10/7/18		Rain in the afternoon.	
			D.H.Q. move to Dug-outs at I 23 A (sheet 57d).	EKL
"	11/7/18		Rain. – The Divisional Commander inspected No 1 Coy.	EKL
"	12/7/18		Rain all day – 1 wheeler detailed from No 1 Coy for temp. duty with 28 Light Mobile Workshop AUTHIEULE.	EKL
			1 HD Bde from No 1 Coy to No 3 Coy	EKL
"	13/7/18		Cloudy – little rain. LIEUT. R. LATHAM. M.C from Hospital.	EKL
"	14/7/18		Cloudy – rain.	
"	15/7/18		Rain heavily at night – Fine during the day.	
			2/Lieut I. J. SIMMS proceeds on leave to ENGLAND.	
			MAJOR. W. P REYNOLDS returns from leave to ENGLAND	
			2/Lieut J. H LUXTON to be BSO 126 Bde (temp) vice 2/Lieut I. J. SIMMS	EKL
AUTHIE	16/7/18		Rain – very hot.	
			Portion of DHQ at SARTON move to AUTHIE. Train H.Q. move to AUTHIE.	EKL
			Whole of DHQ now in AUTHIE.	
"	17/7/18		Fine – little rain in evening.	
			Captains E F SPRECKLEY and J L GRAHAM proceed on leave to ENGLAND.	
			FGCM. Pte DAVIDSON 239 Employment Coy attached No 3 Coy Disobeying an order Finding Not Guilty. At HQ. 126 Bde.	EKL

A7092). Wt. W12839/M1293. 750,000. 1/17. D. D & L., Ltd. Forms/C2118/14.

Instructions regarding War Diaries and Intelligence Summaries are contained in F. S. Regs., Part II. and the Staff Manual respectively. Title pages will be prepared in manuscript.

WAR DIARY

or

~~INTELLIGENCE SUMMARY.~~ EKL

(Erase heading not required.)

Army Form C. 2118.

Place	Date	Hour	Summary of Events and Information	Remarks and references to Appendices
AUTHIE.	18/7/18		Cloudy fine - little rain. Officers & OR leave allotment comes into force. - another 13 leaves to end of July, OR. and 1 officer. Baggage wagons required by 126 & 127 Bdes for relief.	EKL
"	19/7/18		Fine. AA & QMG visited No 1 Coy & DW Troops Dump	EKL
"	20/7/18		Fine - rain in afternoon & evening -	EKL
"	21/7/18		Cloudy -	EKL
"	22/7/18		Fine. 2 Farr. Cpls, 1 Saddle Cpl, 1 Cpl issuer, 8 drivers, & 3 batmen report from Base. Posted 2 Farr Cpls, 3 Drivers } to No 1 Coy; 1 Cpl issuer, 1 driver } to No 3 Coy; 1 Driver to No 2 Coy, 2 Drivers to No 4 Coy. 3 batmen & 1 Driver to Field Ambulances:-	EKL
"	23/7/18		Rain, hard all day. 2/Lt. J. P. BLACKMORE proceeds on leave to ENGLAND.	EKL
"	24/7/18		Fine - but Cloudy - rain during the day.	EKL
"	25/7/18		Rain. Captains G. D. N. WYATT and C. F. SOMERVILLE return from leave.	EKL
"	26/7/18		Cloudy - rain. Surplus Sadd Cpl, 1 Pte Clerk & 1 Pte issuer returned to Base. Lt W. W. YEATS to No 1 Coy (temporary).	EKL
	27/7/18		Rain - 1 Cpl & 1 Dr report from Base - posted to No 2 Coy. Board of officers assembled at No 1 Coy to test shoeing smiths. President MAJOR H.P. WILLIAMS MC ASC; Members { Lt. R. LATHAM. MC ASC; Capt O'NEILL AVC	EKL

A7092). Wt. W12839/M1298. 750,000. 1/17. D. D & L., Ltd. Forms/C2118/14.

Instructions regarding War Diaries and Intelligence Summaries are contained in F. S. Regs., Part II. and the Staff Manual respectively. Title pages will be prepared in manuscript.

WAR DIARY

~~or~~

~~INTELLIGENCE SUMMARY.~~ EKS

(Erase heading not required.)

Army Form C. 2118.

Place	Date	Hour	Summary of Events and Information	Remarks and references to Appendices
AUTHIE	28/7/18		Cloudy - Many NCOs & men struck off strength, return from Hospital & Base, causing surplus in unit. Vicinity of AUTHIE shelled at 7.0 P.M.	EKS
"	29/7/18		Cloudy - Board of officers as follows to audit the accounts of Companies of the Train. President Capt G THURLING-BLACKWELL ASC Members { Lieut. W.W. YEATS ASC { 2/Lieut. T A JAMES ASC	EKS
"	30/7/18		Fine - nil to report	
"	31/7/18		Fine - Farr Staff Sgt & Farr Corporal returned to Base - surplus.	EKS

1st August 1918.

E K Scholtz Capt & Adjt
for LIEUT: COLONEL,
COMMANDING 42nd DIVISIONAL TRAIN, A.S.C.

A7092). Wt. W12839/M1293 750,000. 1/17. D. D & L., Ltd. Forms/C2118/14.

CONFIDENTIAL.

WAR DIARY

42ND DIVISIONAL TRAIN.

A. S. C.

Period 1-8-'18 to 31-8-'18.

VOLUME XVIII

Instructions regarding War Diaries and Intelligence Summaries are contained in F. S. Regs., Part II. and the Staff Manual respectively. Title pages will be prepared in manuscript.

WAR DIARY
or
~~INTELLIGENCE SUMMARY.~~ EKL

(Erase heading not required.)

Army Form C. 2118.

Place	Date	Hour	Summary of Events and Information	Remarks and references to Appendices
AUTHIE	1/8/18	.	Fine – 2/Lt. J. J. SIMMS returns from leave. Major H.P. WILLIAMS. M.C. granted special leave for 1 month to ENGLAND. ACI 2327	EKL
"	2/8/18	.	Rain – Captains E.F. SPRECKLEY and J.L. GRAHAM return from leave to ENGLAND. CAPTAIN E F SPRECKLEY takes over Command of HQ Coy. vice Major H.P. WILLIAMS M.C.	EKL
"	3/8/18	.	Rain – 7 Riders J.I.L.D. arrive from ABBEVILLE – posted to No 1 Coy temporary	EKL
"	4/8/18		Fine – Remounts allotted as follows 3 to No 1 Coy, 1 to No 2, 1 to No 3, 2 to No 4 6 Reinforcements arrive – 4 to No 1, 1 to No 3, 1 to No 4.	EKL
"	5/8/18		Rain – Inspection of 1st Line Transport 126 Inf. Bde by OC Train – Very good Rider stolen from No 4 Coy at 4.30 am – no trace.	EKL
"	6/8/18		Rain – Inspection of 1st Line Transport 127 Inf Bde & 125 Inf Bde by OC Train 2/Lt. J.H. LUXTON to Rest Camp ST VALERY for 14 days.	EKL
"	7/8/18		Fine. Lt. Colonel J. COULSON. D.S.O. proceeds on leave to U.K. Major W.P. REYNOLDS takes over Command – Capt. C.F. SOMERVILLE to be a/S.S.O. 2/Lt. J.P. BLACKMORE returns from leave. A.A. & QMG inspects No 3 Coy	EKL
"	8/8/18		Cloudy – Lt W.W. YEATS returns to No 4 Coy from No 1 Coy	EKL
"	9/8/18		Fine. Major W.P. REYNOLDS lectures on forage to Division, at Theatre BUS-LES-ARTOIS.	EKL
"	10/8/18		Fine – 34 D. horses arrive from PUCHVILLERS – posted to No 1 Coy.	EKL
"	11/8/18		Fine –	EKL
"	12/8/18		Fine. Inspection of 1st Line Transport of 1/2 & 1/3 E. Lancs Field Ambulances by Major W.P. REYNOLDS A.S.C. Lecture by Divisional Commander at Theatre BUS. to all COs & Field officers on C.M.	EKL

A7092). Wt. W12839/M1293. 750,000. 1/17. D. D & L., Ltd. Forms/C2118/14.

Instructions regarding War Diaries and Intelligence Summaries are contained in F. S. Regs., Part II. and the Staff Manual respectively. Title pages will be prepared in manuscript.

WAR DIARY
~~or~~
~~INTELLIGENCE SUMMARY.~~ EKS
(Erase heading not required.)

Army Form C. 2118.

Place	Date	Hour	Summary of Events and Information	Remarks and references to Appendices
AUTHIE	13/8/18		Fine - Inspection of 1st Line Transport of 1/7 Northumberland Fus (Pioneers) by Major W. P REYNOLDS A.S.C	EKS
"	14/8/18		Fine.	
BUS-LES-ARTOIS	15/8/18		Fine - D.H.Q moves to BUS-LES-ARTOIS - T.H.Q moves to BUS-LES-ARTOIS	EKS
"	16/8/18		Fine. Inspection of Transport of 1/1st E Lancs Field Ambulance by Major W. P REYNOLDS A.S.C	EKS
"	17/8/18		Cloudy Nil to report	EKS
"	18/8/18		Fine - Nil to report	EKS
"	19/8/18		Cloudy - Fine - Captain G. THURLING-BLACKWELL proceeds on leave to U.K.	EKS
"	20/8/18		Cloudy - Captain A. F. ARIS proceeds on leave to U.K. 2/Lieut T. H LUXTON returns from Rest Camp at ST. VALERY	EKS
"	21/8/18		Fine - Nil to report	EKS
"	22/8/18		Fine Captain J. L GRAHAM superintends Cutting of Crops - four men & four pairs of H.D. from Train Lt. Colonel J. COULSON DSO returns from leave	EKS
"	23/8/18		Fine - MAJOR W. P REYNOLDS resumes duties of S.S.O - Captain C.F SOMERVILLE resumes duties of R.O.I	EKS
"	24/8/18		Cloudy - Nil to report.	
"	25/8/18		Fine - Railhead changes to BEAUSSART All Companies of the Train move to vicinity of BERTRANCOURT (P 3 d) Refilling Points - no change	EKS
"	26/8/18		Rain - No 1 Coy moves to MIRAUMONT L 35 d - Refilling Point in Camp on the MIRAUMONT-IRLES Road	

A7092). Wt. W128:9/M1293 750,000. 1/17. D. D & L., Ltd. Forms/C2118/14.

Instructions regarding War Diaries and Intelligence Summaries are contained in F. S. Regs., Part II. and the Staff Manual respectively. Title pages will be prepared in manuscript.

WAR DIARY
or
~~INTELLIGENCE SUMMARY~~ EKL
(Erase heading not required.)

Army Form C. 2118.

Place	Date	Hour	Summary of Events and Information	Remarks and references to Appendices
			No 2. 3 & 4 Companies move to vicinity of EUSTON DUMP (K 33 c) Refilling Points 126 Inf Brigade J30 d 4.3 - 125 & 127 Inf Brigades J 29 d 8.5 Fuel Dump K. 33. c. near Sugar Factory. Baggage Vehicles remaining with Units.	EKL
BUS·LES·ARTOIS	27 8/18		Fine - but cloudy. Refilling Points for three Brigades in PUISIEUX AUX·MONT Refilling at 6.0 pm.	EKL
MIRAUMONT.	28 8/18		Rain - D.H.Q move to vicinity of BUCQUOY - T.H.Q move to MIRAUMONT Three Brigade Companies move to MIRAUMONT. Camped in Valley. Refilling Points no change - Refilling at 4.0 PM. MIRAUMONT shelled in the afternoon.	EKL
"	29 8/18		Fine - rain at night: All Baggage vehicles return to Companies Refilling Points for Three Brigade Companies move to MIRAUMONT 125. L 35 c 2.8 126. L 34 d 8.8. 127. L 35 c 3 2 No 3 Coy move their Camp from PYS - MIRAUMONT Road to the Valley Fuel Dump L 35 c 3.8 MIRAUMONT	EKL
"	30 8/18		Fine - MIRAUMONT shelled with H.V & shrapnel, from 3.0 AM to 6 0 P.M. Five Casualties in the train - No 1 Coy & No 3 Coy. - all wounded. Railhead changes to MIRAUMONT - Supplies drawn by H.T. & delivered to Units by H.T., except Divisional Troops who draw by lorry. DHQ move to GREVILLERS. No 1 Coy & No 3 Coy move their Camps on account of shelling. Refilling 3 0 P.M.	EKL

(A7092). Wt. W12839/M1293. 750,000. 1/17. D. D & L., Ltd. Forms/C2118/14.

Instructions regarding War Diaries and Intelligence Summaries are contained in F. S. Regs., Part II. and the Staff Manual respectively. Title pages will be prepared in manuscript.

WAR DIARY
or
~~INTELLIGENCE SUMMARY.~~ EKL

(Erase heading not required.)

Army Form C. 2118.

Place	Date	Hour	Summary of Events and Information	Remarks and references to Appendices
MIRAUMONT	31/8/18		Rain in the morning - fine during the day. Supplies on vehicles dumped in Camp - vehicles proceed to Railhead load dump at Refilling Point, & then deliver supplies dumped in Camp, to Units. This applies to Three Brigade Companies only.	EKL

J. Carline
LIEUT: COLONEL
COMDG: 42ND. DIVNL. TRAIN, A.S.C.

1st September 1918

A7092). Wt. W12839/M1293. 750,000. 1/17. D. D & L., Ltd. Forms/C2118/14.

CONFIDENTIAL.

WAR DIARY

42ND DIVISIONAL TRAIN

A.S.C.

Period 1-IX-'18. to 30-IX-1918.

Volume XIX.

Instructions regarding War Diaries and Intelligence Summaries are contained in F. S. Regs., Part II. and the Staff Manual respectively. Title pages will be prepared in manuscript.

WAR DIARY
or
~~INTELLIGENCE SUMMARY~~.
(Erase heading not required.)

Army Form C. 2118.

Place	Date 1918	Hour	Summary of Events and Information	Remarks and references to Appendices
MIRAUMONT	Sept 1.		Rain in morning cleared later. four Driver reinforcements arrived, posted to Companies as follows 1 to No 1 Coy 2 to No 3 Coy & 1 to No 4 Company MIRAUMONT Shelled in the early morning. Supply train cleared by lorries no wagons required	C.F.S.
MIRAUMONT	Sept 2.		Rain. Supplies drawn from Railhead by H.T.	C.F.S.
MIRAUMONT	Sept 3.		Weather fine. Baggage wagons sent out to units	
WARLENCOURT	Sept 4.		T.H.Qrs. moves to WARLENCOURT M9.a.99 also 3 Brigade Companies. No 1 Company moves to Camp on BAPAUME - ALBERT road map reference Sh. 57C. M6 C.8.3. Major H.P. Williams returns from leave to U.K. & resumes command of No 1 Company. Refilling Points all moved to WARLENCOURT map References Sheet 57C. — Div Troops M11a.8.3. 125 Bde. M10 a.51. 126 Bde. M10 b.4.4. 127 Bde. M10 a 1.6.	C.F.S.
WARLENCOURT	Sept 5.		Div. M.T. Coy moves to BIHUCOURT. Railhead changed to ACHIET-le-GRAND. Fuel Dump moved from MIRAUMONT to WARLENCOURT. M11 b.1.4. No 1 Company move Camp across the road to make room for Field Ambulance. Supplies drawn by M.T. Division comes out of the line & relieved by NEW ZEALAND Division	C.F.S.
WARLENCOURT	Sept 6.		Weather fine. Capt Blackwell & Capt Ames return from leave to U.K. Train Hdqrs move from M9a.99 to M9.a.9.4.. Divisional Reception Camp moved from BUS les ARTOIS to MIRAUMONT. Supplies drawn Railhead by M.T.	C.F.S.
WARLENCOURT	Sept 7.		No 1 Company moved to O.7.C.1. on VILLERS au FLOS – BEAULENCOURT road. Refilling Point at O.7.C.1.1. 3 reinforcements arrive posted as follows:- 1 S/Sgt to No 3 Coy 1 Cpl to No 4 Coy. 1 Driver to No 3 Coy.	C.F.S.

A7092). Wt. W12839/M1293 750,000. 1/17. D. D & L., Ltd. Forms/C2118/14.

Army Form C. 2118.

WAR DIARY
or
~~INTELLIGENCE SUMMARY~~ C.F.S.

(Erase heading not required.)

Instructions regarding War Diaries and Intelligence Summaries are contained in F. S. Regs., Part II. and the Staff Manual respectively. Title pages will be prepared in manuscript.

1918

Place	Date	Hour	Summary of Events and Information	Remarks and references to Appendices
WARLENCOURT	Sept 8th		No 1 Company move to N4 C.4.9. refilling Point to N4 b 4.5. Heavy rain Storm in the evening Several huts in No 4 Company blown down. D'ver STANLEY W Charged with Drunkenness + remanded for F G C M.	C.F.S.
WARLENCOURT	Sept 9th		Capt E K Scholtz proceeded on leave to U.K. Capt C F SOMERVILLE appointed acting Adjutant weather fine.	C.F.S.
WARLENCOURT.	Sept 10th		weather wet. Strong wind. No T1/4828. L/cpl PASCALL A G No 2 Coy proceeded to U.K. to join Cadet Unit for training for Commission in R.A.F.	C.F.S.
WARLENCOURT	Sept 11th		weather wet. E A active about 2 AM several bombs dropped in this area. A/Sergt GLOVER T. No. 1 Coy. attached to 1/8th MANCHESTER Regt. for 1 months probation for Commission in the Infantry.	C.F.S.
WARLENCOURT	Sept 12.		weather wet. very heavy Showers. A/Sergt KING. No 2 Coy interviewed by G.O.C. 126 Bde. after having served 1 months probation with an infantry Battn. for Commission. DADVS. inspected horses of No 2 Company.	C.F.S.
WARLENCOURT	Sept 13.		weather Showery. D.D.R Third Army inspects two horses of No. 1 Coy for casting as dangerous. Lt H LIVINGSTONE-LEARMONTH proceeds on leave to UK.	C.F.S.
WARLENCOURT	Sept 14.		weather fine. No T1SR/761. Driver STANLEY W tried by F G C M on charge of Drunkenness, 2 H D horses No 1 Coy. ~~[illegible]~~ wounded slightly by ~~Stay~~ Shrapnel when on Convoy duty.	C.F.S.

A7092). Wt. W12839/M1293 750,000. 1/17. D. D & L., Ltd. Forms/C2118/14.

Instructions regarding War Diaries and Intelligence Summaries are contained in F. S. Regs., Part II. and the Staff Manual respectively. Title pages will be prepared in manuscript. 1918

WAR DIARY

or

~~INTELLIGENCE SUMMARY~~. CFS.

(Erase heading not required.)

Army Form C. 2118.

Place	Date	Hour	Summary of Events and Information	Remarks and references to Appendices
WARLENCOURT	Sept 15.		Divisional Artillery moved into rest. 2/Lieut J P BLACKMORE met with serious injury being thrown from his horse while out on duty admitted to 1st E L Field Amb. & evacuated to No. 34. C.C.S. A/Cpl Young No 2 Coy interviewed by G.O.C. 124 Bde. reference his application for Commission — Yeomanry. Two E.A. seen to come down in flames at night between 10-30 & 11 pm, weather Showery	CFS.
WARLENCOURT	Sept 16.		Two H.D horses arrived at Railhead sent as follows 1 to No 1 Coy & 1 to No 3 Coy weather fine	CFS.
"	Sept 17.		One H.D horse No 1 Coy killed by Shell fire, while attached to C/210 Bde RFA. Promulgation of Sentence on Dr STANLEY. awarded 90 days F.P. No. 2 & fined £1. One E.A. brought down in flames about 10-45 pm weather fine, very warm.	CFS.
"	Sept 18.		Severe thunderstorm in the early morning between 2 AM & 4 AM. 2 H D horses No 1 Coy sent to M V S. for dispatch Cast by DDR. as dangerous.	CFS.
"	Sept 19.		No 1 Coy ordered to stand to for immediate move. Cancelled later. weather Cool.	CFS.
"	Sept 20.		No 3 Coy moved to I 26 A. 3. 7. from WARLENCOURT. Refilling Point to I 28. b 5 2. Supplies for Div troops & 126 Bde drawn from Railhead by lorry other groups by H.T.	CFS.
"	Sept 21.		Train Hdqrs moved from WARLENCOURT area to YELW area I 36 D. 8. 2. No 4 Coy moved to H 18 Central Refilling Point to I 28 b. 5 2. Fuel Dump moved to I 28 b. 5 3. Supplies drawn by lorry from Railhead for Div troops 126 & 124 Bdes. + by H T. for 125 Bde	CFS.

Instructions regarding War Diaries and Intelligence Summaries are contained in F. S. Regs., Part II. and the Staff Manual respectively. Title pages will be prepared in manuscript.

WAR DIARY
~~or~~
~~INTELLIGENCE SUMMARY~~ EKS

(Erase heading not required.)

Army Form C. 2118.

Place	Date	Hour	Summary of Events and Information	Remarks and references to Appendices
VELU	Sept. 22		Showery – shelling at intervals during the day in neighbourhood. NO 2 Coy moved to I 26 a 3.7 FREMICOURT Refilling Point of 125 Bde I 28 b 5.2 S.S.M. H.G. ROLFE No 4 Coy to ASC Material Unit ROUEN. Supplies drawn by lorry.	EKS
"	23 9/18		Fine – 5 Reinforcements report from HAVRE. 125, 126 & 127 Brigade Dumps move to I 26 a 3.7 Supplies drawn from Railhead by H.T. for three Brigade Groups.	EKS
"	24 9/18		Fine – Reinforcements posted 1 Dr wheeler and 1 Driver to No 1 Coy – 1 driver to each of the other Companies. 9 Remounts posted H.Q. 7 to No 1 Coy, 2 to No 4 Coy.	EKS
"	25 9/18		Fine – Captain E.K. SCHOLTZ returns from leave and resumes duties of Adjutant. Captain C.F. SOMERVILLE resumes duties of R.O.I. 2/Lieut J.A. JAMES proceeds on leave to U.K.	EKS
"	26 9/18		Fine – rain at night – double refilling for three Brigade Groups.	EKS
"	27 9/18		Cloudy –	EKS
"	28 9/18		Cloudy & windy. Railhead changes to YTRES. Refilling Point of three Brigade Groups moves to I 34 c 1.9 near HAPLINCOURT. Supplies for three Brigade Groups drawn by H.T. – Artillery by lorry. 1st Line & Baggage Wagons deliver Supplies to Units. No 1 Coy moves to O 23. a 5.8 BUS BARASTRE Road. Refilling Point in Camp. 42nd Division relieved in the line by N.Z. Division.	EKS
"	29 9/18		Fine – rain during afternoon. No 4 Coy moves to I 34 c 4.9 – Refilling Point no change	EKS
"	30 9/18		Rain at intervals. No 1 Coy moves to P 22 b 8.8 NEUVILLE BOURJONVAL Refilling Point Divl Troops P. 23 c 3.8 Lieut LIVINGSTONE-LEARMOUTH returns from leave	EKS

30.9.1918

J Carlton
LIEUT: COLONEL
COMDG. 42ND, DIVNL. TRAIN, A.S.C.

CONFIDENTIAL.

WAR DIARY

42ND Divisional Train.

A.S.C.

Period 1-X-1918 — 31-X-1918.

Volume XX.

Army Form C. 2118.

WAR DIARY

~~or~~

~~INTELLIGENCE SUMMARY.~~ EKL

(Erase heading not required.)

Instructions regarding War Diaries and Intelligence Summaries are contained in F. S. Regs., Part II. and the Staff Manual respectively. Title pages will be prepared in manuscript.

Place	Date	Hour	Summary of Events and Information	Remarks and references to Appendices
VELU	1/10/18		Fine – Continental time comes into force.	EKL
"	2/10/18		Cloudy – Refilling Points of Three Infantry Brigade Groups move to RUYAULCOURT P9c8.1 First refilling on the 3rd at 10.00.	EKL
"	3/10/18		Fine – cloudy. No 2. 3 and 4 Companies move to RUYAULCOURT. No 2 Coy at P15a3.9. No 3 Coy at P9c4.4. No 4 Coy at P9a Central. Refilling Points – no change.	EKL
"	4/10/18		Fine – Cloudy. Refilling at 09.00 for three Infantry Brigade Groups. Fuel Dump moves to NEUVILLE. BOURJEVAL P22b9.4	EKL
"	5/10/18		Cloudy. Lieut. C. EDWARDS proceeds on leave to U.K. 7 Reinforcements report from the Base – posted 1 Cpl Staff Sgt to No 3 Coy, 1 Pte. issuer to No 1 Coy, 1 Driver to No 2 Coy, 1 Driver to No 4 Coy. 2 drivers to 1/2 EL Field Ambulance, 1 driver to 1/1 E.L Field Ambulance. Winter time comes into force. At 24.59 the time put back 1 hour.	EKL
"	6/10/18		Cloudy – little rain – 1 driver reported from the Base – posted to No 1 Coy.	EKL
"	7/10/18		Rain – Nil to report	EKL
	8/10/18		Rain in morning – M.T. for all Groups – Refilling Points for all Groups move to BEAUCAMP 2/Lieut J.P. BLACKMORE struck off strength ASC 21358/8 dated 4.10.1918 1 H.D. horse arrived – posted to No 1 Coy.	EKL

A7092. Wt. W12839/M1293 750,000. 1/17. D. D & I Ltd. Forms/C2118/14.

Army Form C. 2118.

Instructions regarding War Diaries and Intelligence Summaries are contained in F. S. Regs., Part II. and the Staff Manual respectively. Title pages will be prepared in manuscript.

WAR DIARY
~~or~~
~~INTELLIGENCE SUMMARY.~~ EKL
(Erase heading not required.)

Place	Date	Hour	Summary of Events and Information	Remarks and references to Appendices
TRESCAULT and ESNES	9/10/18		Fine – DHQ moves to TRESCAULT – THQ moves to TRESCAULT. Nos 1.2 3 and 4 Companies move to vicinity of BEAUCAMP Q 11 and 12 (57 B) Refilling Points move to N2 a (57 B) LESDAIN – ESNES Road – Refilling at 0900 hours DHQ and THQ move to ESNES – 15 miles forward from VELU. ESNES shelled during the night.	EKL
ESNES	10/10/18		Rain in morning – fine later. The Three Brigade Companies come under orders of G.O.C Brigades. All Companies of the Train move to vicinity of ESNES N2 a (57 B) No 2 Coy moves to vicinity of FONTAINE AU PIRE I 20 b (57 B) Refilling Points no change – Second refilling at 1600 hours for three Infantry Brigade Groups Fuel Dump moves to N2 a (57 B)	EKL
"	11/10/18		Cloudy – rain. No 3 Coy moves to FONTAINE AU PIRE I 20 b (57 B) No 1 Coy moves to same location. Refilling Points in Camp. R.P. 125 Inf Bde to I 20 b No 2 Coy moves to J 7 c (57 B) CAUDRY – QUIEVY Rd. – R.P. in Camp. Capt W.H TAYLEUR proceeds on leave to U.K.	EKL
BEAUVOIS-CAMBRESIS	12/10/18		Rain – Railhead changes to GOUZEACOURT DHQ & THQ move to BEAUVOIS-CAMBRESIS I 9 d 2 2 (57 B) Pack Train did not arrive till 1600 hours – refilling tomorrow at 0800 hours instead of today. 42nd Division relieves N Z Division in line. 2/Lieut J. A JAMES returns from leave	EKL

A7092. Wt. W12839/M1293 750,000. 1/17. D. D & L Ltd. Forms/C2118/14.

Army Form C. 2118.

Instructions regarding War Diaries and Intelligence Summaries are contained in F. S. Regs., Part II. and the Staff Manual respectively. Title pages will be prepared in manuscript.

WAR DIARY
~~or~~
INTELLIGENCE ~~SUMMARY~~. EKS

(*Erase heading not required.*)

Place	Date	Hour	Summary of Events and Information	Remarks and references to Appendices
BEAUVOIS-CAMARESIS	13 10/18		Cloudy - Rain. 10 G.S. Wagons complete report from 8th A.A (H) Coy ETRES for duty with Division, attached to No 1 Coy. No 4 Coy moves to I 4 a b 5 BEAUVOIS - BEVILLERS Road. Refilling Point I 7 c 2.5 No 3 Coy moves to J 7 c 2.5 LA FOLIE on the CAUDRY - QUIEVY Road. Refilling Point I 7 c 2.5. 150 Rations issued to French Civilians at BERTHENCOURT Refilling at 0800 hours Fuel Dump J 7 c 2.5	EKS
"	14 10/18		Fine - Refilling at 0800 hours. No 1 Coy moves to I 4 c 3 9 - BEAUVOIS - BEVILLERS Road. Refilling Point I 4 a 2.8. Fuel Dump to I 18 b 5.8. Refilling Point for 125 & 126 Bde J 7 c 2.5 for 127 Bde I 4 a. R.O. I collecting vegetables from villages - distributing to Refilling Points - sold to troops, money going to inhabitants. Enemy aircraft very active all day.	EKS
"	15 10/18		Cloudy - Rain. 2/Lieut. J.H. LUXTON proceeds on leave to U.K. 1 Sgt, 1 corporal and 2 drivers report from Base.	EKS
"	16 10/18		Rain. Lieut. R. LATHAM. M.C. proceeds on leave to U.K. Reinforcements posted 1 2 91 to 1/3 (E L) Field Ambulance through No 4 Coy. 1 corporal to No 2 Coy. 2 drivers to No 1 Coy. 3 Riders arrive - posted to No 4 Coy - one held surplus Pack Train did not arrive till 0130 hours on the 17th.	
"	17 10/18		Cloudy - Pack Train arrives 1300 hrs C.O. visits Army.	EKS

A7092. Wt. W12839/M1293 750,000. 1/17. D. D. & L. Ltd. Forms/C2118/14.

Instructions regarding War Diaries and Intelligence Summaries are contained in F. S. Regs., Part II. and the Staff Manual respectively. Title pages will be prepared in manuscript.

WAR DIARY

~~or~~

~~INTELLIGENCE SUMMARY.~~ EKI

(Erase heading not required.)

Army Form C. 2118.

Place	Date	Hour	Summary of Events and Information	Remarks and references to Appendices
BEAUVOIS-CAMBRESIS	18 10/18		Cloudy - Fine later. - Vicinity of BEAUVOIS shelled during the night. Pack Train arrives 1300 hours Baggage wagons sent to units, to be retained by them.	EKI
"	19 10/18		Cloudy - rain at night. The 10 G.S. wagons return to the 8th A.A. (H) Coy. - one H.D. badly wounded and destroyed by V.O. Cpl BRYANT returns from Base - sick. Pack Train arrives 1300 hours.	EKI
"	20 10/18		Rain. - Notified that CAUDRY was to be Railhead, this was cancelled, and railhead remains GOUZEAUCOURT. Reduction of Divisional Trains 1 Sub. Officer, 1 Batman, and 1 Riding horse from each Brigade Company. GRO 5295 17 Oct 1918 Captain C.F. SOMERVILLE R.O.I works under 4th Corps T.M.T Coy, regarding vegetables. 3 loaders from the Train attached to 8 AA (H) Coy for loading vegetables at Corps Dump. Pte DINGLEY No 3 Coy wounded by shell fire. Pack Train did not arrive today.	EKI
"	21 10/18		Rain. Winter Scale of Fuel comes into force Pack Train for the 20th arrives 0830 hours. Pack Train for 21st arrives 1800 hours.	
"	22 10/18		Rain. Pack Train arrives 1930 hours. 1 HD horse No 3 Coy, wounded and destroyed. Lieut. C. EDWARDS returns from leave.	EKI
"	23 10/18		Fine. Railhead changes to CAUDRY. Supplies to be drawn by H.T. Supply vehicles from Railhead for 3 Inf Bdes. Refilling by units (Baggage wagons and 1st Line) Div. Troops no change	EKI

A7092. Wt. W12839/M1293 750,000. 1/17. D. D & L Ltd. Forms/C2118/14.

Army Form C. 2118.

Instructions regarding War Diaries and Intelligence Summaries are contained in F. S. Regs., Part II. and the Staff Manual respectively. Title pages will be prepared in manuscript.

WAR DIARY
or
~~INTELLIGENCE SUMMARY.~~ EKS

(Erase heading not required.)

Place	Date	Hour	Summary of Events and Information	Remarks and references to Appendices
			No 1 Coy moves to CAUDRY - QUIEVY Road J1 a 6 6 Refilling Point J1 a 9.5 57B. No pack train arrives today.	
			N.Z. Division relieve 42nd Division in the line - less Artillery.	EKS
BEAUVOIS-EN CAMBRESIS.	24/10/18 (EKS)		Cloudy - fine later. Pack Train for 23rd arrives at RUMILLY - unloaded there at 1130 hours. - M.T. draw for all groups. Pack Train for 24th did not arrive today.	
			No 1 Coy moves to BELLE VUE E 13 c 7.3 Refilling Point E 13 c 7.3 57B. Refilling 1800 hours.	EKS
"	25/10/18		Cloudy. No 2 Coy moves to FONTAINE AU PIRE - CAUDRY Rd. I 16 a Cent. RP I 16 cent 57B. Baggage Wagons of three Infantry Bdes return to Companies. All three Brigades in BEAUVOIS.	
			Pack Train for 24th arrives 0630 hours. - Train for today did not arrive.	
			3 Riders - 1 from each Brigade Coy. sent to 125 Inf Bde. re G.R.O. 5295 - Authy Q2/582 24 x 18 Saddler sent to D.A.D.O.S. Cpl LIMING to be a/Sgt 127 Bde Dump vice Sgt MILLER to 56th Div. Train.	EKS
"	26/10/18		Cloudy, little rain. Pack Train for 25th arrives 0300 hours - Train for 26th 2000 hours. For 3 Inf Bdes - Baggage Wagons deliver supplies to units for B.H.Q. and Battalions, the rest send in 1st line. Div. Troops no change.	
			Fuel Dump moves to I 4 a 6.5 at No 4 Coy Camp.	
			Lieut W. W. YEATS proceeds on leave to U.K. - Captain G.D.N. WYATT acting O.C. till Captain W. H. TAYLEUR returns.	EKS

A7092. Wt. W12839/M1293 750,000. 1/17. D. D & L. Ltd. Forms/C2118/14.

Army Form C. 2118.

WAR DIARY

~~or~~

~~INTELLIGENCE SUMMARY.~~ EKL

(Erase heading not required.)

Instructions regarding War Diaries and Intelligence Summaries are contained in F. S. Regs., Part II. and the Staff Manual respectively. Title pages will be prepared in manuscript.

Place	Date	Hour	Summary of Events and Information	Remarks and references to Appendices
BEAUVOIS-EN CAMBRESIS.	27/X/18		Cloudy, little rain. Pack Train arrives 1159 hours Inspection of 1st Line Transport 125 Infantry Brigade by O.C. Train at BEAUVOIS. 6 Drivers report from HAVRE. Captain W.H. TAYLEUR returns from leave. Officers surplus to remain for the present. Q.M.G. ASC/21475. 24 X 1918	EKL
"	28/X/18		Cloudy but fine. 6 Drivers posted to No 1 Coy. Pack Train did not arrive today.	EKL
"	29/X/18		Cloudy, fine. Pack Train for 28th arrives 1530 hours – Pack Train for 29th did not arrive today Inspection of 1st Line Transport 1/7 Northumberland Fusiliers (Pioneers) by O.C. Train at SOLESMES Inspection of 1st Line Transport of 127 Infantry Brigade by O.C. Train at BEAUVOIS.	EKL
"	30/X/18		Fine. Pack Train for 29th arrives 1515 hours – Train for 30th did not arrive today Inspection of 1st Line Transport 42 Bn M.G. Corps by O.C. Train at BEAUVOIS	EKL
"	31/X/18		Rain all day. Pack Train for 30th arrives 0330 hours – Train for 31st did not arrive today Presentation of Medal Ribbons to 126 Bde by the Divisional Commander DR (a/L/Cpl) P. GULLY and DR BARTLETT – M.M. Inspection of 1st Line Transport of three Field Ambulances by O.C. Train	EKL

1 XI 1918

[signature]

LIEUT: COLONEL
COMDG. 42ND. DIVNL. TRAIN, A.S.C.

A7092. Wt. W12839/M1293 750,000. 1/17. D. D & L Ltd. Forms/C2118/14.

CONFIDENTIAL.

WAR DIARY.

42ND DIVISIONAL TRAIN

A.S.C.

Period 1-XI-18 — 30-XI-1918.

Volume XXI.

Instructions regarding War Diaries and Intelligence Summaries are contained in F. S. Regs., Part II. and the Staff Manual respectively. Title pages will be prepared in manuscript.

WAR DIARY

~~or~~

~~INTELLIGENCE SUMMARY~~ EKL

(Erase heading not required.)

Army Form C. 2118.

Place	Date	Hour	Summary of Events and Information	Remarks and references to Appendices
BEAUVOIS EN CAMBRESIS	1 XI 18		Cloudy, Fine. Pack Train for 31st arrives 0830 hours – for 1st arrives 1230 hours. Inspection of 1st Line Transport 126 Inf Bde by O.C. Train at JEUNE BOIS.	EKL
"	2 XI 18		Rain. – Pack Train did not arrive today. Inspection of 1/7 Northumberland Fusiliers (Pioneers) for the second time. Lieut V. STEER to hospital 2/Lieut. J.H. LUXTON sick in ENGLAND.	EKL
"	3 XI 18		Cloudy and Rain. Pack Train for 2nd arrives 0100 hours. Pack Train for 3rd arrived at CAMBRAI VILLE at 2350 – Bridge at CAUDRY destroyed by Mine. Normal System of supplies resumed. Baggage Wagons to Units. Lieut E.H. MANNERS proceeds on leave to U.K. Refilling Points of 125 & 126 Inf Bde Groups moves to E. 13 No 3 Coy moves to E 13 C 3 3 on the SOLESMES BELLE VUE Road. 42nd Division relieve N.Z. Division in the line 3/4.	EKL
"	4 XI 18		Fine. Railhead CAMBRAI VILLE. Pack Train arrives 1130 hours. Refilling 1100 hours No 2 Coy moves to E 19 a 2.9 and No 4 Coy on the SOLESMES – BELLE VUE ROAD.	EKL
BEAUDIGNIES AND POTELLE	5 XI 18		Rain all day. Railhead CAMBRAI VILLE. No 1 Coy moves to LE QUESNOY. Refilling Points for all Groups W 23 b. ROMERIES No 2 Coy, 3 Coy & 4 Coy move to LE QUESNOY. Refilling 1000 hours.	

A7092. Wt. W12839/M1293 750,000. 1/17. D. D & L. Ltd. Forms/C2118/14.

Army Form C. 2118.

Instructions regarding War Diaries and Intelligence Summaries are contained in F. S. Regs., Part II. and the Staff Manual respectively. Title pages will be prepared in manuscript.

WAR DIARY
or
~~INTELLIGENCE SUMMARY.~~ EKL

(Erase heading not required.)

Place	Date	Hour	Summary of Events and Information	Remarks and references to Appendices
POTELLE	5 XI/18 continued.		THQ moves to BEAUDIGNIES and to POTELLE CHATEAU. E of LE QUESNOY. Pack Train arrives 1800 hrs.	EKL
"	6 XI/18		Rain all day. Railhead CAUDRY. – Refilling 1200 hrs Refilling Points for all Groups at LE QUESNOY STATION. No Pack Train arriving today – had no rations drawn at AVOINGT. S/Sjt J.H. LUXTON granted 7 days extension. sick.	EKL
"	7 XI/18		Rain. – Pack Train arrives 1400 hrs. – refilling 1200 hrs. – R.P. no change. Lieut R LATHAM. M.C. returns from leave. Nil. Sick have Returns. NO 1 Coy moved to LE QUESNOY STATION. – NO 3 Coy move nearer LE QUESNOY.	EKL
"	8 XI/18		Rain – Nos 1. 2. 3. and 4 Coys move to E of FORET de MORMAL vicinity of LA HAUT RUE. Lieut V. STEER returns from hospital – Lieut C. EDWARDS posted to NO 1 Coy vice 2/Lieut T.P BLACKMORE. Refilling 1000 hrs Advance DHQ to LA HAUT RUE.	EKL
"	9 XI/18		Fine. Refilling 1300 hrs. Refilling Point for all Groups at Cross Roads N36 a FORESTER'S HOUSE. Supplies by lorry to LE QUESNOY, by H.T. DAC and NZ DW. Train to FORESTER'S HOUSE and then on to units by Train Wagons. Rear DHQ to LA HAUT RUE.	EKL

A7092. Wt. W12839/M1293 750,000. 1/17. D. D & L. Ltd. Forms/C2118/14.

Army Form C. 2118.

WAR DIARY
or
~~INTELLIGENCE SUMMARY.~~ EKL

(Erase heading not required.)

Instructions regarding War Diaries and Intelligence Summaries are contained in F. S. Regs., Part II. and the Staff Manual respectively. Title pages will be prepared in manuscript.

Place	Date	Hour	Summary of Events and Information	Remarks and references to Appendices
POTELLE	10 XI/18		Fine – RPs no change. Refilling 1400 hrs until further notice. Method of transhipping - same.	EKL
HAUTMONT	11 XI/18		Fine. THQ move to HAUTMONT. SSO. RoI and Staff at MAISON ROUGE. Hostilities cease 1100 hrs –	EKL
"	12 XI/18		Cloudy - but fine.	EKL
"	13 XI/18		Fine – Refilling Point for all groups U20 Cent (51) BERLAIMONT. Delivery of Supplies by Train Wagons to Units. Staging at Forester's House discontinued. Central Clipping Depot started at HAUTMONT under Lt. Col. the Hon A.G. HENEAGE DSO Six OR including 3 Clippers from the Train sent with Clipping Machines. SSO & RoI rejoin THQ	EKL
"	14 XI/18		Fine. Lieut W.W. YEATS returns from leave. No 4 Coy moves to STREMI. MAL. BATI V3 b a. 1 (51) Pack Train uncertain again.	EKL
"	15 XI/18		Fine – No 1 Coy moves to BOUSSIERES P32 a 9.7 (51) Shoeing Board assembled at No 2 Coy to test shoeing Smiths Pres. Capt G. THURLING-BLACKWELL ASC Members. Capt. WADDELL A.V.C Lieut. V. STEER ASC	EKL

A7092). Wt. W12539/M1293 750,000. 1/17. D. D & I. Ltd. Forms/C2118/14.

Instructions regarding War Diaries and Intelligence Summaries are contained in F. S. Regs., Part II. and the Staff Manual respectively. Title pages will be prepared in manuscript.

WAR DIARY

or

~~INTELLIGENCE SUMMARY~~ EKL

(Erase heading not required.)

Army Form C. 2118.

Place	Date	Hour	Summary of Events and Information	Remarks and references to Appendices
HAUTMONT	16/XI/18		Fine - No 3 Coy moves to JEAN REGNIES - HAUTMONT P22 b18 (51) No 2 Coy moves to HAUTMONT P35 b28 (51) Extract from London Gazette Nov 14th: Temp Lt to be Temp Capt. R. LATHAM MC (Oct 1st) Trains by re punctual.	EKL
"	17/XI/18		Cloudy. Lieut. H. LIVINGSTONE-LEARMOUTH from No 4 Coy to No 1 Coy. 2/Lieut J.H. LUXTON from No 3 Coy to No 2 Coy. CAPTAIN R LATHAM MC to be BSO 125 Brigade. Lieut E.H. MANNERS to be BSO 126 Brigade Lieut V. STEER and 2/Lieut J.J. SIMMS to be supernumerary 2/Lieut. J.J. SIMMS to be Educational Officer for Train.	EKL
"	18/XI/18		Rain. Nil to report.	EKL
"	19/XI/18		Cloudy. Wagon returned to IV Corps M T Coy VIESLY - this wagon was lent for collecting vegetables. Board of Officers assembled at No 2 Coy re Bicycle lost from there President. Captain J.L GRAHAM - Members Lieut. W.W. YEATS - 2/Lieut. J.A. JAMES. 2 HD horses arrived from CAUDRY - posted to No 3 Coy	EKL
"	20/XI/18		Fine. Refilling 1230 until further notice. Lieut. V. STEER proceeds on leave sailing 23rd Board of Officers assembled at No 1 Coy re Bicycle lost from there President Captain C.F. SOMERVILLE Member 2/Lieut J.H. LUXTON. Lieut E.H MANNERS returns from leave	EKL

A7092. Wt. W12839/M1293 750,000. 1/17. D. D & L. Ltd. Forms/C2118/14.

Army Form C. 2118.

Instructions regarding War Diaries and Intelligence Summaries are contained in F. S. Regs., Part II. and the Staff Manual respectively. Title pages will be prepared in manuscript.

WAR DIARY
or
~~INTELLIGENCE SUMMARY~~

(*Erase heading not required.*)

Place	Date	Hour	Summary of Events and Information	Remarks and references to Appendices
HAUTMONT	21 xi/18		Fine – Nil to report	ECL
"	22 xi/18		Fine – 5 Drivers report for duty from 3 A.A. (H) Coy and 1 from Base posted to No 3 Coy.	ECL
"	23 xi/18		Fine. Brigade 1st Line and DAC draw from R.P. and deliver to Units – in order to give Supply Section a rest	ECL
			8 Drivers report from Base – 4 posted to No 3 Coy. 1 to No 1 Coy 2 to 1/2 F.A 1 to 1/3 FA	ECL
"	24 xi/18		Fine – nil to report	ECL
"	25 xi/18		Rain – nil to report.	
"	26 xi/18		Cloudy. Lieut. E.H. MANNERS to be Acting Captain whilst employed as Captain with 42 Div. Train (Oct. 1st 1918) GHQ List 214 17.xi.18	ECL
"	27 xi/18		Cloudy – Pack Train take again.	ECL
"	28 xi/18		Cloudy – Rain. Refilling Points tomorrow for Refilling tomorrow the 29th Div. Troops V.3 Cent 125 Bde P35 b.2.8 126 Bde V.3 Cent. 127 Bde V.3 d.6.9	ECL
"	29 xi/18		Cloudy – Capt. G. THURLING-BLACKWELL 5 days leave in France.	ECL
"	30 xi/18		Cloudy – Nil to report.	

J Coulson [signature]

LIEUT: COLONEL
COMDG. 42ND DIVNL. TRAIN, A.S.C.

1. XII 1918

A7092. Wt. W12839/M1293 750,000. 1/17. D. D & L. Ltd. Forms/C2118/14.

Instructions regarding War Diaries and Intelligence Summaries are contained in F. S. Regs., Part II. and the Staff Manual respectively. Title pages will be prepared in manuscript.

WAR DIARY
or
~~INTELLIGENCE SUMMARY.~~ EKS

(Erase heading not required.)

Army Form C. 2118.

Place	Date	Hour	Summary of Events and Information	Remarks and references to Appendices
HAUTMONT	1 XII/18		Fine Refilling 0900 H.M. The King visits ~~IV~~ Corps Area - Division line MAUBEUGE-AVESNES Road	EKS
"	2 XII/18		Fine Refilling 1400. 4 Remounts HD report. Posted 1 to No 4 Coy 1 to No 3 Coy 2 held surplus at No 3 Coy	EKS
"	3 XII/18		Rain. Refilling 0900 and until further notice.	EKS
"	4 XII/18		Rain 3 surplus drivers from No 3 Coy posted to No 1 Coy. 3 drivers report from HAVRE - posted to No 1 Coy. 1 of 2 surplus HD absorbed by No 3 Coy	EKS
"	5 XII/18		Cloudy - Nil to report	EKS
"	6 XII/18		Fine - Nil to report.	EKS
"	7 XII/18		Cloudy - 60 Bde R.G.A. - 84 Bde RGA attached to Division	EKS
"	8 XII/18.		weather fine. nil to report.	CFS.
"	9 XII/18.		Rain fine later. nil to report.	CFS
"	10 XII/18		Rain nil to report.	CFS
"	11 XII/18.		Some of the Train horses being clipped under Company arrangements instead of at Divisional Clipping Depot.	CFS.
"	12 XII/18.		Rain. nil to report.	CFS.

A7092. Wt. W12839/M1293 750,000. 1/17. D. D & L. Ltd. Forms/C2118/14.

Instructions regarding War Diaries and Intelligence Summaries are contained in F. S. Regs., Part II. and the Staff Manual respectively. Title pages will be prepared in manuscript.

WAR DIARY
or
~~INTELLIGENCE SUMMARY.~~ C F S

(Erase heading not required.)

Army Form C. 2118.

Place	Date	Hour	Summary of Events and Information	Remarks and references to Appendices
~~HAUTMONT~~ HAUTMONT	13-12-18		Second refilling at 1600. for consumption 15th Baggage wagons sent to units owing to Div moving next day. Each Coy supplied with 1 wagon from 8th A A H.T. Coy to assist in move.	C F S.
"	14-12-18		No1. Coy moves to JEUMONT. No2 Coy to MAUBEUGE area No3. Coy to LAMERIES. No4 Coy to ASSEVENT. being first Stage of Divisions move to CHARLEROI area.	C F S
BINCHE	15-12-18		Train Hdqrs moves to BINCH. No1 Coy to THUIN. No2 Coy to ESTINNE au MONT. No 3 Coy to BINCHE No4 Coy to MERBES STE MARIE. Lieut (a/capt) C F SOMERVILLE to be acting adjutant in the absence of T/Capt E.K SCHOLTZ on leave.	C F S
FONTAINE L'eveque	16-12-18		T.H.Q moves to FONTAINE L'eveque. No2 Coy to ANDERLUES. No3 Coy to FONTAINE L'EVEQUE No4 Coy to TRAHEGNIES. Railhead changes to CHARLEROI.	C F S
do.	17-12-18		Division remains in area for one days rest weather wet.	
CHARLEROI	18-12-18		T.H.Q moves to CHARLEROI. No1 Coy to MONTIGNY. No2. Coy to CHARLEROI. No3 Coy to GILLY No4 Coy to MARCIENNES AU PONT. very wet Railhead changes to MONTIGNIES (COUILLET) military Siding	C F S
do.	19-12-18		No. 4 Coy moves to FLEURUS. Baggage wagons returned from units.	C F S

A7092. Wt. W12839/M1293 750,000. 1/17. D. D & L Ltd. Forms/C2118/14.

Army Form C. 2118.

Instructions regarding War Diaries and Intelligence Summaries are contained in F. S. Regs., Part II. and the Staff Manual respectively. Title pages will be prepared in manuscript.

WAR DIARY
or
~~INTELLIGENCE SUMMARY~~. CFS

(Erase heading not required.)

Place	Date	Hour	Summary of Events and Information	Remarks and references to Appendices
CHARLEROI	20/12/18		Supplies for 126 Bde drawn from Railhead by H.T. No 4 Coy moved to LAMBUSART Refilling Point remains at FLEURUS.	CFS
do	21/12/18		125 & 126 Bdes drawn Supplies from Railhead by H.T. 127 Bde refilling Point moves to LAMBUSART	CFS
do	22/12/18		All groups draw Supplies by H.T. from Railhead. T Capt E F SPRECKLEY appointed a/SSO in absence of T/MAJOR W P REYNOLDS on leave to UK. Owing accident on the railway Pack train after not arrive till very late. No Sundries except Candles issued.	CFS
do	23/12/18		Two drivers sent to Corps Concentration Camp for demobilisation as miners. One Sergeant sent for Demobilisation to Corps Concentration Camp. S.S.M arrived as reinforcement posted to 1/1st Field Amb. Pack train did not arrive till early on the 24th No potatoes were received.	CFS
do	24/12/18		Second refilling 1400. 9 reinforcements arrived from Base posted 2 batmen to 1/1st Field Amb 2 batmen 1/3rd Field Amb, 1 Sgt & 1 Driver to No 1 Coy 1 Dr No 2 Coy 1 Driver & 1 Dr Sadd No 4 Coy.	CFS
do	25/12/18		No refilling. Divisional Commander inspected the decorations in the mens dining room at No 1 Coy.	CFS
do	26/12/18		Five men sent to Corps Concentration Camp to be demobilised as Coal miners.	CFS
do.	27-12-18		Brood mares inspected by IV Corps Selection Committee weather wet.	CFS

A7092. Wt. W12839/M1293 750,000. 1/17. D. D & L. Ltd. Forms/C2118/14.

Instructions regarding War Diaries and Intelligence Summaries are contained in F. S. Regs., Part II. and the Staff Manual respectively. Title pages will be prepared in manuscript.

WAR DIARY

or

~~INTELLIGENCE SUMMARY.~~ C.F.P.

(Erase heading not required.)

Army Form C. 2118.

Place	Date	Hour	Summary of Events and Information	Remarks and references to Appendices
CHARLEROI.	28/12/18		DADVS. inspected the horses of No 1 & 2 Companies.	C.F.P.
do	29/12/18		Wet. Pack train did not arrive till 2100. horses & men kept at Railhead as no definite news could be obtained of the train.	
do.	30/12/18		Capt E K SCHOLTZ returns from leave. Weather wet. Pack train again very late. 2100 hours. being time of arrival	C.F.P.
do.	31/12/18		Weather fine. RE material sent to site of 125 Bde Refilling Point to build a Shelter for Supplies. Pack train did not arrive till 2300 hours. No fresh vegetables on the Pack.	C.F.P.

J Coulton [signature]

LIEUT: COLONEL
COMDG. 42ND. DIVNL. TRAIN, A.S.C.

CONFIDENTIAL

WAR DIARY

42nd DIVISIONAL TRAIN

1st January 1919 to 31st January 1919

VOLUME 23

Army Form C. 2118.

Instructions regarding War Diaries and Intelligence Summaries are contained in F. S. Regs., Part II. and the Staff Manual respectively. Title pages will be prepared in manuscript.

WAR DIARY ~~or~~ ~~INTELLIGENCE SUMMARY~~. EKS

(Erase heading not required.)

Place	Date	Hour	Summary of Events and Information	Remarks and references to Appendices
CHARLEROI.	1/1/19		Fine – Pack Train not available for off loading till 1300	EKS
"	2/1/19		Rain. 126 Bde R.P. moves out of GILLY STATION – just outside Wagons of 8 AA.(H) Coy returned to unit at CORBAIS less 1 at No 2 Coy – 1 horse P.U.N. Extract from SIR DOUGLAS HAIG'S DISPATCH NOV 8th 1918 MENTIONED CAPT. (A/MAJOR) W.P.K. REYNOLDS – CAPT E.K. SCHOLTZ – WHLR STAFF SGT DRUMMOND No 2 Coy.	EKS
"	3/1/19		Rain. Extract from NEW YEAR HONOURS LIST. To be O.B.E. (MILITARY DIVISION) MAJOR W.P.K. REYNOLDS.	EKS
"	4/1/19		Rain. The CO. & S.S.O. visit Army H.Q.	EKS
"	5/1/19		Rain – Nil to report.	
"	6/1/19		Fine. Lieut I.T. SIMMS granted 48 hrs leave in FRANCE. Conference at DHQ re Post Bellum Army. Pack Train very late – only part of it arrived.	EKS
"	7/1/19		Fine. Refilling today at 1400. Remainder of yesterdays train cleared. Pack Train for today arrived 23.59. H.D horse stolen from No 1 Coy. during the night.	EKS
"	8/1/19		Fine – Refilling 1400	EKS
"	9/1/19		Rain. Pack Train still coming in late.	EKS
"	10/1/19		Fine – 7600 Kilos Rutabages bought at LAMBASART supplement to Forage Ration. Board of officers assembled at No 1 Coy re H.D. horse President Capt G. THURLING-BLACKWELL Member Lt. I A JAMES	EKS

A7092. Wt. W12839/M1293 750,000. 1/17. D. D & L. Ltd. Forms/C2118/14.

Army Form C. 2118.

Instructions regarding War Diaries and Intelligence Summaries are contained in F. S. Regs., Part II. and the Staff Manual respectively. Title pages will be prepared in manuscript.

WAR DIARY
or
~~INTELLIGENCE SUMMARY.~~ EKS

(Erase heading not required.)

Place	Date	Hour	Summary of Events and Information	Remarks and references to Appendices
CHARLEROI.	11/1/19		Cloudy – Refilling at 0900. Horses of the Train classified by Board for demobilization No 3 Coy. 8900 Kilos Rutabagas bought.	EKS
"	12/1/19		Fine – Refilling 1400. Pack Train to time.	EKS
"	13/1/19		Fine – Refilling 0900 126 Bde at 1400	EKS
"	14/1/19		Fine – Three Reinforcements arrive (drivers) Refilling 0900. Major W.P.K. REYNOLDS applied for by Ministry of Labour – GHQ wired War Office he can be spared.	EKS EKS
"	15/1/19		Rain – Nil to report.	
"	16/1/19		Fine – No 1 & 2 Coy inspected by Vet Board. 3 drivers posted to No 4 Coy. M. DOUCET Belgian Interpreter posted to Train attached T.H.Q.	EKS
"	17/1/19		Fine – Captain G.D.N. WYATT proceeds on leave to UK	EKS
"	18/1/19		Fine – ~~[illegible]~~ EKS S.S.O attends Conference at Army H.Q. – (D.D.S.T.)	EKS
"	19/1/19		Fine – 2/Lieut T. J. SIMMS dispatched to Concentration Camp for demobilization – struck off strength. 1 L.D. Horse of No 2 Coy coming in contact with live wire – electrocuted. Authority received to strike off strength.	EKS

A7092. Wt. W12839/M1293 750,000. 1/17. D. D. & L. Ltd. Forms/C2118/14.

Instructions regarding War Diaries and Intelligence Summaries are contained in F. S. Regs., Part II. and the Staff Manual respectively. Title pages will be prepared in manuscript.

WAR DIARY

~~or~~

~~INTELLIGENCE SUMMARY.~~ EKS

(*Erase heading not required.*)

Army Form C. 2118.

Place	Date	Hour	Summary of Events and Information	Remarks and references to Appendices
CHARLEROI	20/1/19		Fine – No 4 Coy horses classified for sale by Capt WOODS 93 DAC 1 Driver reported from Base – posted to No 3 Coy. 1 Cpl of No 4 Coy returned from Base – 1 Farr Cpl of No 1 Coy returned from Base 1 DR SADD. of No 3 Coy returned from Base.	EKS
"	21/1/19		Fine – The CO visit Army HQ.	EKS
"	22/1/19		Fine – 2/Lt J.H. LUXTON granted three days leave in FRANCE. Shoeing Board assembled at No 2 Coy to test four men from Brigades President – CAPT. J.L GRAHAM. and CAPT. WADDELL RA.V.C. 2 H.D. horses stolen from No 2 Coy (No 1 Coy horses). Extract from Gazette. Awarded the M.S.M. (New Year Honours) No T 19500 Sgt (a/C.S.M.) now T. C.S.M. A.A. GILLINGHAM No 2 Coy " T4/247963 T.S.S.M. F.E. DUTSON. No 4 Coy (late 1/1 E.L. Field Ambnce). War office Jan 1918	EKS
"	23/1/19		Snowing in morning – very cold. AUDIT BOARD assembled at No 3 Coy. President CAPT E.H. MANNERS. and Lieut. C EDWARDS Board re Illegal absence assembled at No 3 Coy President CAPT A.F. ARIS and 2/Lt J.A. JAMES re DR REYNOLDS No 3 Coy. Board of Officers assembled at No 2 Coy re 2 lost H.D. horses. President – CAPT J.L GRAHAM and Lieut. H LIVINGSTONE LEARMONTH.	EKS
"	24/1/19		Cloudy & cold – LIEUT. COL J. COULSON D.S.O proceeds on leave to U.K. – MAJOR H.P. WILLIAMS M.C. assumes Command – CAPT. J.L GRAHAM assumes command of No 1 Coy.	

Instructions regarding War Diaries and Intelligence Summaries are contained in F. S. Regs., Part II. and the Staff Manual respectively. Title pages will be prepared in manuscript.

WAR DIARY

~~or~~

~~INTELLIGENCE SUMMARY.~~ EKS

(*Erase heading not required.*)

Army Form C. 2118.

Place	Date	Hour	Summary of Events and Information	Remarks and references to Appendices
CHARLEROI	25/1/19		Cloudy and frosty. – Extract from Gazette JAN 21 1919 – "The notification regarding LIEUT E.H. MANNERS in Gazette DEC 20th is cancelled.	EKS
			Extract from Gazette JAN 23. 1919 LIEUT. E.H. MANNERS to be CAPTAIN (NOV. 6 1918).	
"	26/1/19		Snowing – 2/LIEUT J.A. JAMES proceeds to join 29th DIV TRAIN for duty at COLOGNE.	EKS
"	27/1/19		Thawing slightly – Nil to report.	EKS
"	28/1/19		Cloudy and cold. – Leave stopped temporarily owing to congestion at CALAIS.	EKS
"	29/1/19		Cloudy and cold – Nil to report	EKS
"	30/1/19		Cold – Nil to report.	EKS
"	31/1/19		Frosty – BOULOGNE – COLOGNE Express suspended owing to congestion.	
			2/Lt. H.H. PELLS demobilized whilst on leave – struck off strength.	
			Leave opened again from the 3rd inst.	
			1 HD horse drawn from Mobile Vet Sect. posted to No 2 Coy	EKS

E K Scholz

for OC CAPTAIN & ADJUTANT, 42ND. DIVNL. TRAIN, A.S.C.

A7092. Wt. W12839/M1293 750,000. 1/17. D. D & L. Ltd. Forms/C2118/14.

CONFIDENTIAL.

WAR DIARY.

42nd Divisional Train.

R.A.S.C.

Period:~ 1-2-1919 – 28-2-1919.

Volume XXIII.

Instructions regarding War Diaries and Intelligence Summaries are contained in F. S. Regs., Part II. and the Staff Manual respectively. Title pages will be prepared in manuscript.

WAR DIARY

or

~~INTELLIGENCE SUMMARY.~~ EKS

(Erase heading not required.)

Army Form C. 2118.

Place	Date	Hour	Summary of Events and Information	Remarks and references to Appendices
CHARLEROI	1/2/19		Snowing hard. freezing – 2/Lieut T H LUXTON reports to BONEHILL WORKS for temporary duty under 5th DIV. Unloading of Barges	EKS
"	2/2/19		Freezing – Authority to strike Capt (T/Major) W.P.K. REYNOLDS OBE off strength of Train. QMG GHQ QP/ASC/22151/44 from 1st 1. 1919.	EKS
"	3/2/19		Frosty – Conference at DHQ re Demobilization	EKS
"	4/2/19		Snowing during the day –	EKS
"	5/2/19		Snowing hard afternoon and evening. 1 LD (GREEK MARE) from No 2 Coy sent to DIEPPE – Breeding.	EKS
"	6/2/19		Thawing very slightly – Capt C.F. SOMERVILLE proceeds on leave to U.K. sailing 8th	EKS
"	7/2/19		Fine but frosty.	EKS
"	8/2/19		Freezing hard during the night – Fine. Capt R LATHAM MC reports to Concentration Camp for demobilization. Capt G.D.N. WYATT returns from leave (5 days extension)	EKS
"	9/2/19		Fine but frosty – 2/Lieut A.D.R GARCIN reports for duty from 61 DIV. TRAIN. – posted to No 2 Coy. Lt Col. J. COULSON DSO returns from leave	EKS
"	10/2/19		Fine but frosty – Major H.P WILLIAMS assumes Command of No 1 Coy. Capt A.F. ARIS proceeds on leave to U.K. sailing 11th	EKS
"	11/2/19		Fine – frosty – Ford Car 53441 with DR WILSON Batman to 2/Lt PELLS reports from C.P.B.	EKS
"	12/2/19		Frosty – Capt G.D.N WYATT to be Div. Troops S.O vice Capt. J.L GRAHAM (leave)	EKS
"	13/2/19		Cold & Frosty – Capt J.L GRAHAM proceeds on leave to UK sailing 14th 1 Artificer and 6 Pivotal drivers to Concentration Camp for demobilization	EKS

A7092. Wt. W12839/M1293 750,000. 1/17. D. D & L. Ltd. Forms/C2118/14.

Instructions regarding War Diaries and Intelligence Summaries are contained in F. S. Regs., Part II, and the Staff Manual respectively. Title pages will be prepared in manuscript.

WAR DIARY

~~or~~

~~INTELLIGENCE SUMMARY.~~ EKS

(Erase heading not required.)

Army Form C. 2118.

Place	Date	Hour	Summary of Events and Information	Remarks and references to Appendices
CHARLEROI	14/2/19		Milder - Thawing slightly - 1 Sgt reports from Base, posted to No 3 Coy.	EKS
"	15/2/19		Thawing hard. 46 "Y" horses sent to Base for U.K.	
			No 1 Coy 6 L.D. 2 R. 11 H.D. No 2 Coy 2 L.D. 12 H.D. No 3 Coy 2 L.D. 1 R. 10 H.D.	EKS
			All bicycles returned to D.A.D.O.S.	
"	16/2/19		Thawing - raining - Refilling 1400 today - Adopt Thaw Precautions from 0900 - half loads to be carried. Fuel drawn from Railhead by H.T.	EKS
"	17/2/19		Cloudy & mild - nil to report.	EKS
"	18/2/19		Cloudy & mild - Captain G. THURLING-BLACKWELL proceeds on leave to U.K. dating 20th. Authority received to strike Bicycle (No 2 Coy) lost 17. 11. 1918 CQMS FELTON to pay 30/-, public 60/- IV Army Q 9/1465.	
			42 DW supplies on 1 Australian Div. Pack.	EKS
			1 Clerk and 2 issuers sent to 3rd Cavalry Division 'D' Supplies X268	
"	19/2/19		Cloudy - Lieut C. EDWARDS from No 1 Coy to No 3 Coy temporary. Resume Normal Traffic, midnight 19/20.	EKS
"	20/2/19		Cloudy - 2 Group 45 B. drivers sent to Dispersal Station for demobilization	EKS
			10 'Z' HD. horses sent to 19 Mob. Vet. Sec. for sale. 4 from No 3. Coy - 6 from No 1 Coy.	
"	21/2/19		Fine - 1 Sgt Clerk - Sgt HARVEY posted to D.D.S.T. office IV Army.	
			32 'Y' Animals dispatched to Base for U.K.	
			No 1 Coy. 8 HD. 2 R. No 2 Coy 5 HD. 1 L.D. 2 R. No 3 Coy. Nil No 4 Coy 11 HD. 3 L.D.	
			Cpl CLIFTEN reports from C.P.B.	EKS
"	22/2/19		Fine - Nil to report.	EKS

A7092. Wt. W12839/M1293 750,000. 1/17. D. D & L. Ltd. Forms/C2118/14.

Instructions regarding War Diaries and Intelligence Summaries are contained in F. S. Regs., Part II. and the Staff Manual respectively. Title pages will be prepared in manuscript.

WAR DIARY

~~or~~

~~INTELLIGENCE SUMMARY.~~ EKS

(*Erase heading not required.*)

Army Form C. 2118.

Place	Date	Hour	Summary of Events and Information	Remarks and references to Appendices
CHARLEROI	23 2/19		Fine – Four drivers reported from Base – posted to No 1 Coy. Six drivers and One issuer posted to Guards Divisional Train. Capt C.F. SOMERVILLE returns from leave.	EKS
"	24 2/19		Fine – rain during night. Drawing at Railhead 1030 onwards until further notice 20 "Y" animals dispatched to Base – No 1 Coy 12 HD. 4 LD No 4 Coy 4 M. HD. 10 "Z" animals sent to 19 M. Vet Sec. for sale. No 1 Coy 2R. 4 HD. No 3 Coy 2R. 2 HD.	EKS
"	25 2/19		Cloudy but fine. 10 "Z" animals to 19 M. Vet Sec. for sale No 1 Coy 1R 1 HD. No 2 Coy 1R. 2 HD. No 3 Coy 2R. 3 HD.	EKS
	26 2/19		Cloudy – Capt E.F. SPRECKLEY proceeds on leave – Capt. C.F. SOMERVILLE to be a/S.S.O. 3 drivers report from Field Ambulances – posted to No 1 Coy.	EKS
"	27 2/19		Fine – rain at night. 3 Drivers report from Base – posted to No 1 Coy. 36 "Y" animals dispatched to Base. No 1 Coy 1R. 1 LD. 32 HD. No 2 1R. No 3 1 HD. SQMS WILKINSON to HQ IV Corps RASC Section S.670 25.2.1919 Capt. A F ARIS returns from leave.	EKS
"	28 2/19		Cloudy – All wagons etc returned to No 1 Coy from Bde Coys and other units except 4 from No 2 Coy Lt C EDWARDS returns to No 1 Coy Sunbeam Car 179791 struck off strength. 1 Z LD returns to No 2 Coy, not sold	EKS

J Carlton

LIEUT: COLONEL
COMDG. 42ND. DIVNL. TRAIN, A.S.C.

A7092. Wt. W12839/M1293 750,000. 1/17. D. D & L. Ltd. Forms/C2118/14.

WO 26

CONFIDENTIAL.

WAR DIARY.

42ND Divisional Train.

R.A.S.C.

Period - 1-3-1919 – 31-3-1919.

Vol: XXV.

Instructions regarding War Diaries and Intelligence Summaries are contained in F. S. Regs., Part II. and the Staff Manual respectively. Title pages will be prepared in manuscript.

WAR DIARY
~~or~~
~~INTELLIGENCE SUMMARY.~~ EKL

(Erase heading not required.)

Army Form C. 2118.

Place	Date	Hour	Summary of Events and Information	Remarks and references to Appendices
CHARLEROI	1/3/19		Fine – 1 HD horse stolen from No 4 Coy – 1 Z Rider returned to No 3 Coy – not sold – 8 drivers report from Field Ambulances, posted to No1 Coy. Owing to animals being sent away, Bdes and Arty have animals to horse vehicles. Summer Time comes into force at 23.00. 27 Y animals for dispatch to Base, returned to No1 Coy, pending further instructions	EKL
"	2/3/19		Cloudy – 1 Sgt and 3 drivers posted to Guards Div Train.	EKL
"	3/3/19		Cloudy – Raining during the day. – Drawing from Railhead 0800. Lt H. LIVINGSTONE-LEARMONTH proceeds on leave. CSM GILLINGHAM MSM. presented with MSM ribbon by Divisional Commander. Divisional Commander inspects No 2 Coy and presents Cup for Transport Competition.	EKL EKL
"	4/3/19		Raining – Drawing Railhead 1030. HD horse stolen from No 4 Coy recovered at Mobile Vet Sec	
"	5/3/19		Cloudy – Fine. Refilling 1400 today only. 26 "Y" animals dispatched to Base – No1 Coy 12 HD. No 2 Coy 9 HD. 1R. No 4 3 LD. 1R. Lt C EDWARDS conducts Divisional party to NAMUR, entraining 6th for CALAIS. 6 Z HD from No1 Coy report to 19 Mobile Vet Sec for Sale	EKL EKL
	6/3/19		Rain – Refilling 1400 today only – 2 ORs from No1 Coy sent to Concentration Camp for demobilization	
	7/3/19		Cloudy – 127 Inf Bde (less MG Bn & 1/1 7 Ambulance) move to CHARLEROI from FLEURES. No 4 Coy moves to GILLY from LAMBUSART. 127 Bde Gpe transferred to 126 Bde Gpe. 17 Z animals sent to Mobile Vet Sec. No1 Coy 1 HD. No 2 Coy 1R 1LD. 4HD. No 3 Coy 1R. 1LD. No 4 Coy 6R. 2HD. Only X animals now with Train.	EKL
	8/3/19		Cloudy. Lieut. C. EDWARDS to Concentration Camp for demobilization. Ford Car returned to M.T. Coy for evacuation. No 24 Bdes RFA rationed by RSO from 9th.	EKL

A7092. Wt. W12839/M1293 750,000. 1/17. D. D & L. Ltd. Forms/C2118/14.

Instructions regarding War Diaries and Intelligence Summaries are contained in F. S. Regs., Part II. and the Staff Manual respectively. Title pages will be prepared in manuscript.

WAR DIARY

or

~~INTELLIGENCE SUMMARY~~. EKS

(Erase heading not required.)

Army Form C. 2118.

Place	Date	Hour	Summary of Events and Information	Remarks and references to Appendices
CHARLEROI	9/3/19		Cloudy – 70 OR sent to Concentration Camp for demobilization No 1 Coy 40 other Coys 10 each.	
			All retainable men and volunteers transferred to No 1 Coy.	
			176 Bde RP closed and units transferred to DW Troops RP	EKS
"	10/3/19		Fine but Cloudy –	
			No 3 Coy attached to No 1 Coy pending reduction to Cadre – No 4 Coy to No 2 Coy.	
			Drawing at Railhead 0800.	
			Capt W. H. TAYLEUR assumes Command of No 2 Coy vice 2/Lt J. H. LUXTON.	
			Capt. E. H. MANNERS to be BSO 175 Bde vice 2/Lt A D R GARCIN.	
			Lieut. W. W. YEATS posted to No 1 Coy	
			All No 4 Coy Animals transferred to No 1 Coy.	
			48 Animals transferred to R.F.A. – RA reforming 24 drivers sent.	EKS
			42 MG Bn moves into CHARLEROI – Reserve Rations to be consumed.	
"	11/3/19		Cloudy – 2 OR. repat from IV Corps Cyclists – posted to No 1 Coy	EKS
			75 OR sent to Concentration Camp for demobilization from No 1 Coy.	
"	12/3/19		Rain – 42 MG Bn reforming 5 drivers wagons and animals sent to them.	
			75 OR sent to Concentration Camp for demobilization No 4 Coy 15 No 3 Coy 10	
			2/Lt J. H. LUXTON to Concentration Camp for demobilization	EKS
			2 OR repat from Ambulances to No 1 Coy, and 2 from 19 Mobile Vet Sec.	
"	13/3/19		Fine – Cloudy. 5 lorries assisting at Railhead 2 for DW Troops 3 for 175 Bde Group.	
			75 OR for demobilization 5 from No 4 Coy 5 from No 2 Coy 5 from 93 RFA. 10 from Ambulances.	
			All animals of the Train with No 1 Coy.	EKS

A7092). Wt. W1289/M1293 750,000. 1/17. D. D & L Ltd. Forms/C2118/14.

Instructions regarding War Diaries and Intelligence Summaries are contained in F. S. Regs., Part II. and the Staff Manual respectively. Title pages will be prepared in manuscript.

WAR DIARY

~~or~~

~~INTELLIGENCE SUMMARY.~~ EKS

(*Erase heading not required.*)

Army Form C. 2118.

Place	Date	Hour	Summary of Events and Information	Remarks and references to Appendices
CHARLEROI	14/3/19		Cloudy-fine. 75 O.R. sent to Concentration Camp for demobilization 7 from Ambulances 5 from 93 RFA 6 from No 2 Coy. 8 Drivers, including 1 L/Cpl sent to 71 AA(H) Coy, all retainable men and volunteers. Major H.P. WILLIAMS. M.C. hands over to Capt A F ARIS.	EKS
"	15/3/19		Cloudy. 2/Lieut A.D.R. GARCIN to Concentration Camp for demobilization (45 a) HQ OHQ reduced to Cadre. Brig Gen JARGUS assumes Command of all troops less RA. 8 OR to Concentration Camp for demobilization. Major H P WILLIAMS MC proceeds on leave to U.K. Capt G. THURLING-BLACKWELL returns from leave extension granted for 8 days. 10 HD x horses to No 8 A.A.(H) Coy from No 1 Coy. No 1 Coy takes over Stores from 19 Mob Vet Sec.	EKS EKS
"	16/3/19		Cloudy 13 O.R. sent to Concentration Camp for demobilization No 1 2 No 2 7 No 3 1 No 4 3	EKS
"	17/3/19		Rain – Nil to report.	
"	18/3/19		Cloudy – Sgt LIMING transferred to IV A.H.Q. 1 Rider to Base from No 1 Coy. The Div Commander vacates Command of 42 Division. 10 OR sent to Concentration Camp from No 3 Coy for demobilization. Sunbeam Car 19791 withdrawn	EKS
"	19/3/19		Cloudy – 2 Drivers (retainable) posted to IV Corps Cyclist Bn Lieut H. LIVINGSTONE-LEARMONTH returns from leave	EKS

Instructions regarding War Diaries and Intelligence Summaries are contained in F. S. Regs., Part II. and the Staff Manual respectively. Title pages will be prepared in manuscript.

WAR DIARY

~~or~~

~~INTELLIGENCE SUMMARY.~~ EKL

(Erase heading not required.)

Army Form C. 2118.

Place	Date	Hour	Summary of Events and Information	Remarks and references to Appendices
CHARLEROI	20/3/19		Raining - sleet. Nil to report.	EKL
"	21/3/19		Fine - Capt J L GRAHAM in Hospital in U.K. 9/Asc/8617 (QMGS)	
			All attached units draw from 125 Bde Dump. - 42nd D.W. units from D.W. Troops dump.	EKL
			24 Drivers attached 210. 211 Bdes R.F.A returned to No 1 Coy	
"	22/3/19		Cloudy - All leave, demobilization etc stopped on account of threatened strikes in U.K.	EKL
			10 OR sent to Concentration Camp for demobilization No 1. 5 No 2. 2 No 3. 2 No 4 1.	
"	23/3/19		Fine. Nil to report	EKL
"	24/3/19		Rain - Capt. E.F. SPRECKLEY returns from leave.	
			The Cadre of the Train as follows Officers LT COL J. COULSON DSO. CAPT E F. SPRECKLEY i/c No1. CAPT E H. MANNERS i/c No2. CAPT. G D N WATT i/c No 3. Lt. W. W. YEATS i/c No 4.	EKL
"	25/3/19		Rain - fine later. 2L. D. Horses transferred to 42 M.G.Bn from No 1 Coy.	EKL
			Leave, demob etc reopened.	
"	26/3/19		Cloudy - S.S.M. MORRIS, 2 corporals 1 wheeler, 1 Saddler and 20 drivers transferred to 21 AA (H) Coy	
			(Authy T 171. 24. 3. 1919)	
			Cadre officers take over respective Company Cadres.	
			6 OR sent to Concentration Camp for demobilization.	EKL
			Summary of evidence taken re DR REGAN. at No 1 Coy office	
"	27/3/19		Snowing - Refilling at 1400. CO. visits A.H.Q. 3 OR to C.C. for demob.	
			Owing to Regular officers under rank of Field officer not being allowed on Cadre - Lieut H LIVINGSTONE-LEARMONTH replaces Capt E.H. MANNERS. No 2 Coy Cadre.	
			Train Rations drawn for 1st Train of Cadre to U.K. All attached units struck off Ration strength to 1 Aust. Div. 210 & 211 Bde RFA on strength again.	EKL

A7092. Wt. W12839/M1293 750,000. 1/17. D. D & L Ltd. Forms/C2118/14.

Instructions regarding War Diaries and Intelligence Summaries are contained in F. S. Regs., Part II. and the Staff Manual respectively. Title pages will be prepared in manuscript.

WAR DIARY

or

~~INTELLIGENCE SUMMARY.~~ EKS

(Erase heading not required.)

Army Form C. 2118.

Place	Date	Hour	Summary of Events and Information	Remarks and references to Appendices
CHARLEROI.	28 3/19		Rain & Snow. 127 Inf Bde Cadres commence entraining - final destination OSWESTRY via ANTWERP. 12 Riders and 22 HD horses sent to RGA 39 56 90 79 83 Bdes 15 drivers sent with them, to remain there till further notice. 125 Bde Dump closes =	EKS
"	29 3/19		Snowing hard - FGCM re DR REGAN at 126 Bde HQ GILLY. 1 OR to CC for demob. 1 Farrier transferred to 21 AA(H) Coy from No 1 Coy.	EKS
"	30 3/19		Fine - refilling 1400. No 4 Coy Cadre i/c LT W.N YEATS entrains. 8 OR. to CC for demob. CAPT E F SPRECKLEY takes over No 1 Coy from Capt. A F ARIS.	EKS
"	31 3/19		Fine - CAPT. A F ARIS transferred to 8 AA(H) Coy at NAMUR (DDST No 4 Area) - taking Command of unit. 8 LD entrain for OUTREAU from No 1 Coy - this leaves 1 animal with Train. Capt. TAYLEUR'S rider. CAPT G. THURLING-BLACKWELL transferred to No 1 Coy.	EKS

[signature]

LIEUT: COLONEL
COMDG. 42ND. DIVNL. TRAIN, A.S.C.

A7092. Wt. W12839/M1293 750,000. 1/17. D. D & L. Ltd. Forms/C2118/14.

42

Army Form C. 2118.

Instructions regarding War Diaries and Intelligence Summaries are contained in F. S. Regs., Part II. and the Staff Manual respectively. Title pages will be prepared in manuscript.

WAR DIARY or ~~INTELLIGENCE SUMMARY.~~ EKS

(Erase heading not required.)

42 D Train

Vol 27

Place	Date	Hour	Summary of Events and Information	Remarks and references to Appendices
CHARLEROI	1/4/19		Fine – Capt G. THURLING BLACKWELL proceeds on leave (special for 14 days) Posted to 66 DIV TRAIN. Authy DDST 4 Area CR 2772 27.3.1919.	EKS
"	2/4/19		Cloudy – 5 Issuers sent to Base Supply Depot CALAIS Authy. X 248 28 3 1919 176 Bde entraining.	EKS
"	3/4/19		Fine – Refilling 1400 until further notice. No 3 Coy Cadre departs i/c Capt G.D.N. WYATT destination OSWESTRY via ANTWERP. Capt E H MANNERS and Capt W. H TAYLEUR posted to 21 AA(H) Coy CR/304. 1.4.1919 Capt G. THURLING BLACKWELL posted to 21 AA(H) Coy – previous posting cancelled	EKS
"	4/4/19		Fine Nil	EKS
"	5/4/19		Fine. Nil.	EKS
"	6/4/19		Fine. No 7 Coy Cadre departs i/c Lieut H. LIVINGSTONE LEARMONTH. Cadre of 19 Mobile Vet Sec 7 OR 1 ?? four wheeled vehicles accompanies it. Destination PREES HEATH via ANTWERP	EKS
"	7/4/19		Fine. Nil	EKS
"	8/4/19		Fine 7 OR sent to C.C. for demob	EKS
	9/4/19		Rain –	
	10/4/19		Fine.	
"	11/4/19		Fine. Capt. J.L. GRAHAM boarded in U.K. & found unfit for service; struck off strength from 12th inst.	EHJ
"	12th		H.Q. & No 1 Coy left for Oswestry via Antwerp.	EHJ

A7092. Wt. W12839/M1293 750,000. 1/17. D. D & L. Ltd. Forms/C2118/14.

Instructions regarding War Diaries and Intelligence Summaries are contained in F. S. Regs., Part II. and the Staff Manual respectively. Title pages will be prepared in manuscript.

WAR DIARY

~~or~~

~~INTELLIGENCE~~ SUMMARY. E.D.

(*Erase heading not required.*)

Army Form C. 2118.

Place	Date	Hour	Summary of Events and Information	Remarks and references to Appendices
Antwerp.	13/4/19		Fine.	E.D.
"	14/4/19		Stormy. H.Q. & No. 1 Coy. Cadre i/c Capt. E.F. SPRECKLEY embarked for Oswestry.	E.D.

[signature]

~~MAJOR~~, A.S.C.

O.C. HD. QRS. ~~COMPANY~~ 42nd DIVL. TRAIN.

A7092) Wt. W12839/M1293 750,000. 1/17. D. D & L Ltd. Forms/C2118/14.

www.ingramcontent.com/pod-product-compliance
Lightning Source LLC
Chambersburg PA
CBHW080807010526
44113CB00013B/2337
9781474520812